LOOKING BACK AT NINETY

DANIEL TYLER

Looking Back At Ninety

SPRING CEDARS

Copyright © 2023 by Daniel Tyler

All rights reserved

First edition, 2023

Cover design by Lauren Zurcher
Book design by Spring Cedars

ISBN 978-1-950484-70-6 (paperback)
ISBN 978-1-950484-71-3 (hardback)

Published by Spring Cedars
Denver, Colorado
www.springcedars.com

Contents

Apologia 1
Rydal, Pennsylvania 5
Brooks School 16
Crystal River Ranch 22
Fountain Valley School 53
Harvard 61
United States Air Force 70
Punahou School 87
Brief Return to Ranching 100
Burlington, Colorado 107
Colorado State University 1 112
University of New Mexico 117
Colorado State University 2 123
Mexico 133
Back in Fort Collins 151
Life With Two Families 173
Early Retirement Years 194
Betty 204
Winding Down 269
Reflections 286
About The Author 309
Notes 310

For my family.

Apologia

Embarking on this memoir has provoked an initial, very basic question: Who am I writing for? The answer determines what I include, what I leave out. For years, I've been thinking about putting my story to paper, pondering how I might use my life as the basis for a novel. But I don't think that makes much sense. First, there has been little angst in my life; no great suffering—yes, the usual disappointments, failures, and successes—but no real tragedies. Second, I don't have a moral lesson to convey; Shakespeare set the bar with Hamlet and King Lear. Other gifted writers have followed his example with tales that have far more drama and complexity than my life. Third, I don't have Hemingway's gift with words nor Tennyson's poetic skills, although I enjoy crafting prose and telling stories.

My good fortune in life has resulted in part from financial security handed down by my family through several generations. My father and my older brother, Sid, who succeeded him as steward of this wealth, believed in preserving and growing the family assets for future generations. I am a beneficiary of that stewardship, as are my siblings and my heirs. The income provided has allowed us to benefit from private school and undergraduate university educations, as well as careers that might not otherwise have been available or advisable. My life story is, at least in part, an aggregate of the many options available to me, resulting from significant financial security.

My father, Sidney Frederick Tyler, managed the assets he inherited with great care. Grampy believed his five children should make their own way in the world after he financed their educations. My generation has pretty much followed his lead with its own children, believing that maturity and responsibility come from living in the world of hard knocks, not from parental handouts. Still, we all recognize that our first-class educations launched us on a privileged path that provided a head start in the race for success.

After graduation from college, I was pretty much on my own. I worked hard to establish myself on various career paths. I wanted to make my own way in the world, and although my direction was sometimes erratic, I was always confident I could compete in any chosen field. During my life, I have felt more comfortable with the *populacho* (ordinary people) than with those who identify with inherited wealth. Grampy, on the other hand, was almost Victorian in his approach to life. He was very much "to the manner born," and he believed in maintaining connections with the "proper" people. Disdain on my part for that kind of social emphasis undermined our relationship at times and propelled me on a course that created friction between us. But in retrospect, I realize that the person I am now is to a great extent the result of Grampy's high standards.

With the exception of underwriting our education and passing out $100 here and there, Grampy's financial generosity to me did not surface again until he sold the Crystal River Ranch in 1967. A few years after that sale was consummated, he divided part of the gain he received among his five children. I was 37 years old with three children, earning $10,000 per year as an assistant professor at Colorado State University and grateful to have extra cash to pay the mortgage. If memory serves, I celebrated with the purchase of an Alfa Romeo sedan. Two decades later, when Uncle Chug died—George F. Tyler, Jr. was Grampy's younger brother—an old family trust vested. Again, I received a substantial amount of money.

I have been exceptionally fortunate: a solid family in which I found security and support; loving parents; reasonable smarts, good health, athletic ability, and hardly any money worries. An asset base of this nature is a propitious setting for a rich life but a poor environment from which to craft nuanced fiction. The novel idea, therefore, is dead in the water.

Instead, this is my attempt at a memoir. When I reflect on the diverse experiences in my life, I feel more comfortable sharing the record with my children and grandchildren, hopefully providing continuity in their lives and perhaps offering insights into perspectives they might not have considered. The focus on their generation is particularly important to me, because I have offspring from two wives: Jean Ames Theopold and Silvia Ruíz Sahagún. Dan, Nick, and Kit, my first three boys, had a much different father than the one Alejandro and Cristina knew. This difference was partly related to the dissimilar nature of their mothers. But it was also a result of my own evolution as a father, family man, and career professional. Dan, Nick, and Kit experienced my unsteady progress from Air Force pilot to teacher, to rancher, to graduate student, and finally, to the faculty of a major university. Alejandro and Cristina, on the other hand, knew me when I was becoming a more confident educator. They grew up at a time when I was focused on making a name for myself as a writer, researcher, and expert in the field of water history. The demands of those different life stages, my gradual maturity, and how I responded to various situations, impacted the relationship between my children and me.

What I write in the following pages is an attempt to recount what has mattered most to me in the past 90 years. I shall try not to appear boastful, apologetic, defensive, or academic. I want to narrate my life as a story, hopefully with a sense of humor. Most of what I say will be remembrances; I don't expect to do a lot of research. This opus will not be subjected to peer review. Although I'll try to keep the facts as accurate as possible, I'm sure my recall is flawed, and what I write will include a certain amount of distortion, possibly on purpose. I hope readers can deal with that. It's a story, after all, and as happens in many cultures, especially Native American, the one who tells the best story is ultimately recognized as the tribal historian.

So, bear with me. I hope what follows makes you smile.

Rydal, Pennsylvania

I was born at Abington Memorial Hospital (now Jefferson Health), Montgomery County, PA, on August 9, 1933. My parents had recently taken occupancy of a small foreclosed estate in nearby Rydal. 1933 was the middle of the Great Depression. As described by Grampy in *A Joyful Odyssey*, the seven acres "contained a dwelling of whitewashed stone, a garage with space for a rental apartment above, a tennis court too narrow to be used, a greenhouse minus most of its glass, an abandoned chicken house taken over by rats, a dairy to accommodate two cows with small pastures to match, a kitchen garden of ample dimensions, and massive tulip poplar trees through which trickled a leaf-strewn stream." My grandfather purchased the property literally for a song and warned my father that he and my mother would have to "work your hearts out for the next 10 years if you want to restore it."[1]

They did, in fact, make many improvements. The greenhouse was repaired, the tennis court enlarged, a swimming pool and adjacent bath houses were installed, the chicken house was cleaned up (sort of—the rats remained), and a massive garden was planted to provide fresh produce. Care and maintenance of this property were the responsibility of a devoted Italian gardener and handyman by the name of Mickel Davanti. We called him Mike, and we loved him. My father enjoyed harvesting wood for the fireplaces, and he did a little gardening, but he wasn't directly involved in restoring the property. Mike did most of the grunt work.

I recall happy years in Rydal. My brothers and I enjoyed Sunday wood chopping with my father. We also learned to hunt on the property with a .410 gauge shotgun. We shot mostly rats, squirrels, and an occasional bird or two. One day, bored and frustrated from having encountered little prey, I fired a shot at a low flying, single-engine aircraft. Brother Sid was with me at the time. I can only assume he reported my indiscretion to Grampy because the next morning at breakfast, my father paused while reading the newspaper out loud to note, "What a shame! Apparently a small, single-engine aircraft crashed yesterday just south of Rydal." He proceeded to read a made-up account of the event. I choked down my cereal and fled from the table, wondering what jail would be like. Nothing more was said.

Rydal's mid-summer heat and humidity were oppressive, although fireflies made the heavy evening air tolerable. They put on a show every night. Sticky sheets and no air conditioning made sleep difficult, but on special occasions, we were awoken around midnight by Gandy and Grampy for a swim in the new pool. It was a special treat, giving us the feeling we were sharing something a tad naughty with our parents. On other warm nights, we would retire to bed on a screened-in porch with a canvas awning overhead. When the rain and thunder came, it was exciting to hunker down under the covers and feel the spray of water as it rolled off the roof and blew through the screens onto our bedclothes. I don't think I ever slept better.

Brother Sid and I rode bicycles about three miles to Meadowbrook School. I was an average student, sometimes chastised for laziness, inattention, carelessness, a tendency to waste my time, and being mischievous—report card comments that most youngsters receive at one time or another. But teachers also commented on my sunny disposition, spontaneous and natural tendency for play, desire to help others, and qualities of leadership. Although I had difficulty with word problems in mathematics, I did well in verbal skills, and I was promoted with honors during my final year. Thanks to my mother's willingness to save memorabilia from our early schooling, I still have the box in which she kept my report cards and letters.

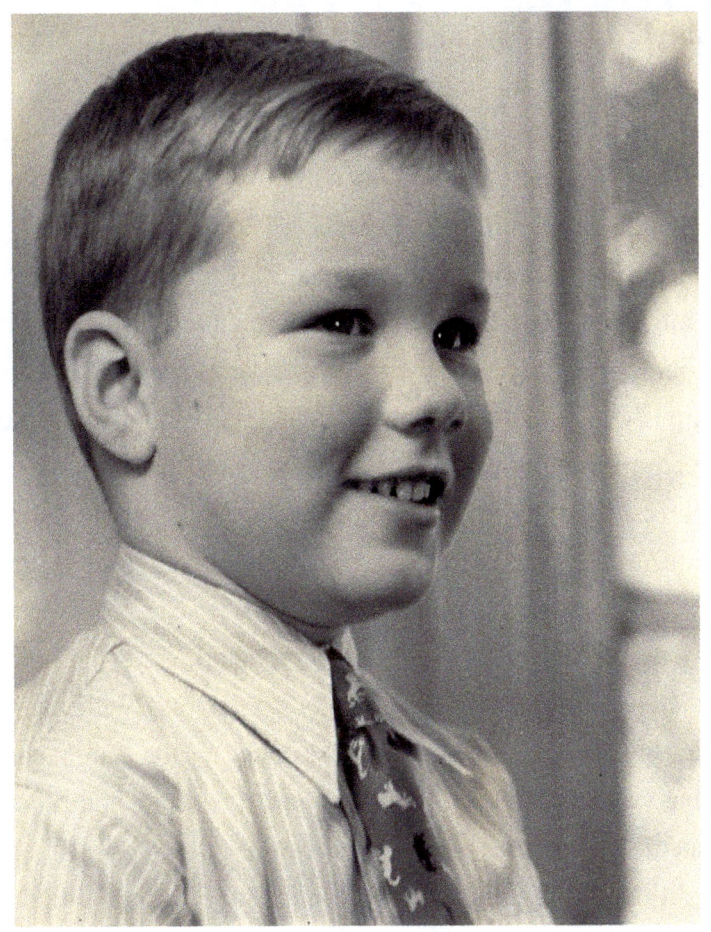

Headshot, 1938

In contrast to today's parents, Mum and Dad were not involved in school life. My father used to make fun of the headmaster, Mr. McEachron, to whom he referred laughingly as Mr. McKeeKee. My mother rarely took an interest in my teachers, but she liked coming to sports events with her 16mm movie camera. I played baseball and entered the track and field competition in the spring. I won a lot of competitions, because I could run pretty fast. My classmates teased me about a big butt which stuck out when I ran. Anything I said in response seemed to invite gleeful iterations of the same jibe. It wasn't until I was a freshman at Harvard that I finally had an adequate comeback. Uncle Dick Harper, Mum's younger brother, said to me, "Just tell anyone who teases you that you can't drive a spike with a tack hammer." From that day on, I had all the rebuttal ammunition I needed.

During the summers of 1941 until the end of the war, Sid and I were either on Cape Cod near Mum's relatives or attending camps where outdoor activities and sports were the principal occupations. At Camp Choconut in Friendsville, PA, I competed in swimming and developed an interest in playing the trumpet. At Camp Wyanoke in Wolfeboro, NH, I discovered the ukulele. Dad was in the army at that point. My letters home were occasionally directed to him. One letter described breaking my arm after another camper tripped me. I was so frustrated by not being able to participate in camp activities, I asked if I could come home so I could at least play with the cat. But my request fell on deaf ears. I returned to the same camp the following year. Swimming, tennis, riflery, canoeing, and other sports dominated our summers in New Hampshire.

At home, I organized a football team. We had a nice lawn at the house for practice. Seven or eight players of all sizes and abilities showed up from time to time. I think I had the only ball. We rode our bikes to the train station—Rydal's only public building—looking for others who might be interested in a game. We were never defeated, because we rarely found anyone to challenge us. But the disappointment of not finding combatants was eased by finding balls in the long grass off the fairway of a golf course. Something

Camp Wyanoke

Rydal football team (bottom row, second from left)

fascinated me about golfers, especially because they were so eager to buy back the balls they had just lost. I didn't know it then, but golf would later become something of an addiction in my life.

Dad authorized construction of a skating pond where a stream flowed through the lower end of the property. It held water for the most part, and it froze enough for us to have skating and hockey from time to time. Tennis was obligatory—the gentleman's game. For my father, it was as much a lesson in manners as it was a sport. Being prankish, I once made a smart aleck remark during a game. It did not sit well with my father. He banished me from the field of battle. I retired to the nearby pool feeling injured and listened half-heartedly while my mother tried to explain that the best outcome for everyone would result from an apology to Grampy. I did not know then that such apologies would improve her life too. But I didn't know what to apologize for, and I was stubborn. My presence on the tennis court was not requested for a while.

During the winter, my brother Sid and I were supposed to participate in wrestling matches which Dad organized. He renovated a room over the garage, bought a large mat, and hired an instructor. I didn't like the sport at all. My older brother was too good at it; I was not. Furthermore, I didn't like the smell of another body sitting on me and soon decided to look for alternate forms of entertainment. Sid didn't appreciate my attitude. Our sisters and brother Rob were too small for wrestling, and his only victim was bailing out. I can't be sure, but I suspect that's why he decided to heave a wrench at my head, causing a spectacular fountain of blood, lots of wailing on my part, and lavish amounts of attention and sympathy from our mother. I felt victorious. The scar served as a protective shield, reminding everyone that my brother should be watched closely lest he attempt to do me additional harm.

Flanked by Sid (left) and Rob on the pool diving board, 1943

The Rydal house and grounds still hold many warm memories. In the fall, we raked those immense tulip poplar leaves into large mounds and enjoyed leaping into the fragrant piles; we had apple fights with rotten and sometimes not-so-rotten apples; we watched the coal truck fill the basement with fuel for the furnace; and we marveled at the strength of the ice man who brought fresh ice for the ice box. Indoors, we had black dial telephones that required speaking to a female operator who connected callers through a switchboard. Television wasn't invented, so we listened to radio adventure series after school: Captain Midnight, The Green Hornet, The Lone Ranger, Flash Gordon, Jack Armstrong, Superman, and Dick Tracy. We cut off the tops of cereal boxes which we mailed, along with a dime, to a remote address where special gifts from our heroes were mailed back. Waiting for that return mail was filled with keen anticipation followed by disappointment when the item we had ordered turned out to be chintzy.

Most evenings we joined Mum and Dad while they had cocktails in the living room. At times, Dad would read from *The Hollow Tree Snowed-In Book* by Albert Bigelow Paine, first published by Harper Brothers in 1910. Paine was Mark Twain's secretary, and he knew how to tell a good story. Dad loved these stories, especially the rhythmic prose in which Paine wrote. I remember warmly the animated way in which he read to us.

Dad also liked his gin. He kept a case or two in a bathroom off the living room. One night the family dachshund knocked over and broke a gin bottle. After lapping up part of the spill, the dog staggered into the living room and entertained us. With its low center of gravity and wobbly legs, the poor critter executed gyrations a sober dog would have found infeasible. That should have been a warning to Sid and me when Dad offered us a small martini. I accepted, because it was offered in the spirit of family conviviality. I had no idea what the gin would do to me, but at the age of ten, I soon learned I had little tolerance for booze. Even though today's parents might be shocked by the early age I had my first drink, I have always been grateful that my father showed me how vulnerable I was to alcohol. Sitting at the dinner table after a martini while trying to act normal was a challenge, especially when Dad decided to play a spelling game called Ghost. Success in the game depends on one's ability to spell creatively, so words don't end on one's turn. With each failure, a player is penalized one of the five letters in GHOST. After five words end on a player, they become a ghost who is then forced to remain silent for the remainder of the meal. I failed more than most, but having words end on me was the best way to get out of the game and retreat into my own inebriated condition. Once declared a ghost, I could not speak or be spoken to. Peace.

The Rydal house was a tranquil place. Sid and I lived on the third floor where we could roughhouse and enjoy our own games. Rob and the girls lived on the second floor where they were cared for and supervised by Erica "Sass" Habluetzel, a Swiss lady who helped my mother and who remained with the family many years. My father played classical music on the piano after dinner. The sounds of Rachmaninoff, Tchaikovsky, Beethoven, and Chopin rising to the third floor were comforting. I loved the music but lacked the discipline to stick with the lessons Dad provided. Maybe it was the teacher. Ironically, I did take piano lessons later in life, and I recall my father telling me how relaxing it was to hear me play Beethoven's *Für Elise* on his piano in Tucson. Payback!

Mum loved holidays, especially Christmas. She engaged all of us in decorating a large tree. My job was throwing tinsel on the tree. The crowning moment was placing an angel on the very top. She wrapped all the presents, even those she put in our stockings, and she was careful to make sure we were treated equally. Like most children, I believed in Santa Claus until my demonic older brother broke the news that Mr. Claus did not exist. I remember where I was when my bubble was popped. I spent a long time trying to understand how it could be true, when I had clearly seen Santa and his sleigh from my third-floor bedroom window one Christmas eve. Seeing is believing, or is it the other way around?

Mum and Dad were not religious. Christmas was essentially

a secular holiday. We were together in church for only one or two occasions. I often felt that Mum would have preferred to attend church more regularly, possibly for social reasons. Consequently, I knew nothing about organized religion while growing up, and when I did have occasion to attend various services, I felt awkward.

Two other memories of that time stand out. The first stems from a home visit by the family doctor. We did not go to clinics or doctors' offices in those days. Doctors made house calls. We were given a polio vaccination; it was probably in 1946 or 1947. Dr. Jonas Salk had begun work on a dead virus form of the vaccination, but it would not be approved until 1955. We were actually vaccinated with a live, weakened form of the virus, an experience I now look back on with horror. The second event occurred at Meadowbrook School. I was in class in the late spring of 1945 when a newspaper circulated showing a picture of an atomic bomb, the weapon which annihilated Hiroshima and Nagasaki and ended World War II in the Pacific. I was old enough to grasp the horrors associated with that weapon.

The war had been unsettling for our family. Although we children were aware of what was happening in Europe, it was not until December 7, 1941, that we realized how deeply Dad was going to be involved. On that Sunday morning, while Sid and I were cutting firewood with him, we learned of the Pearl Harbor attack while listening to the Philadelphia Orchestra. I recall how quickly Dad dropped his saw and raced to the house. Not long after, he was commissioned as an officer in the Army Air Force. From 1942 until the war's end, he wasn't home very much, but his experiences during the war ultimately affected our lives profoundly.

Dad was posted to several duty stations in Kentucky and Washington, D.C., but he wanted an overseas assignment. In the fall of 1943, he was sent to Algiers to serve on the staff of British

Lieutenant General Bernard Montgomery. Monty was an inspirational military commander who led the Eighth Army forces against then undefeated German tanks under the command of Field Marshal Erwin Rommel at the second battle of El Alamein in North Africa. This battle turned the tide of the war in North Africa. Egypt was saved from the Axis advance, and the Suez Canal was no longer threatened.

Dad saw in Montgomery many of the British traits he admired. His service in North Africa was challenging and meaningful. At the same time, his long absence proved difficult for Mum. She had help, but five children, a large home to manage, and the uncertainties associated with war-related rationing created stress. As a boy, I still did what boys do, probably more mischievous than normal, because the Chief Disciplinarian wasn't around. I recall making a wisecrack to my mother one evening as I was walking up the stairs, and she hauled off and slapped me in the face. Shock and awe! She never hit us. From that moment on, I was more aware of her worries, although it was impossible to know what she really felt. I was too self-absorbed.

When Dad returned from North Africa in 1945, he and Mum decided to send Sid and me to Brooks School, a boarding school in North Andover, MA. Dad was a graduate of St. Mark's School for which he had great affection. But he heard that Brooks had a strict headmaster by the name of Frank Ashburn, and he was convinced that Sid and I needed the discipline which had been absent during the war. Ashburn had worked with Endicott Peabody at Groton, and he brought the same rigid set of rules to Brooks in 1927, remaining there as headmaster until 1973. Boarding at Brooks was supposed to bring us back into line.

Brooks School

I was only 12 in 1945 when I enrolled at Brooks. I knew nothing of boarding school culture. Along with the other first formers (7th grade), I felt miserable for several months. But like incarcerated prisoners, we developed bonds with each other. Participation on sports teams helped diffuse homesickness and produced strong friendships.

I played baseball under the tutelage of Leo Joseph Cronan. Rumor had it that he was associated with the Red Sox organization, but I can't find any evidence of that. It's likely that the rumor's origin evolved from confusion with Joe Cronin who played with the Sox from 1935 to 1945. Leo was a great coach. I think he saw in me just enough talent to warrant his personal attention. He encouraged me to play catcher behind home plate. It was a dirty job. Few players competed for the position, because foul balls caroming off opponents' bats tended to land on exposed skin and bone. But I liked the job. The catcher had a leadership role. He worked with the pitcher, saw the whole field in front of him, and handled the ball on almost every play. Following Leo's advice, I played catcher in high school, college, and for several summers, in a semi-pro, fast-pitch softball league when I was working in Burlington, CO.

Winters were cold in North Andover. I disliked basketball, so when the ice froze on the outdoor hockey rink, I grabbed stick and skates and joined the melee. It was pretty wild. A lack of boards on the side of the rink allowed the puck to slip into adjacent snow drifts. If we couldn't find it, one of us chose a suitable rock which we banged back and forth until it broke or someone got hurt. Those free-for-alls were fun and dangerous. But I suspect the Brooks School teachers (masters) were delighted to see us expend all that energy so we would be more malleable in the classroom and dormitories.

We also experienced ice boating on nearby Lake Cochichewick. A few of the masters had boats with runners. They were fast and could turn over unexpectedly when the blades hit an uneven surface. But the feeling of wind-powered speed was euphoric, and when I was unable to get a ride in a boat, I found a friend to help me attach a sheet to two hockey sticks so we could be blown by the wind at what felt like warp speed on skates.

Coming back from the lake, we often encountered students engaged in major snowball fights. Large forts were constructed from blocks of snow within which worker bees (us younger students) rapidly crafted the missiles to be used against the enemy. Armed with snowballs, intrepid snow knights (upper classmen) would then sally forth, retreating only when ammunition ran out. For the most part, we only threw snow at each other. But few battles went by without someone inserting a rock in a projectile. Playing fair was not a requirement for 13-, 14-, and 15-year-olds. Each one of the six forms was passionate about defending its honor against other classes under all circumstances and with whatever weaponry was required.

The Brooks teachers were a mixed bag. For three years, I took Latin from Doc Scudder. He motivated me to do translations of Latin texts. When I got it right, I felt like I had solved a puzzle. Doc was a character, and he gave a lot of homework, but thanks to him I developed a better understanding of the roots of Romance languages. I was third out of a class of 18, brother Sid being first. My history teacher, on the other hand, did not inspire. He believed in rote memory. Because his class was so boring, students paid scant attention to the subject. The teacher spent much of the class period scolding us. I was a terrible student and occasionally disrespectful, the penalty for which was a blow on the back of the hand with a ruler. It was painful, but it made me even more determined to distance myself from Plantagenet royalty. In addition to the teacher's shortcomings, I was a very poor reader. My eyes and brain seemed out of sync, and reading most school materials seemed like a lot of work. I might have had a form of dyslexia, but in those days a ruler on the knuckles was the accepted response to slow learners. Consequently, I was a poor history student all the way through high school and college. Given my career as a university historian, how could that be? Read on!

First and second form students lived in large rooms divided into cubicles with a curtain for a door and no ceiling except that which covered the entire room. We could hear every snicker, grunt, snore, sigh, fart, belch, laugh, and crying jag of our classmates. Each cubicle contained a bed, desk, and bureau. Because adolescence is the age of sexual awakening, my first acquaintance with bodily changes and emotions took place in this open-air environment. Girls and their mysteries were ever the topic of conversation, and "dirty" magazines appeared from nowhere to be purchased by the highest bidder. After one reader had his fill, the item of interest would be resold, launched over a cubicle wall in the dark of night, and enjoyed by the next buyer until another sale materialized. These prurient works would change hands all night long.

We were an adolescent zoo, helpless in the face of anything remotely sexual. We heard that the school was doctoring our food with saltpeter (potassium nitrate) to neutralize our sexual appetites. I didn't see or feel any diminution of sexual energy in myself or anyone else during my three years at Brooks, and from what I have learned since, I doubt that any educational institution would have used saltpeter. It is a principal ingredient of gunpowder that could have given us gastroenteritis, kidney disease, anemia, and high blood pressure. Brooks School would not have wanted to explain such consequences to tuition-paying parents. The rumor was, indeed, a rumor.

Instead of using saltpeter, teachers and coaches tried to wear us out. Even when we got sick and had to spend time in the infirmary, the old nurses were proactive about muting our sexual awakening. Anyone caught with an erection would receive a sharp blow on the offending appendage by a nurse who knew that a well-aimed strike with a stick would prove both painful and effective, at least for an hour or so.

Back among the healthy, I enjoyed acting in several plays. They weren't as much fun as playing Peter Rabbit or Chanticleer at Meadowbrook School, but I liked the feel of stepping into different personalities. I can't explain it psychologically, but there was satisfaction in pretending to be someone else for a short period, and that same gratification was available to me as a teacher when I developed historical characters which I presented in class to my students.

I also learned to box. Because I was quick, I did reasonably well—much better than wrestling. But following a few smart aleck remarks demeaning wrestlers in general, the wrestling coach offered to spar with me. He put on gloves, I threw jabs, and the next thing I knew, I was lying on the mat. I was unaware that I had a glass jaw and a mouth that would get me in trouble if I wasn't more careful.

My letters home from Brooks detail a mixture of accomplishments and emotions. I was wildly enthusiastic when Dad informed us that we might soon leave Philadelphia for a ranch in the West. "You made my mouth water," I wrote Dad, "when you spoke of the Wild West. My life ambition has been a western life, and there would be nothing nicer in the world you could do for me." I kept thinking about specific items I would need, requesting that Mum and Dad set them aside for the summer trip to Wyoming in 1946: my sheath knife, deer antlers, canteen, and ten-gallon hat. Horses and cowboys dominated my imagination, and when I wasn't complaining of homesickness, bullying prefects, and boring teachers, I wrote frequently about my enthusiasm for life in the West.

I also wrote about discovering fencing, developing my own pictures in a darkroom, setting up a shoeshine business, experiencing jock itch, and playing golf. I mentioned theatrical performances in which I had minor parts, one being a stage production of *A Bell for Adano* in which THE Anthony Perkins held the role of Margherita. Little did we know that Tony would become such an accomplished actor. In other letters I also noted rhetorically, "I don't know what has gotten into me, but I certainly am anxious for girls." And in a letter to Mum, I admitted that I finally confessed to interested upperclassmen that the picture of the good looking girl on my dresser was actually my mother, not my sister.

Dad decided to remove us from Brooks at the end of the 1947–48 term. It is not clear why he did this, but by then, the family headquarters were in Carbondale, CO, at the Crystal River Ranch. The move from Rydal was complete. Mum and Dad also had a home in Tucson where sister Hope was attending school and getting medical attention for her asthma. Dad felt that Colorado would be a better locale for our secondary education. He might have had a falling out with Headmaster Ashburn, or he might have wanted us closer to home.

Whatever the reason, we learned of our fate from Ashburn himself. I was actually quite disappointed. I had made very good friends and had been invited to their homes. The frustration I felt

Brooks School, 7th grade, far left

erupted shortly before leaving the school. Knowing I wouldn't be returning, I helped a friend empty his room literally: Once he packed his personal possessions, we ejected every piece of furniture out of his third story room to the ground below. What remained looked like kindling. I was called to Ashburn's office in short order and dressed down for my inexcusable behavior. This was not a good way to end three years of schooling, and I am still embarrassed by my out-of-control antics. Perhaps there is a reason why in 2014 the Brooks School archivist could find very little in the way of records on the Tyler boys.

Crystal River Ranch

Dad purchased the CRR in November 1946. The decision to leave Pennsylvania came as a surprise, but I don't recall asking many questions. The Wild West meant horses, something I had dreamed of for a long time. Dad had been considering a move prior to his discharge from the Army Air Force. His last commanding officer, who saw the possibility of a real market for beef after years of rationing and a mutton diet in the United States, provided a ranching contact in Wyoming. Mum and Dad visited this family and decided to rent cabins in nearby Story, WY, for the summer of 1946. They planned to look for a ranch to buy while we played.

Dad's decision to move to the West was viewed by friends and family with skepticism. He had been an investment banker before the war, had little experience with agriculture or livestock, and was admittedly incompetent on horseback and with tools. On just about any farm or ranch, animals and machinery are the essence of every operation. Although my grandfather George Frederick Tyler had developed Neshaminy Farms, a thriving operation for beef and dairy cattle, there is no evidence that Grampy had anything to do with the business.

But the war changed everyone. Dad returned home determined to branch out on his own and to provide a home environment for his five children that would keep us all together, out of trouble and engaged in a shared enterprise. More than anything, he believed Mum would enjoy ranch life. She loved outdoor activities and made friends easily. After four years of running the family by herself, she was entitled to an adventure that suited her personality. Dad had confidence in himself as a businessman and thought he could make a working ranch profitable. It was a naive assumption; acting on it took courage. But Dad was determined to reunite the family, and he was especially focused on getting sister Hope into the West's drier air.

There was one other ingredient in Dad's decision to leave his Philadelphia background so abruptly. Described openly in *A Joyful Odyssey*, it had to do with the 14 months he spent in North Africa. The long separation from Mum resulted in his having an affair with a lady from Nebraska who was stationed at the same base. We have no way of knowing how Mum took the news when she was informed, either by mail or when Dad returned home. But Dad insisted on driving to Nebraska to visit the woman so Mum could hear and see for herself that the affair was over.

I was shocked to read about this in *A Joyful Odyssey*, not because I was surprised it had happened. It was wartime after all, and the stress of loneliness and uncertainty about the war's end resulted in a multiplicity of behaviors. But I was surprised that Dad felt compelled to write about it, possibly causing embarrassment for Mum in the process. That she was able to move forward and look to the future was evidence of her upbeat and forgiving spirit. Dad's decision to move to the West, I suspect, was in no small way influenced by his conviction that keeping five children busy and outdoors during adolescence would free her up to do more of the things she enjoyed. In sum, I think we ended up on the Crystal River Ranch to a great extent, because Dad wanted to do something for Mum. The burden she bore caring for the five of us during the war and his North African indiscretion contributed significantly to this decision. Obviously, my opinion is subjective.

The summer in Story went fast. We rode horses, fished, packed into the back country with cowboys, and entertained occasional visitors from the East. We lived in rustic cabins, experienced extreme weather, and suffered an invasion of miller moths and electrical failures that taught us the joys of wood stoves and kerosene lanterns. For me, it was a summer rich with new experiences, including an innocent romance with a young lady who also loved horses and spoke of growing up to be a cowgirl. T'was a lovely infatuation.

Toward the end of the summer, Mum and Dad invited Sid and me to accompany them on a trip to see the Crystal River Ranch in Carbondale, CO. Located 12 miles south of Glenwood Springs on the road to Aspen, the CRR was originally a potato farm. Irrigation water was diverted from the Crystal River to the ranch by way of a seventeen-mile ditch called the Sweet-Jessup Canal. Without this water, the 1,600 acres of deeded ranch land could not grow meaningful crops. Average rainfall was too restricted to sustain anything but pasture. The ditch was the ranch's Achilles' heel.

When we first visited the ranch, the old potato lands were growing alfalfa, oats, and corn. W.D. Farr, the owner, explained to Dad the importance of the Sweet-Jessup Canal, known to everyone as "the ditch." Dad certainly seemed to understand its importance. But he didn't fully comprehend how vulnerable ranch operations could be when gully washers roared down the surrounding hills and took out roads, fences, culverts, and ditches in their path. We were so enthralled by the verdant beauty of the ranch, the peaceful livestock grazing in pastures, and the scenic background of Mt. Sopris, that it was hard to imagine the possibility of any natural calamity. The principal house had been modernized by the Metropolitan Life Insurance Company, owner of the ranch prior to W. D. Farr. Barns, corrals, and fences were maintained, tack for riding and work horses was in good shape, and the bunk house was more than adequate for a work force of 10–15 men hired specifically for the haying season. Ranch ownership included grazing rights on the White River National Forest. Bureau of Land Management lands were adjacent to ranch boundaries and were utilized for driving cattle and sheep to and from the National Forest in spring and fall.

W.D. Farr had owned the ranch for four years, but he was ready to return to his cattle feeding operation in Greeley. He offered the CRR to Dad for $325,000, and a deal was consummated in November 1946. Farr later told me he didn't make much money on the sale, especially when factoring in the expenses of keeping water flowing in the ditch. He advised Dad to retain foreman Homer White, who knew both cattle and farming. Homer was not particularly polished or submissive, particularly when dealing with a new boss from the East. His manner rubbed Dad the wrong way. They soon parted company, resulting in the very problems Farr had foreseen.

In 1947, Sid and I returned to Brooks for one more year. When school ended, we came to our new home with great enthusiasm, anticipating a life that would be filled with the kind of excitement that Rydal simply couldn't offer.

My introduction to that life began with the doctoring and branding of calves born in February, March, and April. On my first work day, I wore shiny, new blue jeans, a straw hat, leather gloves, and cowboy boots. This was going to be the life! The real cowboys roped calves and dragged them close to the fire near the center of the corral. I was the designated flanker. Grabbing each end of the calf, I was supposed to pull up and knee the animal at the same time. If the timing worked, the calf would land on its side with a thump, at which point I would take hold of a leg, remove the lariat, and sit on the animal until the branding, castration, and vaccination were completed by other cowboys. When I wore out, I rode my horse into the pens to bring out more calves.

Playing cowboy

I began this work with zest. The smaller calves were easy to throw, once I got the hang of it. But some weighed upwards of 200 pounds, and they kicked. Frequently, they got the best of me, much to the amusement of the cowboys. When we broke for lunch, I staggered back to the house with a torn shirt, mud and shit on my pants, feeling a mixture of exhaustion and pride. All in all, it was a rough indoctrination to ranch life. But I was hooked.

As the weather warmed, the alfalfa grew. This "hay," along with oats and chopped-up corn (ensilage or silage), would become winter feed for cattle, horses, and sheep. Haying was our principal summer activity. Determining who did what job was the responsibility of the ranch foreman. Irrigation of the fields was done by men who had experience moving water. They went to the fields carrying a sharpened shovel and several canvas dams. They set the dams in the small lateral ditches at the high point of fields and made cuts in the ditch bank, allowing water to flood a section of the pasture or hay meadow. Alert for dam breaks, runaway water, and occasional animal activity, good irrigators were on the move constantly, always concerned that the precious water would get out of control. This was not a job given to neophytes. It was hard work, and it required experience.

Likewise, skill was essential to the operation of haying machinery. Mowing with a sickle bar attached to a tractor required vigilance and mechanical aptitude. Rocks and other impedimenta could damage the seven-foot-long cutting bar. Blades riveted to the bar had to be sharpened and replaced regularly. Raking the hay was less demanding, but knowledge of how to make good windrows—segments of dried, rolled-up hay ready to be baled—was imperative. Operating the hay baler was a specialty left to one or two individuals.

Unqualified for irrigating or operating machinery, I was assigned a tedious job I soon learned to hate. Balers were pulled by a tractor whose driver followed windrows of hay that had dried in the sun to an ideally cured moist and crisp consistency. These rows were fed through the baler which compressed the hay into rectangular, wire-tied cubes weighing 50 to 80 pounds. Unfortunately, the baler ejected bales indiscriminately, especially at the ends and corners of fields where sharp turns were required. My job was to align these bales so that a half-ton truck with side loader could navigate a row, forcing bales to ride up the loader onto the truck bed where one or two men would arrange them in a stack four or five levels high. When the truck was fully loaded, it would leave the field and drive to an area where the bales were unloaded and stored until needed for winter feed.

In order to align the bales on the ground, I was armed with a metal hook, which I used to penetrate and pull the hay into rows. The job was lonesome and monotonous. I envied all the other ranch hands who were driving machinery. I became easily bored. Occasionally, a nest of field mice under a bale would provide amusement, but for the most part, the work was pure drudgery from 7 a.m. to 6 p.m. For entertainment, I occasionally created parallel rows or lined up bales head to tow on sharp turns, causing mayhem for the men standing on the back of a truck as the bales came at them like shot from a cannon. I usually got an earful when we convened again at the shop, but being the boss's son, I never really got what I deserved. I liked the men on the hay crews. Many were alcoholics who worked just long enough to be able to afford another drink. When they showed up at the shop in clean city clothes, asking for their paycheck, I was always disappointed. I hoped they would come back. A few did, but the majority drifted away to find another job

Heading out to line bales.

which would pay for another spree. They were replaced by others who shared jokes, lies, stories, and experiences that kept me in awe. We were worlds apart, but I always felt these humble men provided me with an education I could never have gotten anywhere else. I learned to appreciate the lives of rootless, laboring men, most of whom were humble, grateful for a job, and worldly in ways I could not have imagined.

At times, I even tried to disguise my privileged upbringing to appear more like my fellow workers. I wanted to fit in, so I laughed at their jokes, massaged their biases, and even reworked my vocabulary to speak like them. When Mum and Dad went off on a trip one summer, I ate my meals at the cookhouse where conversation was a rarity. Everyone focused on the food prepared by the cook. She was a large woman, and she insisted on good manners from anyone who partook of meals in her kitchen. Because I thought I could use the language we shared in the fields to be accepted by the men I worked with, I once requested in a loud voice, "Please pass the fucking chicken." The men snickered but didn't say anything. They knew what was coming. In less than a minute, the cook was standing by my side with a rather large instrument in her hand. "I don't care if you's the boss's son or not; I ever hear that language again in my kitchen, you gonna feel some pain." The men tried not to laugh; I wanted to hide under the table. What a stupid thing I had done. All I heard the rest of the summer was, "You gonna feel some pain."

Being the boss's son was interesting. Dad would occasionally ask for my advice about ranch activities or my view of certain employees. Because I felt loyal to those with whom I worked, my opinions were usually not what he expected. I considered myself part of the hay crew, so when the men refused to work one morning, demanding a salary increase to $5 per day, I stood with them. Dad came over to the shop from his office to determine why no one had left to work in the fields. Eventually, he gave in to their demand, but there were uncomfortable moments. I was making $250 a month at the time, roughly $100 more a month than the hired men. Even though they were getting free room and board, I fully supported their request for an increased daily wage.

Dad ran the ranch from a large office he added onto a building where Sid, Rob, and I bunked. He surveyed ranch operations through large glass windows with binoculars. But the hay fields extended a mile north of headquarters, requiring Dad to make a daily drive, usually in the afternoon, to check on what was going on. We knew he was coming when someone would spot a plume of dust rising in the air from the dirt road. Work shifted into high gear. The men were happy to see him; always polite and courteous when he asked questions.

I had mixed feelings about my role. The men respected Dad, because he owned the ranch, but they couldn't relate to him. I wanted Dad to be more of a hands-on leader, but it was naive of me to have that expectation. He had practically no experience with physical labor. Additionally, his eyesight was bad, and he had been raised with nannies and servants. He saw himself more as a business manager than a hands-on rancher. On horseback, he was a lump in the saddle, although he did have his own steed, Jake, which the men saddled for him when he wanted to join a cattle drive. For exercise, he built a tennis court near the main house which became the subject of frequent jokes from the very men I wanted him to impress. He even insisted on players wearing white. I was mortified.

To his credit, though, Dad did not interfere with the relationship between his sons and the foremen who assigned us work. We were treated like any other hired hand, and if we made mistakes, they were reported to the boss. We showed up at the shop at 6 a.m., worked the same hours as everyone else, and enjoyed isolated days off. When the hay was ready to cut and bale, or the corn and oats were ready for harvest, or the cattle and sheep were ready for sorting and marketing, we followed the same schedule as everyone else. Dad was pleased we were learning how to work. Physical exhaustion kept us occupied and free from the usual teenage mischief—exactly what he and Mum had hoped to accomplish.

But I'm sure my siblings would agree that we were very privileged. We gathered as a family for supper in the evenings. Mum and Dad enjoyed a drink or two before dinner. We ate together at a table and talked to each other. There was no television at the ranch, and the only radio station we could occasionally pick up came out of Del Rio, TX. When dinner ended and the dishes were done, we entertained ourselves with a variety of games, mostly Hearts and Mah Jong. Occasionally, we tried playing musical instruments, but the sounds we produced soon led to frustration. Curiously, Dad did not play the piano at the ranch. When our family band convened, he would hum the melodies on a comb wrapped in toilet paper.

Because Mum was the family photographer, we frequently had showings of her 16mm films, which were digitized in 2016 and shared with my siblings. But when all is said and done, family gatherings at night were restricted by the need to rise and shine with the sun. We were usually in bed by 9 p.m.—a practice I continue as an old geezer, albeit for different reasons.

The CRR was a happy place. It was a lot more than a business; it was a real family home. Ranch life served in many ways to develop the personalities and characters we came to be. It was a place with which we identified and from which we hoped never to be separated. The first question I always asked Dad when he came to visit us at Fountain Valley School was, "What's the latest ranch news?" We couldn't wait to get home.

These feelings became increasingly intense as the years passed. We saw ourselves as ranchers, not immigrants from the East. Experiences of the first years had caused us to wonder if we would ever be accepted in the Roaring Fork Valley. Locals were openly displeased when they saw an eastern gentleman move in, especially when they became aware he was running sheep along with the cattle. Although violence between sheepmen and cattlemen was a thing of the past, the old cowmen of Carbondale continued to erroneously believe that grazing sheep destroyed vegetation for cattle. For me, this bit of history came into focus at the age of 14, while I was sitting on a bench in front of the local drug store eating an ice cream cone. Parked on the same bench was a grizzled, old cowboy. "You one a' them Tyler boys?" he asked.

"Yessir!" I replied.

"Understand your Pappy's running sheep up there," he said.

"Yessir!" I confessed.

"Well," he warned, fixing me with a well-practiced stare, "you oughta know we used to hang sheep people around here."

"Yessir!" I croaked, swallowing the rest of my ice cream in one giant gulp and making tracks for the vehicle that brought me to town. From then on, I committed to being a rock-ribbed, card-carrying, bona fide cattleman. Brother Sid would have to handle the sheep.

In fact, W. D. Farr had run sheep on the CRR for the same reasons Dad was running them. In the mercurial world of livestock prices, sheep were a hedge against sudden declines in beef prices. Additionally, sheep produced two crops: lambs and wool. As things turned out, we didn't have sheep every year. Dad experimented with different stock combinations, varying the numbers and breeds of animals according to his best analysis of fall markets. Memorably, he bought truckloads of wild turkeys one year. They were driven into the gulches near ranch headquarters with the expectation they would get fat and be ready for sale around Thanksgiving. If you can imagine cowboys swinging their ropes and yelling at a bunch of turkeys flying from tree to tree, you will know that this bizarre experiment had a short lifespan and unintended consequences. The turkeys that never got rounded up that fall, multiplied over the years in a habitat they found especially friendly. They now frequent the back yard of the main house, because Sue Anschutz-Rodgers, present-day CRR owner, insists on feeding them.

The CRR's primary focus was a herd of about 1,000 cows and 25 bulls. Dad tried Angus and Hereford cows and crosses between the two breeds. It took a few years before the Carbondale locals recognized Dad's commitment to quality, but when he brought back blue ribbons from the Denver Stock Show, they embraced the ranch and the good name it was bringing to their community. The graffiti and sign damage that had plagued our early years ceased.

After several years of lining bales, I was promoted to raking the mowed hay. I drove a Johnny Popper (John Deere) tractor attached to a revolving rake whose tines were cantilevered and rotated by two outside wheels that caused the hay to be lifted and folded over into a windrow. The Johnny Popper had two cylinders, ran on diesel fuel, and was started by manually rotating a wheel adjacent to the crank case. On a chilly morning, numerous rotations were required to make that Johnny pop. Once under way, I had to ensure the rows were straight enough for the baler that would follow. I carried a grease gun for the rake, replacement tines, and extra fuel for the tractor. As enjoyable as it was to be doing something other than lining bales, I soon learned that farm machinery breaks all the time. I also learned that good repairmen had to be creative. We didn't have duct tape in those days, but we carried baling wire, pliers, wrenches, and an assortment of nuts and bolts. The ranch shop had a forge, acetylene tanks for welding, grinders, and just about any tool one might need. We made many of our own parts. Although I never developed the mechanical skills of brother Rob, little by little, I learned how to keep things running. When I left the ranch, I knew just enough about plumbing, electricity, reciprocating engines, welding, and hydraulics to be dangerous.

I also recognized that while farming had its rewards, I really wanted to ride with the cowboys. Cows and calves spent summers on National Forest lands on either side of the ranch itself. I wanted to be with the men who looked after these animals, riding, roping, distributing blocks of salt, doctoring, fixing fences and corrals, and doing it all with real cowboys. Sid was with the sheep. I felt superior, being associated with the romance of punching cows.

I got my chance one summer in early June. This was the time the cows and calves were driven about 30 miles from the home ranch to grazing lands on Cottonwood Pass in the White River National Forest. Over a period of two days, we nudged the animals along roads up into the high country, spending one night at the Haff Ranch where the livestock rested. Most of the animals started out well from the CRR about 4 a.m., but as the sun came up and temperatures rose, they sought shady spots under trees, in gulleys, and in thick brush. I was assigned to ride drag—the dusty, dirty position at the rear of the herd. My job was to make certain the laggards didn't get too far behind, which meant I had to cajole, whip, yell, push, and beat the exhausted mamas and their three-month-old babies. I even carried them on my saddle. It was a tiring job, and once we left the state highway onto the narrow, dirt county roads, things became even more difficult. A greater variety of hiding places came into play, along with three-wire roadside fences whose decrepit condition allowed tired cattle to escape and hide on private property.

Eventually, we made it to Cottonwood and for the next three months, the cows reveled in the abundant, high altitude grasses. Calves frolicked and gained weight. We moved the herd around National Forest permit lands by changing the location of salt blocks, and we checked the herd daily to make sure they hadn't tangled with barbed wire, porcupines, or gopher holes. Doctoring was occasionally required, but there were few dangerous predators, and the calves were big enough to run from trouble.

I spent parts of several summers riding the Cottonwood range, living in a one-room line shack with a couple of cowboys. Supplies came to us weekly, usually delivered by Mum. The food variety she provided was welcome. Cowboys could fry meat, bake bread, and boil up a pot of beans. Vegetables and fruits were relatively unknown. Flour, rice, and cereal containers were frequently left open in our haste to begin work in the early mornings. In our absence, legions of mice feasted on the grain. The mice disappeared when we returned, but when the sun set and the kerosene lanterns were extinguished, they rushed back in. Sleeping on the floor on an air mattress, I could testify to the large number of mice who scurried over and around me in their eagerness to get at the available food.

Some cowboys brought their own horses, but the ranch provided a string. Because he was determined to save money, Dad decided one year to replace the aging animals with wild horses captured in South Park. We trucked several to Cottonwood where they were to be broken and trained to herd cattle. It was a crazy plan.

These outlaw horses were six to nine years old; they had never been under saddle or bridle; recently gelded, they were ornery. Free to roam all their lives, their fighting instincts were intuitive and easily aroused.

Our plan for taming these outlaws was to saddle a well-trained horse at first light. The next step was to rope and ear down one of the broncs while a saddle and halter were thrown on. One of the cowboys would mount his horse, grab the lead rope of the outlaw horse, and dally it around his saddle horn as someone (me) got on the outlaw. We would then proceed out of the corral at warp speed, heading directly for the nearest stand of quaking aspen. The objective was to teach the outlaw that he had to watch where he was going and obey commands from his rider, or he would get bruised when he hit the trees.

The ensuing adventure was generally wild and unpredictable for all concerned. One morning when we were making pretty good time through the trees, my outlaw horse decided that he had enough. He bucked, raising his head so fast and hard that the cowboy leading me lost control of the lead rope. Gyrating back and forth, up and down, busting dead branches and doing all he could to loosen me from the saddle, that outlaw horse was determined to regain his freedom. On one hop he launched me into the air, and before I landed, his front hooves were coming up again, nicking my face as my body obeyed the laws of gravity, pulling me in the opposite direction. When the dust settled, I was a mess with a broken nose and mild concussion. We had no phones at cow camp, so the cook took our only vehicle and headed for the nearest ranch 15 miles away. My mother appeared later in the day. She took me to the doctor who decided I would mend with rest. I hurt, but my pride was intact, and I felt I had earned a battle ribbon as a fledgling cowboy.

The outlaw horse didn't fare as well. He was named Banjo because of his ability to pluck a tune on the posterior of anyone who tried to ride him. By the end of the summer, he was on his way to the horsemeat factory.

I returned to Cottonwood after a few days of healing, packing a .22 caliber Smith & Wesson pistol in a holster and a pouch of Beech-Nut chewing tobacco in my shirt pocket. I had decided to live in the image of the very cowboys I admired. The realities of that life turned out quite differently. The sweet-tasting Beech-Nut chew produced savory juices I endeavored to spit in a nonchalant manner, but I dribbled on my chin, stained my shirt, and nearly passed out as the nicotine entered my stomach, causing nausea and dizziness. The pistol flopped around on my hip, creating unwelcome discomforts. It wasn't long before neither the pistol nor the Beech-Nut were part of my accoutrement.

The only time I used the pistol was on a ride back to the cabin one evening. Circling around a small reservoir, I spotted a young buck taking a drink. When he saw me, he raised his head and stared. I unholstered the pistol and fired a single shot that nailed him between the eyes. The buck went down like a sack of cement, but the cowboy in me was too green to know what to do next. I raced back to the cabin to report the kill. This was not deer season, so my colleagues were more than a little apprehensive about game wardens. We drove back to the reservoir where the men immediately cut open the animal from breast bone to anus, exposing all its slimy innards. As I kneeled down to assist, one of the cowboys put his hand on the back of my neck and shoved my face into the animal's guts. This was my initiation into the brotherhood of hunters. It happened fast, and it wasn't pretty. Enveloped by the stink and taste of a dead animal, I did my best to continue with the rest of the butchering, but that experience convinced me I would never again shoot a game animal. In short order, my image of the heroic cowboy life had been seriously eroded.

For the most part, I rode ranch horses. Dad provided saddles to us as Christmas presents. We did not know at the time that these saddles actually belonged to the Crystal River Corporation. I wanted my own horse to go with the saddle I thought I owned, so when the foreman told me about a two-year-old black Morgan filly for sale, I jumped. She was beautiful. Sleek, coal black, and unbroken, she communicated a welcoming disposition. I bought her on the spot and called her Midnight. For several weeks, I worked her in a corral, first with a halter, followed by bridle and saddle, and eventually mounting her for brief periods as she became accustomed to me. We seemed to have a good partnership. Her disposition was excellent, and she was beginning to trust me, when I was called back to Cottonwood for work with the cattle.

Midnight

I turned Midnight into a pasture by herself near the main house. When I returned to the ranch, she was lying down, apparently unable to move. A freak electrical storm had passed overhead while I was away. She was struck by lightning and paralyzed. We had to shoot her. There was no possibility of recovery. I was devastated. It was like being in love and losing your lover. I didn't own another horse until many years later when I returned to the CRR in the '60s.

While ranch life involved constant work, Sid and I found ways to squeeze in some recreation. The Diamond J guest ranch in Basalt was owned by Fred McLaughlin. Operating also as a cattle ranch, it attracted visitors who were enamored of the fishing on the Frying Pan River. By the 1950s, the Diamond J was purely a dude ranch. It represented our best chance to find young ladies. Because we worked long hours and most weekends, the McLaughlins considered us unavailable for socializing. We were seldom invited to the dances and other entertainments.

Finding ourselves free one Saturday evening, Sid and I decided to drive up to the Diamond J for a little mischief. We loaded up the trunk of Dad's Buick with rotten apples and headed for the dance. Arriving at dusk, we parked the car on the road overlooking the outdoor dance floor. It was decorated with Japanese lanterns, and we could clearly see the young couples beginning to prance around the dance floor about 75 yards away. For the next minutes, we launched apples at the dancers below, reveling in the squishy sound they made as they landed on the wooden surface.

Our amusement was short lived. We noticed a trail of dust heading our way from the ranch house. Whatever it was, we had to get out of there in a hurry. Sid and I jumped into the Buick, turned it around on that narrow road and headed out. When we hit the main washboardy, dirt road to Basalt, we could see a pair of headlights through the plumes of dust behind us. We were being followed. Gradually, as our own speed rose precariously to 85 mph, the lights appeared less frequently, and by the time we reached the hard surface Highway 82 back to Carbondale, our pursuer was nowhere to be seen. We had escaped.

Almost! It was well after 10 p.m. by the time we arrived at the CRR. We parked the car and retired to the bunkhouse to get a few winks before the next day's work at 6 a.m. Everything seemed normal as we returned to our haying chores the next day. We laughed about our miracle get-away until we saw the tell-tale dust rising from a vehicle coming down the dirt road to the hayfields. It was still morning; not the usual time for Dad to be making a visit.

Uh-oh! Apparently, Fred McLaughlin had seen enough of the Buick to suspect who the party crashers were. He called Dad, who wasted little time putting the facts together. "Think you know why I'm here," he announced.

"Yes sir," we replied in chorus.

"Well, you can return to the house, change your clothes, and go apologize to Mr. McLaughlin. You will be docked two days' pay."

We did just that. The encounter in Fred McLaughlin's living room was tense. He was mad. It took a lot of creative apologizing before he let us off the hook. Sid was better at apologizing. I still nursed a grudge against the Diamond J for not inviting us to their dances. But what we did was reprehensible. There was no adequate explanation, and I knew we would be persona non grata at the Diamond J for the rest of the summer. Dad never mentioned the incident again. He wasn't a great admirer of Fred McLaughlin, and I always suspected he was somewhat amused by what we had done.

I say that because on other occasions, he seemed to get a kick out of our mischievous behavior. Two examples may illustrate the point. On our first trip west after Dad's return from military service, we passed through the little town of Pagosa Springs—Mum and Dad, Sid and me. We spent the night in a rundown motel which was so dilapidated that when Sid and I roughhoused on the bed, it broke. We jumped on it to complete the destruction. Dad thought this was amusing, because he thought the motel had overcharged us for its rundown condition. On another occasion, we took a picnic trip to the old mining town of Ashcroft, above Aspen. After eating, Sid, Rob, and I proceeded to tear down the old houses that were barely standing. Historic preservationists would have had a fit, but at the time, it seemed a fitting and fun family activity. Dad was amused. Perhaps his inner child was being allowed freedom after a very rigorous and formal upbringing.

With the Diamond J off limits, I found other ways to meet girls. Shortly after Sid had been presented a new 1950 Chevy Belair two-door coupe from Granny Tyler, Mum and Dad surprised me with a 1927 Model T Ford. This was a very nice gift. I was 17, nuts about girls, and fascinated by a piece of machinery that was both historic and eye catching. The engine overheated, the drive bands slipped, and the magneto malfunctioned with regularity. But on a Saturday night in Carbondale, I had my pick of ladies who wanted to "go for a ride." I installed a ten-gallon can on the roof with a hose to cool the radiator, and I carried bands for the transmission to replace those that heated up and slipped. Throttle and spark were both on the steering column, the clutch, reverse, and break pedals were on the floorboard. That Mountain T required constant coordination from two feet and two hands, but it moved right along and had a great horn that I leaned on with impunity.

The biggest challenge was getting back to the ranch after a night of carousing. After crossing the Crystal River on a bridge, the

1927 Model T, Rob on fender, David Lowry hanging on door, 1950

road home ascended a 500-foot hill to the mesa top. Because the forward drive gear bands were smoking hot by the end of the evening, and it was too dark to install replacements, I usually turned the T around and headed home in reverse. The reverse bands were cool and worked fine, but backing up that long hill and continuing about a mile on the straight road to the ranch headquarters required agility at night, especially if I was in a hurry. Curfew was 11 p.m.

"What can you possibly do after the bowling alley closes?" my mother used to ask. Assuming she really didn't want to know, I never answered that question, but I did make an effort to return on time, and that meant I was usually going fast and erratically in reverse as I covered the last mile home. Mum waited at the large glass window of the main house which overlooked the county road on which I had to return. With binoculars she could make out my red light, weaving back and forth erratically. She was convinced I had been drinking. In fact, I was just trying to meet our agreed upon curfew. I was driving backwards, for Pete's sake!

I ended up with different girlfriends each summer. One of them, a Mormon gal from Utah who visited a local family just below the ranch, frequently found her way to the hay fields with a friend. She was attractive, buxom, and flirtatious. We had a few dates in Carbondale, and when she had to return to Salt Lake City, I took her to the train station in Glenwood Springs. Surprisingly, Mum and Dad allowed me to visit her in Utah when the summer was over. I knew nothing about the Church of Latter Day Saints, but the family's lukewarm hospitality suggested that I wasn't entirely welcome. In their eyes, I was a Gentile, so nothing would ever come of the infatuation. But it was a heady experience for me that was followed by a six-month exchange of letters. Hers were perfumed. When they arrived, I knew I was in love.

Another girl I dated worked in a restaurant in Glenwood Springs. We came to know each other the summer I took flying lessons at the local airport. We dated regularly. I had one objective in mind, the pursuit of which was probably my parents' greatest worry. After picking her up from work one evening, we went to a campsite called Grizzly Creek. I was determined to lose my virginity, and I had enough sense to use protection. After ejecting the evidence out the window of my parents' car, I returned my date to her house. We said goodbye in the car, and she entered her home alone. I headed back to the ranch.

After returning the car to the garage, I went to my bedroom in the bunkhouse, hung up my clean clothes, and jumped in bed. Early the next morning, I put on my work clothes and headed over to the shop. When I returned to wash up for lunch, I saw that my mother had been in my room tidying up and gathering laundry as she did on occasion. To my horror, I also noted that my clean jeans were still hanging in the bathroom with a condom stuck to the back pocket. Apparently, the car window had been closed when I tried to toss out the condom. Instead of finding a home in a bush, it landed on the edge of the front seat and stuck to my pants. As embarrassed as I was at the thought that my mother might have seen this, I was relieved to have escaped even greater embarrassment: I might have gone into my date's home with the damn thing stuck to my pants, or I might have left the condom on the seat of my parents' car. Both possibilities left me with the realization I would have to be far more prudent in the future. Characteristically, Mum never said anything.

Ranch life in general did not allow for a regular social life. I enjoyed the work—haying and cowboying—and I learned a lot during the summers I was employed at the CRR. But there were a few summers I did other things.

In 1948, Granny Tyler offered to take Sid and me, along with first cousins, Molly and Winky West (children of Dad's sister, Molly and her husband Harry West), to Europe. I didn't want to go. Travel abroad held no interest for me, although I was always happy to be around Winky. She had a good sense of humor and just enough mischief to be a lot of fun. So I agreed to go.

Travel arrangements were not restricted by a budget. Granny was accustomed to being attended by servants. Her butler, Frederic Banks, came along with us. Our itinerary was simple and elegant: depart New York with first-class accommodations on the *Queen Mary;* visit Paris, Montreux, and London; return on the *Queen Elizabeth.*

Readers will recall that WWII had ended only four years previously, but because the purpose of the trip was for Sid, our cousins, and me to experience European culture, we saw no signs of that devastating conflict. Instead, we went to Versailles, the Tuileries gardens, the Eiffel Tower, London's cathedrals, Westminster Palace, and the viniculture of Lake Geneva. Granny also escorted us to the

Folies Bergère. A cabaret performance launched 80 years earlier, it featured mostly nude dancers. I was enthralled, but I had a hard time enjoying the performance, because I was sitting next to my grandmother. Fantasies emerged in my head but disappeared quickly.

Sid and I managed to get away by ourselves on occasion. We visited bars, drank too much wine, and got ripped off by cab drivers who knew we had no idea where we were most of the time or what a franc was worth. Banks accompanied us on occasion, leading us to the watering holes he had frequented in earlier years as a young Englishman sowing his oats. The explorations were memorable, but during the three weeks we were in Europe, we rarely encountered signs of the upheaval that had nearly destroyed European civilization. Ours was a tour of *privilège*.

Because the summer had been shortened by our sojourn in Europe, I decided to study for my private pilot's license and work at the Glenwood Springs airport when we returned to Colorado. Airplanes had always fascinated me. As a child, I made dozens of balsa wood models powered by rubber bands. When I was sick and forced to stay in bed, my mother would bring me what I needed to design my own crafts, build the frame with toothpicks, and cover the body with toilet paper.

With Dad's approval, I took flying lessons in a Piper PA-18 Super Cub. It was a two-seater, fixed-wing aircraft. My instructor sat in the rear seat. We flew together two or three times a week, doing chandelles and lazy eights, emergency landings, spins, and short cross-country flights to Basalt, Aspen, and Gypsum. When not flying myself, I gassed up visiting aircraft, kept the hanger clean, and responded to any and all service requests from pilots and maintenance people. It seemed like a soft life compared to ranch work: 8 a.m. to 5 p.m. six days a week with time off to go into town or swim in the Roaring Fork River.

PA-18

I soloed near the end of the summer. Without the weight of an instructor in the back seat, that little Piper Cub felt like someone was trying to push the tail skyward. But I did well with my three solo landings and soon prepared for a cross-country flight. This would be the last obstacle before earning my private pilot's license. I chose a triangular route from Glenwood Springs to Montrose to Grand Junction and home. I was required to land in each place and have my logbook signed. I departed Glenwood Springs early in the morning to avoid cumulonimbus clouds that built up during the day and to take advantage of the denser morning air. I had to fly over several peaks in the Elk Mountain Range that reached 14,000 feet. Warm air and altitude were not friendly to that little Super Cub.

I chose a cruising altitude of 16,000 feet to be safe. The FAA now requires planes to carry oxygen when they exceed 10,000 feet. That rule may have been in effect in 1950, but my instructor didn't appear concerned when I shared my flight plan with him. The Super Cub has a service ceiling of 19,000 feet, but it gets a little wobbly 3,000–4,000 feet below that, and the heater doesn't work very well.

Consequently, I arrived over Montrose an hour after takeoff, shivering from the cold. I tried to lose altitude quickly, but the lift on the wings of that little plane made rapid descent difficult. I didn't have flaps to increase my glide angle, so I orbited the Montrose airport for a very long time. When I was ready to touch down on the runway, I had so much airspeed, the Super Cub just bounced.

Montrose tower: "Yellow Super Cub, are you planning to pay us a visit, or are you doing a low level fly by?"

Me: "Gonna go around, sir, and try again."

Montrose Tower: "That would be advisable. This is not a race track or a basketball court, and we would be charmed to have you pay us a real visit."

Me: "Roger sir. I can do that."

Montrose Tower: "That remains to be seen. We won't hold our breath, but if you are serious, we recommend a reduction of speed and commitment to a full stop landing."

The go-around and landing were just fine. I had been well trained. I parked the plane, endured teasing from the good ol' boys who had been having fun at my expense, got my logbook signed, and readied myself for immediate takeoff. I was way behind schedule for arrival in Grand Junction, 50 nautical miles to the north.

Grand Junction was a busier airport, but I was cleared to land by the tower and came to a full stop without incident. Parking at the gas pump, I noticed that the clouds had built up in the vicinity of my route back to Glenwood Springs. Some were showing moisture-laden tops, and pilots in the area were reporting light hail. Without any instrument training, I was skeptical about a VFR (visual flight rules) return to base, so with tail squarely between my legs, I called my instructor and asked him to come get me. He arrived an hour later, not in a particularly good mood. It was pretty quiet in that

Super Cub as we dodged storm clouds on the return flight. We arrived at the airport safely. My instructor gave me a passing grade, but I was embarrassed and determined to be a better judge of weather in the future. Not until my Air Force training did I have the opportunity to fly IFR (instrument flight rules), but even then, I made a cross-country blunder that was even more mortifying.

A few weeks after the Grand Junction-Glenwood Springs debacle, I received my private pilot's license. I could take passengers, and Dad insisted on being the first. He had flown in many different aircraft during the war, and although he was a good judge of airmanship, he knew nothing about FAA (Federal Aviation Administration) regulations. Consequently, soon after we took off, Dad wanted us to get down to 500 feet off the ground and proceed to the Crystal River Ranch so he could observe the haying operations. I was nervous about flying so low. The minimum safe altitude for private aircraft was 1,000 feet above the ground, but that rule applied to congested areas. We would not have been in violation of FAA regulations at 500 feet as we flew up the valley, but I was apprehensive about a possible engine failure and eager to return my father to *terra firma* without mishap.

We stayed about 1,000 feet off the ground, just high enough for convection currents to throw us around. Chatter from the back seat dissipated as the Super Cub bounced relentlessly. After a few passes over the hay fields, I decided to return to the airport. Dad was by then a bit queasy. He didn't object, and his condition didn't improve when we entered the landing pattern for the Glenwood Springs airport. Because the valley is quite narrow, and because we were landing to the south, it was necessary to fly close to Red Mountain on the downwind leg. With rising temperatures and a west wind, we were bounced spectacularly close to that sandstone formation before turning onto final approach. Conversation from the back seat ceased entirely, and after a pretty good landing, Dad got out of the plane, murmured something about lousy air, and headed for the men's room. That was our one and only flight together.

The other diversion from summer ranch work occurred after I had completed my junior year at Harvard in 1954. A uranium boom had just begun on Colorado's West Slope. Mining companies were looking for laborers to work as muckers in the mines. At $14 per day, more than twice what Dad paid for ranch work, a mining job seemed a worthwhile adventure. I applied for a job with Gadget Almy, a friend from Harvard. We offered our services to a company that had just developed new mines at Dead Horse Point on the Colorado River, not far from Moab, UT. We were accepted on the payroll with the understanding we would work a cycle of 10 days at the mine, followed by four days off.

Our principal function was to load the muck (ore) into wheelbarrows after each dynamite blast, dumping the loads outside the mine entrance onto large piles where the material was assessed for radioactivity. The deeper we went into the mountain, the longer the distance from the mine face to the dump pile. And the faster we shoveled up the muck, the sooner another round of holes could be drilled, packed with dynamite, and ignited. There wasn't much time for rest. The mine had no fresh air supply, and the chunks of rock we sat on to eat our lunches made the Geiger counters bleep like rattlesnakes, a result of Alpha and Gamma radiation. The mine shafts in which we worked were only occasionally supported by timbers, and sometimes, only six or seven of the eight holes drilled would explode, leaving us on the lookout for undetonated blasting caps. But working inside the mine wasn't all bad: we enjoyed a reprieve from the outside heat that soared well over 100 degrees. Besides, we were

Mining camp, Dead Horse Point, Colorado River

building muscle, making good money, and participating in a Wild West uranium boom.

Dead Horse Point was located in the Utah desert, several hundred feet above a gooseneck on the Colorado River. In the evening, after the sun went down, the heat radiating outward from the surrounding rocks and sand remained stifling. Inside our tents and mosquito nets at night, sweat was a constant companion. Bathing in the river provided temporary relief, but the Colorado was so loaded with silt that a bath amounted to an exchange of one layer of dirt for another.

We were generally innocent about the risks of our job. Exposure to high levels of radiation could have caused sterilization or cancer. Thrusting a shovel into a detonator cap might have resulted in loss of a limb. Cave-ins were always a threat. But the time we were at greatest risk occurred one day after lunch when we were settling in for a nap in our tents. Almost everyone had left the mess hall for a siesta. The one exception was the bulldozer driver who continued clearing boulders off the road up to the mine, about 250 feet over our heads.

Shortly after beginning our naps, a ten-ton boulder was loosened above us. It came crashing down through the camp, narrowly missing us, and ripping a path through the middle of the mess tent. The cook was apoplectic. All of his equipment was ruined. He marched up the hill with a knife in each hand, determined to rip the heart out of the dozer operator. Fortunately, he was restrained, but his intended victim had to be removed from camp to avoid a possible homicide.

Exiting mine with a load of muck

Fountain Valley School

In the fall of 1948, Sid and I enrolled at Fountain Valley School in Colorado Springs—Sid as a junior or Fifth Form, me as a sophomore or Fourth Form. Dad didn't want us to attend Carbondale schools, and he no longer wanted to send us back east to Brooks. Francis "the Duke" Froelicher, who had been FVS headmaster since the school's founding in 1930, was an impressive figure. He had been lured to Colorado from the Avon Old Farms School in Connecticut by Elizabeth Sage Hare and Spencer Penrose. They wanted a school that offered a progressive education, one that focused on learning by doing, problem solving, group collaboration, social responsibility, democracy, and life-long learning skills. Compared to traditional college preparatory curricula that focused on classical studies, the FVS program was more experiential, suitable to the varied outdoor activities available in the Rocky Mountain West. Originally known as the Lazy B Ranch, Fountain Valley's 1,600 acres and buildings were converted from a polo pony operation to classrooms, dormitories, and playing fields. Designed by architect John Gaw Meem, an aficionado of the American West's Pueblo Revival architecture, FVS was home to approximately 160 male boarders in grades nine to twelve.

When Sid and I arrived, the school had been growing steadily since its founding in 1930. Many of the teachers had been hired away from Avon Old Farms by Froelicher. There was little turnover. The Duke was admired and looked up to—literally. Well over six feet, always impeccably dressed in coat and tie, he was a unifying figure for faculty and students. Visible most days with the school's mascot, a Great Dane (also called Duke) at his side, the Duke perambulated around the campus, showing particular interest in sports. He led mountain-climbing expeditions, attended football, baseball, and hockey contests, and he taught both history and public speaking. He was soft-spoken, thoughtful, and erudite. He was a good teacher, but what I remember most about him was the power of his quiet presence. Although he occasionally appeared austere to students, he was approachable, interested in our lives, and gentle. His example had a profound impact on my own life and the values I continue to espouse. His leadership style was one I have tried to embrace most of my life.

Unfortunately, the Duke had a drinking problem. We could smell the alcohol when he came to class at 8 a.m. in the morning to teach public speaking. It didn't concern us at the time, but the student chatter was embarrassing to the faculty. Word soon got out to the trustees that the headmaster was drinking. They fired him in the middle of my senior year. I was president of the student council at the time. With the school's leader gone, the faculty anticipated trouble from the student body. But most of us realized that FVS was a lot more than its headmaster. After a short period of instability, students rallied to help the faculty get through the remainder of the school year. It was an interesting period for me, because I had to learn how to accept and understand the faculty's responsibilities while preserving the loyalty of my classmates. I was challenged, but I learned a great deal about leadership from the experience.

I was happy at FVS. Classes were small, teachers were house parents, coaches, and tutors. The athletic program was well developed, giving me an opportunity to play football, hockey, and baseball, The school had traditions and formalities, but it was far more relaxed than Brooks. Its western orientation was preserved through the continuation of ranch operations: haying, cattle raising, and horses. Students assisted with ranch chores and participated in competitive gymkhana, the highlight of which was the annual

With Dave Lowry #21 and Grampy

FVS hockey starters

competition with the Thacher School of Ojai, CA. Event times were exchanged via Western Union telegrams to determine winners.

I captained the baseball team, co-captained the football team with brother Sid, and played hockey at the famous Broadmoor Ice Palace.

In baseball and football, we competed with small schools and with the B teams of larger schools. But in hockey, a sport just coming into its own in Colorado, we faced off with three other high schools and the Colorado College junior varsity. Practice times were often very early or very late, because the Broadmoor had the only sheet of ice south of Denver. But going to the Broadmoor, where girls from Colorado Springs often came to watch us practice and play, was a real bonus for FVS boarding students. My first serious girlfriend, Viola "Vi" Ryder, came into my life as a result of hockey.

Vi risked a lot by dating what her male classmates at Palmer High School referred to as a "Fountain Valley Fairy." She had a great sense of humor and was more than willing to join her friend Hanna Langdon (daughter of a former FVS teacher) on trips from town to FVS so we could sneak out for a few hours. Hanna dated my best friend, David Lowry, who later married cousin Winky West. Vi and Hanna came to our games, invited us to their homes, and were our "steady" companions throughout the FVS years. We double-dated frequently.

Academically, I was a very mediocre student. History was my worst subject. I didn't enjoy reading, and I was bored by the dynastic histories of European nations. One of my instructors, E. J. Smith, was a prince of a guy who had married Betty Froelicher, one of the Duke's daughters. He tried everything he could think of to make me a better student, but I was too immature. In class, he was boring, overly intellectual, and distant. Because his classroom was on the ground floor of the old ranch barn, we had access through open windows. After Mr. Smith took roll, one of us would sneak out

With F. Martin Brown and Jean Tyler, 1970s

the window and re-enter class through the door. The first reappearance of a student he had already marked present clearly confused Mr. Smith, but the second and third times it happened usually prompted punishment. The prank got old after a while.

I did like geomorphology. The subject was taught by F. Martin Brown, who had come to FVS with the Duke in 1930. He was a curious scientist with a great deal of energy. When he taught us how to read geological maps with stereopticons, I was hooked. He also told good stories about his wartime experiences, and how he and the school's first students built a glider on FVS grounds that actually flew. He was a brilliant entomologist, paleontologist, and cartographer. The hands-on learning he incorporated into teaching outside of class reflected the progressive educational philosophy embraced by the school's founders.

I became president of the student body, because my classmate, Rod McWhinney, had been caught drinking in Colorado Springs. He would have been the students' first choice, but he was suspended for his sins. I was next in line and was very glad to get the job. I embraced leadership. As head of the student body, my behavior required improvement, but my classmates were schemers. Not many days went by without a prank being played on someone. My nickname was the Deal, because I was known for planning legal and illegal escapades well in advance of the weekends when we had no sports-related responsibilities.

The Deal heading out.

A group of football team jocks started The Gridiron Club in the basement of an old ranch house located on the backroad to the school. There was a lot of drinking, about which I was quite aware. Other classmates contacted girlfriends in town and persuaded them to drive to the school at midnight for joy riding. On more than one occasion, I witnessed students shinnying down a tree after lights-out so they could meet these ladies on the backroad. Because the school nurse was young and attractive, she was visited regularly by several "sick" students who wanted a lot more than medication. Her reluctance to be firm was viewed as encouragement. I heard stories about what happened in the infirmary, but I was unable to corroborate them. In my new role, I tried to turn a deaf ear to the shenanigans, but in a relatively small community, that proved difficult. Being a prankster myself, it was difficult to ignore what was going on, but I knew I had to separate myself from these extracurricular activities in order to preserve a nexus between myself as representative of the student body and the faculty. Fortunately, the man who assumed leadership of the school after the Duke was fired was Dwight Perry, the French teacher. He was a very buttoned-down, proper, and principled individual. He also possessed an uncanny sense of student behavior. He knew very well what was happening and how my job was made difficult by a student body looking for excitement. He encouraged me to be non-judgmental with my peers and to seize on every occasion to promote a good image of FVS. He knew that success would require tiptoeing around things that shouldn't be happening while trying to set a good example for those who would listen. I was flattered by the confidence he showed in me, the gentle manner in which he allowed me to figure things out for myself, and his warm support when we scored small victories. From him, I learned even more about what good leadership entails.

A fortnight prior to graduation, Mr. Perry called me into his office to tell me that I would not receive the school's highest honor, the Colgate Cup. That award had been bestowed on Sid the previous year, and I was hoping to follow in his footsteps. I was devastated by the news. But one of the criteria was academic excellence, and my grades were barely mediocre. In fact, Mr. Perry had suggested to Dad that I not apply to Harvard; even if I was accepted, he argued, the work would be too difficult for me. The Colgate Cup was for those who excelled in all phases of school life. I had no right to expect it. Still, the news hit me hard. I was unable to comprehend at the time that Mr. Perry was doing me a favor. I would have been hurt far more had I gone to graduation believing that I would be honored with the school's highest honor. Instead, I could go to graduation without having my expectations dashed. What happened that day was far more memorable for me. Before any awards were handed out, Mr. Perry got up to say that we had had a tough year with the loss of Froelicher. The school suffered a blow from which recovery was not easy. He went on to say that the student body held together and surpassed behavioral expectations as a result of my leadership. It was such a personal, profound, and unexpected expression of gratitude that I almost burst into tears.

That moment was very powerful for me. It still stands out in my memory. Ever since, I have tried to honor and acknowledge the merits of other people, especially when their good deeds might have been overlooked or forgotten in the rush of daily life. Mr. Perry's little speech was a nice ending to my three years at FVS. I have never regretted not receiving the Colgate Cup.

Harvard

Disregarding Dwight Perry's recommendation, Dad insisted I apply to Harvard. For him, the Harvard experience would enable his male children to maintain appropriate connections through education, clubs, and the Boston social environment, all of which would establish credentials for entry into "the proper circles." I thought I could compete in sports at a smaller school. I was accepted at Williams College, the University of Virginia, and Harvard. At the time, I was sure that Dad had paid off the Harvard admissions people, but he always denied it. And when I told him I preferred Williams, he made clear his position: if Williams was my choice, I would pay for the experience myself. He would only pay for Harvard. Sid was there, and it would be nice to have his guidance. But to this day, I do not understand how I managed to be accepted. In all likelihood, the window was still open for legacies like me. Harvard expected to receive a substantial donation from Dad, which they received at the time of his death. Rejecting me might have jeopardized that gift. I also represented a small percentage of students from the West which Harvard was trying to woo in order to diversify the dominant eastern boarding school population. Whatever Harvard's admissions used as criteria for my acceptance, it has always puzzled me that my children and those of my siblings who applied were not even awarded space on a waitlist. They are far smarter and were more qualified than I was when they applied. But then again Harvard never received from me a promise of future donations.

As Mr. Perry predicted, I struggled with many aspects of my first year at Harvard. I was assigned to Matthews Hall, one of the old houses on the Yard that date back to the 18th century. My roommate,

Doc, was the son of a liquor dealer in Little Rock, AR. We hit it off well enough, but he was a night owl, and I was—and still am—a morning person. We didn't have a lot in common. The third-floor room was spartan and breezy. A common bathroom was at the end of the hall, and the noises from above and below persisted until late at night. My classes were large and of little interest. The one subject I expected to do well in, Latin, turned out to be way over my head. By the end of the first semester, I thought I might not make it. But I got the hang of things after Christmas break. I reunited with an old friend from Cape Cod days, Phillips Perera, and soon found myself with a new circle of friends. Phil's parents lived in Boston. He drove a 1948 Cadillac that could carry large numbers of besotted classmates. We attended parties in Boston, went duck hunting and skiing, and traveled to surrounding colleges in style. I also had a car. Granny Tyler gave new cars to her grandsons and coming out parties to her granddaughters, a gift selection that would surely cause resentment today. My car was a 1951 black and yellow Chevrolet Bel Air two-door hardtop with a six-cylinder engine. It was reliable transportation between Colorado and Cambridge, and it carried me all over New England. But when friends gathered, Phil's Cadillac was our vehicle of choice. With gas selling at 27 cents a gallon, we weren't concerned about operating costs.

Phil and I decided to room together in Leverett House our sophomore year. My grades were passing, I made the freshman baseball team, and I finally felt comfortable in the Harvard community. As we began what would be a three-year residency in Leverett, Phil and I decided to seek membership in the Fly Club, one of Harvard's final clubs. For several generations, Tylers had belonged to the Fly; Sid was already a member. As with most final clubs, the Fly had once been a national fraternity. Its original function was to provide a place where students could get better food than what was served by the university. But along with this pragmatic goal, the clubs organized to preserve a certain lifestyle known mostly to eastern prep school students and children of the Boston, Philadelphia, and New York Social Register. When Phil and I launched ourselves into the "punching season," we gave no thought to the club's policies against admitting women, Jews, or Blacks. The decade of the '50s was not known for intense social reflection regarding equality, justice, and opportunity. We reveled in the post-war economic boom and desired only the good times that privilege made possible. Harvard's student body was more diverse than that of Yale or Princeton, but it was all too easy for sons of the wealthy to isolate themselves in groups made up of their own kind.

The Fly Club invited Phil and me to join. We accepted. With a comfortable clubhouse that provided a library, billiard tables, great meals, and a full bar, it was a place where about 40 members enjoyed intense camaraderie that turned into lifelong friendships. I parked my car at the club, studied in the library, and met alums who became contacts after graduation. I was elected president in my senior year. Although I would now suggest that present-day Harvard sophomores think twice about belonging to a final club, I look back on my own association with The Fly as one of great pleasure and intellectual stimulation.

Academically, things improved toward the end of my sophomore year. I chose political science as a field of concentration. I had heard that it required a certain understanding of law. At the time, I was thinking ahead to possible careers I might pursue, and law school was in the back of my mind. As part of Harvard's tutorial system, I was assigned to Fred Holborn, a young instructor who was completing his Ph.D in political science. His tutorial was made up of

The Fly Club

five students, all of whom were taking much the same classes. We met with Fred weekly to go over course material and to prepare for exams. When I first met him, Fred was also writing speeches for a Massachusetts state senator by the name of Jack Kennedy. One member of our tutorial, who never showed up, was Jack's brother, Teddy. In fact, Teddy was absent from most of his classes. He was a year ahead of me and known as something of a playboy. I remember clearly when he was suspended from Harvard for paying people to take his exams.

    Fred taught me the meaning of engagement in teaching. I soon realized that his personal interest in each one of us extended far beyond the classroom. He invested intellectually and emotionally in our success, and when I did well on a final exam in constitutional law, he came to my room in Leverett House and left a warm note of congratulation on my door. I probably did not realize it at the time, but Fred was a role model for my decision to become a teacher.

>   Winthrop G-22
>   January 31st
>
> Dan,
>
>   I cannot let this day slip away without setting
> down these few lines which very inadequately express
> the heartening pleasure your almost breathless
> visit this noon brought me. Amid the tedium and
> seemingly wasted hours of exam blues your news
> did perhaps as much to raise my spirits as they
> did yours.
>
>   Grades in themselves mean but little and are
> soon deservedly lost epitaphs. This grade in 124,
> however, is surely emblematic of something a
> little bigger for you--of hopes and efforts rewarded,
> knowledge of a job well done, appreciation of a
> hard challenge surmounted. This is also the kind
> of moment that reassures the fellow at the teaching
> end that he is in the best and most satisfying
> profession. Small as this event was on the
> surface, it was nevertheless one of the highspots
> of my short career. Long shall I remember the
> quick gait and broad grin that marked your coming
> this noon--just as all term we have all immensely
> enjoyed our association with you.
>
>   I cannot commend you enough for this fine
> achievement. I only wish my own small efforts
> could have measured up half as well.
>
>   Congratulations!
>
>   *Fred*

Fred Holborn letter

I look back on Harvard as a formative period in my life. I should have been far more grateful to my father for insisting that I matriculate in Cambridge, but youth and wisdom are seldom easily conjoined. As a freshman, I was far too immature to take advantage of everything the college offered, but the high quality of undergraduate teaching, the diversity of the student body, and off campus opportunities afforded by the Boston community made for four memorable years. Additionally, Harvard was a connecting point to other learning experiences. I learned how to crew on an oceangoing yacht, skied the famous Tuckerman's Ravine in New Hampshire's White Mountains, experienced urban life in Boston, New York, and Philadelphia, and dated several interesting 'Cliffies, one of whom was Toni Paepcke. She was the daughter of Walter Paepcke, founder of the Aspen Institute, the Aspen Skiing Corporation, and the Aspen Music Festival. Toni was smart and beautiful, a graceful skier, and a woman I always felt would remain just out of reach. I took her on a ski trip to New Hampshire where I realized she was far more "woman" than I was prepared for. We went our separate ways, but I always had fond memories of our brief romance.

The Harvard experience also gave me an opportunity to develop an avuncular relationship with the children of Dick Harper (my mother's younger brother) and his wife Anne Bullivant Harper in Milton, MA. My nieces and nephews ranged in age from two to ten, and I visited their home on weekends, not only to provide free babysitting, but to occasionally dress up and serve dinners as the family butler. The home environment was a nice break from college. For Dick and Anne, my visits provided occasional assistance with the chores of raising four children: Virginia "Cookie", Patty, Rick, and Stuart.

In my junior year, Dick and Anne orchestrated another important event in my life. They told me about an attractive woman who often came to visit friends nearby. She was about my age, they surmised, and her name was Jean Theopold. She was completing training to become a Registered Nurse. We arranged a meeting and began dating shortly thereafter.

Jean was the second of five girls in the Theopold family. Her father, Philip, was a Harvard graduate and successful investment banker in Boston. He was affable, welcoming, and fun to be around. I am so pleased that one of my grandsons now bears his name. Sadly, I recall wishing that my own father had Uncle Phil's personal qualities. We got along well, and I enjoyed every minute in his company. Jean's mother, a superb tennis player, was a bit austere, opinionated, and occasionally sharp-tongued. The family had a commodious home in Dedham and a farm in New Hampshire where I loved to go in the fall for quail hunting, hikes in the woods, and an occasional ski trip.

Mum and Dad were pleased I had met a lady of "proper" lineage. Dad had not been enthusiastic about my relationship with Vi, and I rarely shared information regarding friendships with other ladies because of his critical attitude. He worried, of course, that I might end up with a woman who was not, in his view, socially acceptable. As silly as this may seem today, that mark of social respectability was important to him and even to Mum, although she tended to be a lot less critical. I was relieved that I had found someone I liked whose family would be acceptable to my parents. Even though I now realize I was far too young to think about marriage, I proposed to Jean believing I was in love and that I would have parental blessing. We were engaged in the spring of 1954 and married on June 18, 1955, two months before my 22nd birthday.

Looking back 68 years later, I realize how naive I was about marriage and family at the tender age of 22. But the wedding celebration in Dedham was a festive and harmonious family occasion that launched the two of us on a journey lasting 20 years. We honeymooned at the Hotel Hana Maui, traveling to the Hawaiian

Islands on the Matson Company's luxurious liner, *Lurline*. It was the same ship on which I had traveled previously with my parents when I was about five years old. Jean confessed to being homesick but got over it, and we enjoyed a 10-day Hawaiian vacation before coming back to an apartment we had rented in Dedham. Just days prior to the wedding, I had received an officer's commission in the United States Air Force, but due to a lack of immediate openings at any of the flight training schools, I was forced to fill the interval with a job my father-in-law helped me secure at the First National Bank of Boston.

At the bank, I was charged with the responsibility of burning the coupons of expired bonds. Every day for six months, I showed up for work in coat and tie, rolled up my sleeves, and headed for the basement furnace. With relatively few breaks, I heaved enormous quantities of bonds into the fire. Older employees took time to teach me certain aspects of their jobs, but for the most part, I was relegated to a dead-end job. As the months passed, I became increasingly annoyed. To me, it felt like lining hay bales all over again. Why couldn't a Harvard graduate be given more responsibility? I wrote a letter to the bank president, a close friend of my father-in-law. He replied politely, noting that I had offered no indication that banking might be a career for me and that if I had changed my mind, he would be delighted to start me on a regular training program. He was right. My goal was to be a fighter pilot. I looked down on banking as a career, and it showed.

Fortunately, I soon heard from the Air Force. I was told to report for primary flight training at Graham Air Base, Marianna, FL, in the spring of 1956. It would be a while before I realized that the banking experience had provided me with a much needed and overdue lesson in humility. The first of many.

Wedding, June 18, 1955

United States Air Force

Jean, already pregnant with Dan Jr., and I arrived at Graham Air Base in March. The Air Force had contracted with civilian instructors to teach us how to fly propeller driven aircraft: T-34 and T-28. Not far from the Alabama border, Graham was in the heart of the South. For both of us, this was a first experience living in a culture quite distinct from New England. We rented a house not far from the base and settled in for a six-month stay.

My instructor, Mr. Green, was capable and engaging. He oversaw a table of four students: three cadets and me. He treated us equally and with respect. I had confidence in him and was able to make good progress. The only pending worry was the birth of my first child. I became increasingly nervous, slept poorly, and worried that the birth might occur when I was in the air. I even went to the base doctor, only to be told that I had "First Fatheritis," words that were actually written on my medical records. Apparently, there was no cure, so I did the best I could. A week or so after visiting the doctor, I was flying solo north of the base when I got a call from Graham Tower telling me in a ho-hum voice to return and land. No need to ask why! I landed without incident, drove to the hospital, and welcomed Dan Jr. to the world on July 3, 1956. Jean was fine, and I was most relieved. A new routine for us both commenced with few glitches. Jean was an excellent mother and dedicated wife. She enjoyed the Air Force life.

The remainder of my time at Graham was filled with flying and ground school. We studied aircraft mechanics, navigation, meteorology, safety, and USAF protocol. We flew dual and solo missions, learned basic maneuvers—chandelles, lazy eights, spins,

United States Air Force | 71

T-34 Graham Airbase

T-28 Graham Airbase

With Mr. Green and three cadets, bottom left

stalls, acrobatics, emergency landings—and ventured away from the base on cross-country flights. We flew both day and night. I was apprehensive at first about night flying but gradually came to enjoy the warm glow of cockpit lights, the occasional moonlit landscape, and the steady hum of the engine. It was actually easier to identify major ground features at night, because they were framed by lights, but the first times I went up solo, I was nervous.

Prior to graduation, all students were given a chance to choose the next stage of flight training. Options included single-engine jets, bombers, or helicopters. I chose single-engine jets. I graduated fifth in my class and felt pretty cocky about the next phase of training. The Air Force assigned me to flight training in the T-33 at Webb Air Force Base in Big Spring, TX.

At Webb, all personnel were in uniform. Instructors were a mix of men with varied experiences. The seasoned veterans who had

T-33

been combat pilots in Korea felt deflated by having to serve a few years in the Training Command, and their attitude was negative. They hated the assignment and made no secret of their superiority. Others were young graduates of pilot instructor schools who had never been in combat. My first instructor, John Pratt, was an Annapolis graduate. He was very gung ho and an excellent pilot. He made up for a lack of combat experience with an enthusiasm that was contagious. Fifteen years later, I ran into John again as the chairman of the English department at Colorado State University. What a coincidence!

I still remember my first flights in the T-33. This aircraft was a two-seater version of Lockheed's P-80 Shooting Star, the first jet fighter used in combat. Wearing an oxygen mask for the first time, traveling at much greater speeds, and learning the idiosyncracies of the jet engine were challenges that initially undermined my confidence. There was a lot to get used to, and I had plenty of moments of doubt. But with Pratt's help, I soloed on schedule, passed my instrument test, and thoroughly enjoyed the acrobatic capabilities of the T-Bird.

Webb Air Force Base class, right

Pratt's sense of adventure provided extra thrills. On a dual navigation training flight from Big Spring to Albuquerque, we flew at 500 feet off the ground with a ground speed approaching 400 knots. As the landscape flashed by below, I watched herds of sheep scattering to the sound of the aircraft passing overhead. Herders shook their fists in anger as we roared by. The need for constant elevation adjustments became obvious as we proceeded west. We were too low to benefit from navigational aids. It was an experience in dead reckoning that kept me on my toes. And it was a blast.

But I didn't retain the dead reckoning lessons of that flight. A week or so later, the flight commander, assigned himself to me for a second cross-country trip, this time to New Orleans. Smitty was a hard ass. One of those Korean War vets who disliked every aspect of the Training Command. He was especially hostile toward ROTC (Reserve Officer Training Command) officers in flight training. He had gone through the program as a cadet, an experience he considered far more rigorous than what second lieutenants like me endured. His principal entertainment was to abuse college-educated students whom he viewed as spoiled and privileged. And being a Harvard graduate made things worse.

Aware of his bias, I prepared especially well for the trip. He said little as we took off, arrived at an altitude of 23,000 feet, and established a course for the Big Easy, 800 miles east. I was feeling pretty smug when Smitty's gruff voice on the intercom fractured the steady whoosh sound of the jet engine and wind. "Where are we, Tyler?"

"On course sir," I replied. "Twenty-three thousand feet, heading zero nine zero, estimating the Naval Air Station in one hour." I was on top of everything, I thought.

"I said, where are we, Tyler?" Smitty repeated, impatiently.

I didn't know what else to say, but I had little time to speculate.

"I've got the plane," Smitty announced. The next thing I knew, we were on our backs looking down at the ground. "What the hell do you think that is down there?" he yelled. "It's the damn Mississippi River."

I had not been paying attention to where we were in relation to the ground, i.e. dead reckoning. I had been cozily checking all the instruments, relying entirely on these electronic aids to tell me all I needed to know. Not good.

"You're busted, Tyler."

I was devastated. I made a great landing at the Naval Air Station, but nothing could remove the angst of having failed a flight with the one person who seemed determined to wash me out. And I had to fly back to Texas with him. Not much sleep that night.

When Smitty and I met on the flight line the following morning, I could tell that he was sporting a major hangover. He was grumpy and uncommunicative. When I strapped on my oxygen mask, I knew who would be flying the plane home. The stench of alcohol from a shared oxygen system was so strong it made me queasy, but I sensed that I would not hear from Lt. Smith for a while.

I was right. The return flight was uneventful and without conversation. But had the sleeping giant awoken, I was prepared to identify any and all landmarks as we flew west. The Mississippi River lesson would remain in my mind when I became an instructor pilot. When we landed at Webb, Smitty mumbled about my having passed the checkride. I felt in no way triumphant and fully expected our paths to cross again. Sooner than I would have liked.

I had difficulty with the formation phase of jet pilot training. Flying in close proximity to other aircraft requires a delicate touch on the controls. You have to anticipate movements of the aircraft you are following, and you have to avoid at all cost a mid-air collision. Flying in formation is very graceful, but the experience can be stressful, especially at night or in rough air. I had the tendency to overcorrect. Pratt did his best to smooth me out, but he wasn't successful. He handed me over to Lt. Smith for a checkride. I failed, but I had one last chance with another instructor chosen at random. The Air Force invests a lot of money in its pilots. Being booted out is not only hard on an officer's morale, it is also costly for the government, especially after almost a year of training.

I was nervous. Fortunately, I was assigned to ride with an instructor to whom I had taken a particular liking. He was loose and funny. The Sunday we met for what might have been my last ride in an Air Force jet, he was visibly hung over. I should have expected this. Drinking and flying are mirror images for fighter pilots. Once again, sharing the same oxygen source convinced me I needed to be on my game. When we lined up on the runway, just behind and to the right of the lead aircraft, he said, "Okay lieutenant. You've got it. Show me your stuff."

It was an encouraging tone of voice. I knew he wouldn't sleep, but I felt that he was expressing confidence in me. And I believed we might be in trouble if I couldn't fly the plane. The psychological impact was immediate. I figured out how to be gentle on the controls. I stayed in tight formation the entire flight and best of all, I received an unqualified pass at the end of the ride.

I was ecstatic. My best friend and college roommate, Phil Perera, had washed out of pilot training, because he couldn't fly on instruments in bad weather. I didn't want to follow him into a meaningless assignment for the remaining two years of my Air Force career. I wanted the wings bestowed on pilots at graduation. Flying formation soon became one of my favorite pursuits, and when I transferred to the Army National Guard in Hawaii, I took it upon myself to teach those fixed-wing propeller pilots what they had missed in their own training. For the most part, they were horrified by the experience.

The remainder of my stay at Webb was uneventful. Because my overall grade average had been knocked down by the additional checkrides, I ended up far down the graduation list when the time came to choose a duty station. The most desired gunnery schools were snapped up quickly. When my turn came, I could select between F-86Ds (all-weather fighter interceptors) in Alaska or Instructor Pilot (IP) School in Selma, AL. I chose the latter. I wanted to learn more about the T-33, and the prospect of teaching students how to fly was enticing. Furthermore, the vision I had of flying out of Alaska in foul weather and sub-zero conditions was not compelling. As things turned out, my assignment to Craig Air Force Base in Selma was life-changing. I was proud of the shiny new wings on my chest, eager to improve as a pilot, and looking forward to teaching other students to fly.

Graduation with wings

The biggest change I encountered at Craig was learning to fly the T-Bird from the back seat. Students usually flew that aircraft from the front seat, because they were in training to fly single engine, single-seat fighters. Instructors taught from the back seat. They had all the same instruments and controls, but in the T-33, forward vision was impacted by the presence of the front ejection seat, which extended to the top of the plexiglass canopy. With a helmet on, the instructor pilot in the back seat had limited forward vision. At first, I found this very disconcerting, but I soon realized that in the aft position, the instructor had a better perspective of the plane's yaw and pitch. No wonder my instructors could complete so many acrobatic maneuvers better than I could when I was learning how to fly.

At night, on the other hand, backseat instructors were practically helpless when coming in for a landing. They had to trust student judgment. As the aircraft flared out prior to touchdown, instructors could see absolutely nothing except runway lights zipping by. I soon learned why my instructor at Webb AFB had told me on my first night flight that I was doing really well and could shoot touch-and-go landings myself without the need for a demonstration. Little did I know he was practically blind during the last moments prior to landing.

The back seat had other benefits. Peripheral vision was better. Formation flying and daytime landings were facilitated by being able to see more of the aircraft. On days when the cumulonimbus clouds were relatively small and puffy, we would fly up to them, pull up sharply, roll the jet over, and cruise over the tops upside down. It was great fun—and dangerous. Unseen aircraft in the area might have been attempting the same maneuvers. I never taught my own students to have so much fun, but I continued to play with the clouds even when I flew L-19 aircraft over the Hawaiian Islands. I did have a close call in Hawaii while flying over the Ko'olau Range and from then on, I kept my distance from the fluffy white stuff.

After graduating with an IP (Instructor Pilot) rating from Craig AFB, I was assigned to the 3530th Pilot Training Wing at Bryan AFB just west of College Station, TX. Home of Texas A&M University, College Station was an established community with a diverse population. We rented a house not far from base and made friends, some of whom remained in our lives long after my Air Force assignment ended. The student Aggies were required to say "Howdy!" to everyone they passed on the street. Jean and I were amused by their "Howdy! Howdy!" as they walked by, punctuated by a third "Howdy!" after they realized several steps past that we had Dan Jr. with us. Not too long after we arrived, Nick was born, so we qualified for a fourth "Howdy!" As Jean filled her time raising two boys, I began my first real teaching stint at the base, overseeing students in a T-33 training program identical to the one in Big Spring from which I had graduated a year earlier.

For each class I trained, I was given a table of three students. Their aptitudes varied from naturally good pilots to stiff and mechanical. They were all aviation cadets, not officers, and they led a very disciplined life on base. I had a lot of power over their future, and I was often humbled by their dedication, discipline, and determination. In most ways, they were far safer and easier to fly with than the senior officers who came to the flight line looking for an active-duty pilot like me with whom they could fly in order to qualify for flight pay. They only needed four hours of flight time a month. Most of them had been pilots in WWII or the Korean War. Although they had logged many hours in various aircraft, their reaction time and overall judgment were pathetically lacking. But if I was called to fly with one of them, I had to go. I was always outranked, but I flew in the back seat and was in charge of the aircraft. An awkward arrangement at best.

I was subjected to irresponsible behavior. On one outing, four senior officers requested IPs for a two-hour flight. I was one of the IPs chosen. We rendezvoused in four aircraft over the base and immediately put ourselves in trail position, i.e. the planes were lined up nose to tail. My senior officer and I were number four. All I could see in front of me was the tailpipe of number three. I could feel g-forces as we did loops and rolls, but I had no idea what we were doing until I noted a commercial airliner slide by as we looped over it in trail formation. My senior officer, unable to maintain position, had long since given me control of the aircraft, so I was inadvertently engaging in an illegal and dangerous maneuver. When we returned to base, the IPs were in shock, but the good ol' boys thought it was hilarious. That night at the Officers' Club, I heard them boasting and making fun of us "nervous ninnies." For me, the experience launched a questioning period in which I reassessed my interest in making the Air Force my career.

On another occasion, a senior officer wanted me to join him on a cross-country flight to Oklahoma. When we arrived within radio range of Tinker AFB, the major called the tower for landing instructions. He proceeded to fly us into what he thought was Tinker's landing pattern, but he actually entered the air space of the commercial airport. I decided to say nothing, hoping he would figure it out himself, but when he lined up on final approach going the wrong way, I had to interject. "Excuse me, major," I said, "I'm taking control of the aircraft." I jammed maximum power to the T-33 and made a hard turn right over Will Rogers Airport. About the same time, a voice on the radio from Tinker AFB said they did not have us in sight. The major had reported we were on final approach. True, but at the wrong airport. The major had committed a dumb mistake, but my situation was very delicate. I had to do my best to make sure that he wasn't embarrassed, so I told Tinker we were on our way and would explain upon landing. The major took part of the blame, so he saved his hide. But he left me hanging by implying that he got bad advice. Again, I had to conclude that the quality of the top brass in the USAF was not what I had expected. Compared to those bozos, my students were angelic aces. With them I had only two serious emergencies.

The first occurred on a routine formation flight. I flew the lead aircraft with a student in the front seat, and my other student flew solo on my wing. We climbed to altitude without incident, but when we leveled off, my solo student was nowhere in sight. As a result of his nervous jockeying of the throttle back and forth to remain in good position, the linkage had broken. Automatically, the throttle returned to idle, so he lost speed and fell back. We had radio contact, and he told me he had managed to establish emergency power of 65%, barely enough to maintain altitude as he headed back to base. Although I was unable to see the student, he told me he was on his way home, hoping to have one shot at a landing. Because of the emergency, we changed to a multi-channel radio frequency that allowed everyone in the area to hear our conversation. For the most part, the exchanges were calm. I finally spotted him about five miles from the airfield. He was able to make a large, circular pattern over the base, ending up on final approach with enough altitude to cut the power completely, and descend for what turned out to be a superb dead-stick landing. I was very proud of him. But when I landed, all hell broke loose. The base commander had listened to our 15 minutes of dialog in the air and had determined that I was at fault for not following proper procedures after takeoff. Where he came up with that idea was beyond me, but I soon realized his anger resulted from a fear that an accident would blemish his career and deny him the chance to make general. Shortly after his tirade, the mechanics reported the broken throttle linkage. I was exonerated, but the angry base commander decided he wanted his pound of flesh. He appointed me snack bar officer, a job that required me to keep a refrigerator stocked with his favorite snacks. I did what I was told, bit my tongue, and drifted even farther away from my dream of staying in the Air Force.

A second incident with a student occurred in the winter when we were returning from a cross-country flight in formation with another T-33, piloted by a good friend and his student. About 30 minutes from landing at Bryan AFB, I noticed that the fuel indicator on my reserve tank was beginning to drop. The tank only held 80 gallons; T-Birds burned 180–200 gallons per hour. Normally, a two-hour flight allowed for a reserve of 200 gallons, but the main wing tanks were not feeding, and I was concerned. Actually, I was really worried. I reported the situation to my friend in the other jet. I waggled the wings and did a few maneuvers to see if possibly a float valve was stuck, but to no avail. At 25,000 feet and 200 miles from base, we had a problem. My fellow IP contacted Air Traffic Control noting we had a minor emergency. "It's either an emergency or not an emergency," ATC responded. Everything in the Air Force was based on procedures that differed according to circumstances. "An emergency," we declared. A forced landing or bail out were the only options if we did not get the fuel flowing. No other airfields capable of accommodating a T-33 were available to us any closer than Bryan AFB. Hoping to find a highway or pasture that would suit our needs,

I initiated a slow descent on the wing of the lead aircraft, not wanting to give up any more altitude than necessary, but hoping to get down into warmer air. Passing through 10,000 feet, I saw the fuel gauge on the reserve tank stabilize, then begin to rise. The main tanks were feeding again. Hallelujah! Apparently, the sub-zero temps had caused ice particles to block the main lines. We climbed back to altitude, thanked ATC, and landed at Bryan without further incident. My heart returned to a normal rhythm.

I had other minor incidents, one time thinking I might have to eject when a fire warning light came on. I was near the base, so I returned to have mechanics tell me the problem was in the circuit. False alarm. No sweat…

On another occasion, I was flying to Florida one night with a student in the front seat. As we neared our destination, the weather got nasty. Thunderstorms rose on all sides, and lightning flashed so brightly, it was hard to remain focused on the red light blinking off the left wing of the plane with which we were in formation. In fact, my student couldn't handle the combination of turbulence and disorientation. I had to take over and didn't do much better. By the time we got through the weather and landed, I was soaked in sweat. The experience shook me up.

But I was also gaining confidence the more I flew and in many ways, I felt increasingly at home in the air. I think I probably became a little cocky. Not a good thing because I caught myself cutting corners in a profession where everything goes by the book for a reason.

On a cross-country flight to California with a student, I landed at Albuquerque for a pee break. When my student and I returned to the refueled aircraft, the mechanic told me that one of the plane's two alternators was down. He did not have a replacement and could not get one installed until the next day. As commander of the aircraft, I could override a crew chief's suggestions, but when he wrote in the plane's log that a piece of equipment was out of order, I could not legally take the plane off the ground.

Foolishly, I erased what the crew chief had written, signed the log, and took off for California. I didn't want to wait around Albuquerque with a student I didn't know very well, and I fully believed one alternator was all I needed to get me to California and back home to Texas.

The remainder of the trip went well. I reported the bad alternator when I landed at Bryan and thought I was in the clear. I had not expected the mechanic in Albuquerque to contact my base commander at Bryan. I was surprised to get a call to report to his office ASAP. Having already had an altercation with this officer, I was prepared for the worst. He threatened me with a court martial under Article 231 of the Universal Code of Military Justice. I had broken an Air Force regulation, and I had no defense. Furthermore, in the eyes of a grizzled war veteran who had little patience with an Ivy League ROTC-trained lieutenant, I was dead meat. My punishment was to be assigned as the duty officer at the Officers' Club. This meant I would have to close the club three nights a week at 2 a.m. when the only patrons were the base commander and his toadies. For a young family man who was expected on the flight line at 8 a.m. every morning, this was, indeed, punishment.

For weeks, all went well. But one night, I arrived as usual with an armed MP (Military Policeman) accompanying me. At 2 a.m., I politely advised the officers at the bar that the club was closing. "Sure, lieutenant," they replied. "We'll just have one more drink." I waited until about 2:30 a.m. The senior officers at the bar showed no signs of abdicating their thrones. I was tired and needed sleep. I asked the MP if we could force the closing. "We can do it, lieutenant," he responded, "but you might not like the consequences." I considered what sort of revenge my seniors could manage and ultimately decided that I was in the right and they could only embarrass themselves if they resisted my order to leave the club. From past experience, I had concluded these men were not good leaders. "Kick them out," I ordered the MP. As the men retreated, they glowered at me and uttered obscenities. I really didn't care. For all practical purposes, my dream of an Air Force career was over.

For the next week, I awaited a call from the base commander. It never came. Instead, the base put out a general announcement to the effect that the Air Force had decided to close Bryan AFB. I was given a choice of getting out of the service or being reassigned to Fürstenfeldbruck, a German Airforce base near Munich. I was really excited by this offer. Had I been single, I would have jumped at the opportunity, but with a family to support and a growing lack of respect for Air Force leadership, I decided on a discharge.

Almost immediately, I looked for a high school faculty job. The experience of teaching students to fly convinced me that I could do as well in the classroom as I had done in the cockpit.

Punahou School

I'm not 100% certain how we ended up choosing Punahou School in Honolulu, but I vaguely recall perusing magazines and running across an ad requesting Ivy League graduates to apply in all disciplines. I didn't have a teaching credential required to be able to apply at public schools. Jean and I agreed that eastern preparatory schools would probably view my mediocre Harvard academic record with suspicion. Hawaii, on the other hand, was still a territory in 1958. The private schools were essentially unencumbered by regulations. Although in retrospect I was still young and naive, we felt that our combined experiences—Jean's nursing, my ranching and military service—would be viewed in a positive light by school administrators, allowing us to learn on the job in a place generally considered a paradise. I had memories of at least one Waikiki visit with Mum and Dad in the '30s, and Jean and I had been on Maui for our honeymoon. When Punahou headmaster John Fox sent back a letter saying I was hired, we were ecstatic.

We arrived in June 1958, barely in time for me to teach a summer class of European history. We were provided temporary housing on school grounds in an airy bungalow we learned to share with well-fed cockroaches and mice. I walked a few hundred yards to meetings and classrooms. I soon learned that Fox had hired a total of five young Ivy League graduates: two from Yale, two from Princeton, and me. One of the Princetonians, Bob Torrey, became a very good friend and godfather of our third child, Christopher "Kit" Lii, who was born in Hawaii in October 1962.

Bob and I taught separate classes of the same subject. We were both more enthusiastic than knowledgeable, essentially trying

With Nick, Jean, Bob Torrey, and Dan Jr.

to learn a textbook chapter a day in advance of teaching it to the students. We used every gimmick imaginable to entertain the students: audio visual aids, guest lecturers, skits, geographical puzzles, and anything else we could think of to mask our inexperience. I even took my students out of the classroom with a tape measure to mark the boundaries of the Great Sphinx as if it had been located on the Punahou campus.

    Bob was actually a history major. I had been a terrible history student, both at Fountain Valley and Harvard. My political science background was helpful, but historical interpretation and analysis were absent from my classes for several years as I built up the basic knowledge I should have absorbed during my formal education. I partly corrected the enormous gaps by taking classes at the University of Hawaii. They were helpful. But if I succeeded at all as a young, first-year, high school teacher, it was probably because I was eager and hopeful and able to help the students understand how to learn. Watching Alejandro teach a math class at Arapahoe High School in 2014, I was reminded by his subject knowledge and skill, how poorly prepared I was to teach teenagers.

Punahou was founded in 1841 as a school for the children of missionaries. It had been both a day and boarding school until just before I arrived. Classes were offered from kindergarten through 12th grade, and although other private schools provided high-quality education (Mid Pacific, Iolani, Kamehameha), Punahou was king of the mountain. The facilities then and now are equal to that of a small private college. Some of the old stone buildings have been well preserved; the school's endowment and its loyal alumni have made sure they are well maintained and in first-class condition. Graduates of Punahou attend the best colleges and do well academically and athletically. Bob and I worked together and enjoyed a marvelous friendship. He remained at Punahou longer than I did and taught Barack "Barry" Obama in the years leading up to his graduation in 1979. Bob died in 2021.

I felt challenged in many ways at Punahou. My immediate supervisor was Walter Curtis, principal of the high school. He was a lovely man, tolerant, and patient to a fault. He visited my classes once in a while, never really offering much in the way of advice. He was always kind, reassuring, and helpful. The only criticism I remember was his telling me to take a pack of Lucky Strike cigarettes out of my shirt pocket. I had taken up smoking in the Air Force. The Surgeon General had not yet required warning labels.

After a year living on campus, Jean and I bought a home in Manoa Valley about three miles from the school. If memory serves, we paid $30,000 for the house. Dad provided cash so we could make the down payment. Keahi Place was located where sunny skies generally gave way to clouds and rain. The house could be chilly. Walls were constructed of single pieces of tongue-and-groove pine which bowed back and forth when the wind blew. Because of the dampness, we had our share of scorpions crawling around. Big ones! And we also had a fireplace we used regularly.

But it was a first home and it served our needs. We paid for the construction of protective lava rock stone walls to hold back the moist soil. They were built by stout Samoans. That the walls still stand today with little erosion is testimony to the workmanship of those skilled South Pacific islanders.

At home on the Punahou School campus

I rode a Vespa scooter back and forth to school, sometimes taking Dan Jr. on the back with me as he attended kindergarten and first grade. We also owned a Hillman Minx. Large enough to accommodate all of us, it was a good size for the roads on Oahu which were narrow and windy with posted speed limits of 45 mph.

In addition to my job at Punahou, I transferred from the USAF Reserve to the Army Reserve so I could continue flying. The Air National Guard on Oahu had just received supersonic F-102 interceptor aircraft. This single engine fighter with a maximum speed of Mach 1.25 (almost 1,000 mph at sea level) was more machine than I wanted to deal with on a one-weekend-a-month basis. In contrast, the Army National Guard had several observation planes called Bird Dogs. A fixed-wing aircraft with a single reciprocating engine, this two-seater L-19 had a maximum speed of 115 mph and could land in 50 yards. It was designed by the Army as a spotter aircraft, the pilot "observing" artillery rounds as they exploded near a target. Pilots who flew these aircraft in Vietnam were referred to as "ten second men" due to their vulnerability once the enemy realized who and what was determining the accuracy of the ordnance.

Jim Doole, dean of students at Punahou, was a member of the Army National Guard, and he encouraged me to join. We flew together on Monday nights and one weekend a month. I met other pilots whose company I enjoyed, and I learned about flying fixed wing aircraft in support of ground troops.

During weekends when soldiers were involved in simulated combat maneuvers on the ground, we were expected to fly overhead, dropping quarter-pound sacks of flour to give the grunts a feeling they were being attacked from the air. It was a ridiculous sham, but when I rode in the back seat with a dozen or so bags of flour on the floor, I took the mission seriously. Attempting to hit

L-19 en route to Kilauea Iki volcanic eruption

Piloting the L-19

exposed vehicles by dropping the "bombs" out the plane's open window was a blast.

I did my job well. Too well! After one weekend's exercise, my co-pilot and I were called on the carpet for targeting the Army commander while he was directing his troops in a mock attack. He was paying no attention to the skies, and we nailed him with one of our quarter pounders. From 500 feet, that little bag of flour picked up considerable speed. Apparently, the commander was knocked right out of his Jeep. Humiliating! We received no further requests to "bomb" the troops.

I taught the Army pilots to fly close formation, and they taught me how to land an airplane on a postage stamp. During one ride I had with a major in the back seat, I tired of being chided for the type of landings the Air Force taught me, so after a go-around with the major muttering undisguised obscenities about Air Force pilots, I determined to stick the two front wheels on the first part of a dirt runway just beyond a gaping ditch marking the landing strip's perimeter. I landed as planned, but the aircraft stalled just as we passed over the ditch. The tail wheel did not quite make the runway. The resulting jerk on the rear section of the aircraft caused the propellor to nick the ground as the metal covering on the tail section realigned itself in response to the crash. The major didn't say much. When the plane stopped, almost immediately, he got out, put his foot on the prop to straighten it a bit, kicked the tires, and announced that we were ready to fly home. Not me! I called a cab. The major flew back by himself, probably cursing me all the way. It was the last time the Army made fun of my short field landings.

Jim Doole and I flew together often. One afternoon, we headed over to the island of Hawaii, 180 miles away. Kilauea Iki, one of the smaller volcanoes on Mauna Loa was erupting. It took us

Kilauea Iki crater

Kilauea Iki eruption, 1959

an hour and a half to get to the eruption site. When we got there we joined a pattern of other aircraft who were orbiting the volcano. The view was spectacular. Yellow-red lava was spewing into the air up to 1,000 feet. When I lowered the side window of the Bird Dog to take pictures, the heat was palpable. I was able to take several color pictures, but we only circled once because of the heat and rough air.

Most of my flights took place on the Island of Oahu. I didn't relish flying between the islands over the Pacific in a single engine plane with no emergency equipment for a water landing. In fact, I remember having a panic attack flying solo to Maui when the engine sputtered and I was halfway there over water. Fortunately, the engine settled down as did my heart, but after that experience, I decided it was more enjoyable to buzz workers in the pineapple fields, cruise down the Manoa Valley over my house cutting the engine off and on as a "hello" to my family, and pretending to be a glider on the Kailua side of the island where the winds out of the north and east hit the Ko'olau Range and produced such strong updrafts that the L-19 floated in the air and gained several hundred feet of altitude with the engine in idle.

After a year at Punahou, I thought seriously about improving myself as a teacher, hoping to someday achieve mastery of my craft. I asked my father-in-law, Philip Theopold, if he might have any leverage to get me into a graduate program at Harvard. He wrote Bob Watson, Harvard's dean of students, asking for advice. Watson's reply dated November 1959 has served as motivation for me whenever I have attempted something a bit out of my comfort zone.

"Dear Phil," Watson wrote. "For college teaching, and I honestly don't think Dan is academically strong enough, he would have to work first for an M.A. and then a Ph.D. Frankly, I would discourage him from trying this." Instead, Watson suggested I pursue a Masters in Teaching, which is exactly what I did four years later at Colorado State University, only to be told by a senior faculty member that I would have to start from scratch and that my five years of teaching experience at Punahou counted for nothing, because I had probably been doing it all wrong. What a smug and arrogant attitude! His response belied everything we know about how to encourage students. I left his CSU office in a hurry.

But I'm getting ahead of myself. The lesson for me, and one that was becoming increasingly a part of my psyche, is that sometimes, you just have to believe in yourself, follow your dreams, and prove the naysayers wrong. In 2002, when I retired to Steamboat Springs, I framed Watson's letter so each of my children and grandchildren could read it. They have all climbed steeper mountains than I, and they have all arrived at the top. As I say to Cristina on occasion when she faces a challenge, "Monument!" This little challenge reflects a time when she was getting bullied in a soccer game at Monument, just north of Colorado Springs. Of her own volition, she decided enough was enough and determined to knock the bully on her keister. I was very proud of her.

Meanwhile, back at Punahou for the remainder of 1959 until the summer of 1963, I continued to teach European history, mostly to freshmen. The student body was diverse. Many families on the island had intermarried with other races, so the White population, while still a majority among the student body, was increasingly losing its dominance. The Hawaiian, Japanese, Chinese, Samoan, Portuguese mixture produced an outstanding blend of academically talented, athletic, and handsome offspring. I had to work hard to keep up with them.

As part of my responsibilities, I was required to participate in Punahou's high-level athletic program. I could not claim enough experience to be a coach or even an assistant coach of the major sports, so I was offered the job of athletic trainer for the football team. With very little understanding of training room treatments, I once again learned something new. At times, I felt that the image I was trying to project as a professional teacher was at odds with the job of athletic trainer. Taping ankles, cleaning out the whirlpool jacuzzi, providing ultrasound treatments for an assortment of injuries to athletes, some of whom were my students, felt awkward. But I did it for two years and enjoyed my relationship with the coaches. I also learned basic first aid.

I left a more permanent mark as a soccer coach. At the time, Punahou did not have a soccer team. Bob Torrey and I asked if we could start one. The Samoans we had in class loved to kick balls around with their large feet. Training them to follow the rules of soccer was a greater challenge than we thought, especially because neither Bob nor I had played soccer. I believed the game was similar to ice hockey, and that's the way I taught it. Bob thought we would win all our games just because our players were big and could kick the ball a long way.

We had success, but our best feature proved to be intimidation. The players thought it would be more fun to run over, not around, opponents, so games were constantly interrupted by referee whistles. I wasn't sure we would be allowed to promote the sport a second year, but it happened, and we improved. Punahou has continued to play soccer ever since.

Hawaii is a good environment to raise children, enjoy the outdoors, and learn about other cultures. We all benefited from the experience. But it takes time to become a *Kama'aina* (native) and for mainland *Haoles* (White guys) there is always the feeling of being a visitor in Hawaii. We had lots of friends through Punahou and our

Manoa Valley neighborhood. We also had a longing for seasons and mountains and real snow. These emotions surfaced when Dad shared his frustrations with the ranch's farm operation. I expressed an interest in helping him out. He was quite eager. Mum warned me that to be able to work with Dad, I would have to be very careful with what might become a delicate relationship. "Of the three of you [Sid, Rob, and me]," she suggested, "you probably have the best chance of making it work, but before you abandon what you have in the Islands, you should give considerable thought to the possibility of unintended consequences."

What a smart lady! I think in many ways she viewed Dad and me as having similar temperaments—an observation I used to choke on—but she also felt that my sensitivity and what some might call ESP would allow me to defuse tensions and conflicts before they turned nasty. At least that was her hope. She too was excited about the possibility of having a child and grandchildren at the ranch. She just didn't want to see anyone get hurt.

Sometime during the winter of 1962–63, I told John Fox we would not be returning for the next school year. He was quite upset, not so much because he thought he would be losing a star teacher, but because he had always believed it took four to five years before neophyte faculty earned their pay. He also suggested that I was leaving a profession where I had a bright future. Returning to the family ranch, he argued, was immature on my part, akin to giving up on my goal of self-support. That upset me somewhat and made me all the more convinced I was doing the right thing. Returning to the ranch where I had experienced so many rewards during my own growing up seemed the perfect scenario for Jean and me and the three children who would benefit the most. Additionally, the move tendered the possibility of a real give-and-take relationship with my father based on mutual respect.

Punahou School | 99

Just before departing Hawaii

Brief Return to Ranching

We left Hawaii for Vancouver by ship in June 1963, connecting with a train that eventually brought us to Denver. Dad gave us an enthusiastic and emotional welcome when we disembarked at the train station in Glenwood Springs. His expectations were sky high.

I did not know it then, but Dad viewed other humans in two categories: wonderful, proper people; or uncultured sloths with whom he refused to waste his time. There was little room in the middle for average folks, and if he ever sensed that he was being made fun of or criticized, his temper knew no bounds. When he hired foremen, he viewed them as miracle workers until the reality of their humanity revealed frailties. When he fired them, he did so in anger. But at the Glenwood Springs railroad station, in the warm sun of a June afternoon, the farthest thought from my mind and his was that our "noble experiment" might end in the same sort of disaster. We were both guilty of expecting our new relationship to be perfect.

Mum and Dad had fixed up the old Shorty Wald place for us, on the south end of the Crystal River Ranch. It was located about a mile south of the main road to the ranch, connected by a winding, hilly, muddy, and often icy road to headquarters. The house itself had been abandoned for a long time, but Mum and Dad had cleaned it up and made it habitable for the five of us. It had new appliances—stove, refrigerator, washer-dryer—and basic furniture. But it was still rustic: no screens on the windows, chickens running around the yard, a water system that barely worked, dust blowing inside and out, and seasonal critters sharing our space. It was home, and Jean did her level best to make it comfortable. But Kit had terrible nightmares, and the drive Jean faced to get from our house to the main road once school was in session brought back memories of easier times in Hawaii.

I was far less disturbed by conditions at home, because I was spending 10–12 hours a day learning the ranch ropes. The agricultural season was in full bloom. I was focused on learning about new machinery, irrigation patterns, half a dozen men who were supposed to take instructions from me, and all the repair and maintenance challenges that accompany ranch life. Duane Gilfry, the foreman, was a good teacher. I enjoyed a close relationship with him, although there was always a certain edginess about our friendship. He suspected I had been brought in to take his job once I was trained. We never discussed this fear openly, but I knew it was there. All I could do was work as hard as possible to learn as much as I could in as short a time as possible and assist Duane with all his duties. When the time came for me to assume some of his responsibilities, I wanted to be master of the jobs he knew so well, and I wanted to be credible in the eyes of the men who would look to me for leadership.

Dad was not openly opposed to my focus on learning ranch work, but he wanted me to show more interest in the business side of things. In short, he wanted to train me to do the books, the filing, the payroll, the buying and selling, etc. I had no objections to learning the business. It was, after all, the essence of good management. But my first priority was learning how to do what we were asking the men to do. I saw no other way to be a good leader. Therefore, Dad and I started out in the very beginning with different priorities. Our leadership styles were in opposition. He ran the ranch from his office; I wanted to run the ranch as a knowledgeable participant in all its activities in the field. This essential philosophical difference eroded the high expectations we had espoused earlier with such enthusiasm.

Throughout the summer and early fall, we tolerated one another. There was tension, but I concentrated on the ranch, hoping the ill will and suspicion would evaporate. Jean knew I was frustrated. She did her best to make things work on her end, building a fence for the pony Dad had bought for Dan and planting a garden. When fall came, she drove the boys to school, sliding off the road several times in the process. Dad became increasingly short-tempered with both of us. When the corn had been cut in October, the calves weaned and taken to market, Mum and Dad packed up and departed for Tucson. We viewed their departure with relief and hoped the wounds would heal while Dad baked in the sun, smoked cigars, and read *The Wall Street Journal*.

But I was naive to think things would get better. I reported to Dad regularly on cattle feeding, machinery repair, or the weather without receiving much in the way of a response. I went all out to be a good employee. When March came, the new calves began to drop. Spending brutally cold nights around expectant heifers was a surreal experience. To preserve heat, they hardly moved. Their collective breath rose toward the bright overhead lights like steam from a coal-fired powerplant, vaporizing in the frigid air. When a heifer went into labor, she became restless and easy to spot. My job was to ease her toward a sheltered area where clean straw and respite from the cold provided improved birthing conditions.

Older cows usually gave birth seamlessly. They knew the drill. But first-time heifers were spooky, especially if their calves were in breech position. To save a calf, it was sometimes necessary to rope the heifer, snug her to a pole, and use a block and tackle to extricate her baby. No one showed me how to do this, and my first attempt resulted in pulling the calf apart. A truly awful night. I was embarrassed by my lack of skill and the loss of life. It was a learning experience, but it gave me nightmares. Suffice to say, I did not report this debacle to the *gran jefe*.

Possibly, Dad found out through Duane. They spoke regularly on the telephone. I never heard about it, because Dad was more focused on the declining egg production of about 50 ranch hens. Duane, the quintessential cowboy, thought it was beneath him to have to bother with chickens, but he sent Dad the declining monthly egg report. I was charged with the responsibility of fixing the problem.

Dad had a certain affinity for the chickens. He liked to be able to offer free eggs to ranch families. But he also had memories of chickens at Neshaminy Farms. To him, the declining egg production was serious; fixing the problem would constitute a measure of my worth. I determined to do everything I could to find the cause, seeking guidance from the experts at Colorado State University, asking local vets what I could do, and checking the hens for disease. Everyone I spoke to thought a solution was attainable through nutritional changes. We tried vitamins, proteins, and new feeds. I visited the hen house regularly to make sure conditions were sanitary. Duane teased me in a good-natured way about my preoccupation, but I was determined to find a solution.

Unfortunately, egg production continued to drop. Dad became convinced I wasn't taking the matter seriously. His communications became increasingly critical and unsettling. I took umbrage at his lack of appreciation for what I was doing and fired back with a little heat of my own. By the time spring was in full bloom, we were not speaking to each other. I thought he might actually fire me. Jean and I decided we should move on. Our good friends, Bart and Mary Strang were running a cattle operation across the valley on the Big Four Ranch. They combined ranch operations with a camp for teenagers who helped with chores in exchange for horseback riding, pack trips, fishing excursions, and other activities. It was a happy and bustling community of work and play, the teenagers providing the Strangs with a small amount of extra income. When I told Bart about our circumstances at the Crystal River Ranch, he offered a small house in return for whatever assistance I might be able to provide with haying and cattle operations. Jean and I jumped at the opportunity to exit the tension that had been building in our lives.

Without attempting a final discussion with Dad, I saddled up my horse with the saddle Mum had given me, unaware that it was owned by the Crystal River Corporation, and rode off the ranch to the Big Four, crying like a baby. Fanny, my loyal Australian sheep dog, followed along, most certainly aware of my emotions. It was a terrible moment in my life. Something I had wanted so much to succeed had come a cropper in far less time than I had imagined, even in my most pessimistic moments. Jean followed me with the three boys and the bare essentials of our household possessions. We didn't look back, but I knew Dad would have a hard time living with our precipitous departure. In a way, I felt sorry for him; more for Mum. And I knew my relationship with Dad was pretty much over. The Roaring Fork Valley was an intimate community. Word of my departure would spread rapidly. Dad would feel humiliated. But I was determined to move on with my life, and the Big Four provided us all with a much happier and healthier environment.

Fanny and I helped on the Big Four wherever we were needed. She was an amazing companion, willing to do anything I asked of her and loyal to a fault. Anyone who got too close to me would be eyed with suspicion and growled at. She could gather up 20 bulls in a large pasture simply by my command. I would see her run off and then watch as the tall grasses betrayed her position while she circled around the grazing animals. Gradually, the bulls would move toward me, never in panic but with a steady and collective understanding that any laggards would be nipped in the heel. Fanny was always so proud of herself when her job was done. I took her everywhere I went, even to the Post Office to get mail. On one occasion, I stayed in the driver's seat of the Jeep as the boys jumped out the back to get the mail. Fanny went with them. When the boys returned and hopped back into the Jeep, I asked if everyone was in—no seatbelts in those days. Hearing a yes from each, I backed up right over Fanny. She had not jumped in and had waited for me to call her. She was dead in an instant. All I could think of doing at the time was driving to the mountains with the boys to bury her. It took a long time to recover from my grief. I have never owned another dog, but as I write this, Cristina's husky, Cashew "Cash," has stolen my heart, and I find myself enjoying his affection and loyalty as much as Fanny's devotion.

At the Big Four, we were happy. The boys had lots of teenagers to befriend, and Jean had a good relationship with Mary Strang. Jean's only bad experience on the Big Four occurred in the late summer when a lightning bolt struck an underground water pipe not far from the house we occupied while she was doing dishes in the kitchen. The electricity traveled along the pipe into the house, bursting through the sink, and connecting with Jean's metal belt buckle. The voltage knocked her to the floor. No damage was done, but the experience was a reminder that we couldn't stay at the Big Four through the winter. It was time to find employment. I wanted to stay in ranching, so I posted ads in various livestock and agricultural journals.

Branding calves on the Strang ranch

Burlington, Colorado

Mr. Reed, a sugar beet farmer and cattle feeder in Burlington, CO, answered my ad. He told me he was looking for someone to manage his operation. His only son had decided to look elsewhere for work, even though he remained in town. Reed wanted someone to learn the business and eventually manage it for him. He recognized I might not have all the requisite skills, but he liked the fact we were a young, educated family, and he assured me that I could be trained to do what he needed. He had a house and would help with the move. Jean and I decided to give it a try, unaware of the enormous difference between ranching in the mountains and feeding cattle on the high plains. We were still young, we could work hard, and we were naively optimistic about succeeding under any circumstances.

Burlington is a small town almost entirely dependent on agriculture. There are no rivers nearby. Farmers have to draw water from the Ogallala Aquifer, using powerful V-8 engines that pump water to the surface which is distributed into ditches running across the high points of irrigated fields. In the 1960s, there were no center pivots. Crop irrigation was done by laborers setting 3/4" aluminum tubes in the ditch which sucked water up and over the bank, through the tube, and down into a windrow. As windrows became saturated, workers would move the tubes down the ditch until the entire field was irrigated. The noise of those diesel engines sucking water from the aquifer blended with the constant shriek of wind drying out the landscape. It wasn't a sustainable operation, but unless extreme drought or violent hail storms destroyed the crops, sugar beets and wheat were usually profitable.

Reed did his best to show me all facets of sugar beet farming and cattle feeding. He was clearly disappointed that his son had turned his back on the operation, and it wasn't long until I felt that I was being used as bait to bring him back. In the meantime, we tried to make a home in the house Reed provided. It was old and drafty. When the dust blew, which was almost every day, a fine film covered everything indoors. When the boys arose from naps, the outline of their bodies could be seen on their cots. The propane refrigerator worked, but it shot out a flame when it turned on, scaring away hordes of flies that shared our living space.

We decided to invest in a 12-foot-wide, 60-foot-long house trailer which was delivered to the Reed farm. I hooked up one of his tractors and took it to a trailer park on the east end of town. For the remainder of our stay in Burlington, this was our home. It was cozy and relatively functional. Jean worked at a nearby nursing home. Dan and Nick started school.

When it appeared that we had settled into our new lives, Reed greeted me one morning at the shop to say that his son had decided to return. His strategy had worked. The son feared I might replace him as successor owner-operator of the business. Reed was apologetic. He connected me with Rex and Kenny Hitchcock who were also sugar beet farmers and cattle feeders. Kenny was interested in using me to keep his books and pay his taxes. He had established a small machinery manufacturing business, building "incorporators" which enabled farmers to plant and fertilize beet seed in one operation. Not being a numbers person, he was delighted to hand over the books to someone else. As in the past, I concluded I could learn anything, and I liked the idea of a job that would tax my brain part-time, but I knew nothing about bookkeeping or tax preparation.

Northwest Kansas Technical College, a small college 35 miles east in Goodland, KS, offered a course in double entry bookkeeping. I attended several nights a week during the winter of

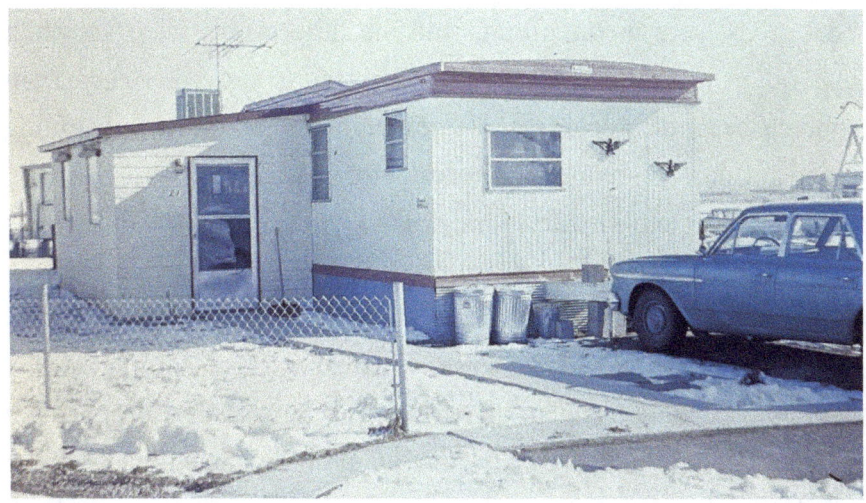

Burlington trailer home

1964–65, experiencing white-knuckle drives with blowing snow and freezing temperatures. I also took a course in bead and acetylene welding offered at the local Burlington high school. With these skills, I hoped to be of use to the Hitchcock brothers.

    In many ways, our year in Burlington was positive. Jean was much appreciated at the nursing home. The aging farmers and their wives enjoyed her upbeat attitude and energy. When the boys and I visited her, the old-timers regaled us with stories about earlier times, especially the Dust Bowl days of the '30s and '50s. Life in our trailer home was intimate and efficient. The one Christmas we spent there was simple and enjoyable. We had very little money, but we made enough to pay the bills. Everyone was safe and secure, and I had the feeling we were building something as a family. The 18-wheelers that shifted gears as they headed out of town made plenty of noise, but we got used to it. I look back on this year as one of the best in my life.

    At work, Kenny proved to be a demanding boss, very unforgiving of mistakes in his shop or in the field. Accounting work was interspersed with whatever chores he assigned me. Once the beet seeds were in the ground and the little shoots were showing, cultivation of the long rows was necessary to prevent weeds from robbing beets of precious moisture. On one windy day with roiling clouds of dust billowing in the west, Kenny assigned me to a tractor and cultivator and instructed me how to go down the half-mile rows at a turtle's pace. The tractor didn't require much steering, but the slightest deviation would cause the cultivator to wipe out beet plants. I did fine until that dust storm wrapped its arms around me. I couldn't see either end of the field. The temperature dropped 20 degrees, and I had difficulty staying properly positioned on the windrows. Several times, I became disoriented, zig-zagging back and forth. Kenny couldn't see my "detours" because of the reduced visibility, but the next day, he greeted me in a very bad humor. I had wiped out quite a few beet rows, costing him a lot of money. But no one else was willing to cultivate. It was a boring job which under decent weather conditions was not difficult. I climbed back on the tractor and did the best I could, passing the time memorizing doggerel to keep me from going nuts: *The Face on the Barroom Floor, The Dark Town Poker Club, Runt.*

    I also had time to evaluate the entire Burlington experience. It wasn't going anywhere, and the sugar beet culture was anathema to me. I drove cattle trucks on occasion and did feeding, but the cow-calf operation with which I had grown up on the Crystal River Ranch was still out of reach. Jean and I decided I needed additional education that would enable me to become involved in ground-breaking work being done in cattle breeding. Colorado State University's animal science department was highly touted. We decided to move to Fort Collins with the house trailer so I could get a master's degree in artificial insemination. I think the Hitchcocks already knew I was a short-timer. They shrugged their shoulders when we said our goodbyes.

The house trailer almost didn't make it to Fort Collins. The tow truck driver was sloppy and unprofessional. He neglected to unhook the water lines when he drove off, creating a spectacular fountain. During the 200-mile journey to Fort Collins, he experienced such severe winds, he almost lost the trailer. But our three-bedroom home finally arrived at a trailer park southeast of Fort Collins, near the intersection of Harmony Road and College Avenue, about four miles from the university. I installed skirts around the bottom of the trailer to keep water pipes from freezing and built an enclosure and storage area that protected the main door. Once settled, I searched for work that would help pay bills and tuition. In fairly short order, I was accepted as a salesman for the Encyclopedia Britannica. I also found work as an hourly helper with North American Van Lines. Then I went to the animal science department to establish a plan of study.

Sugar beet planter and incorporator

Colorado State University 1

In 1965, Fort Collins was a sleepy town of about 40,000 people, including 15,000 college students. Originally a land grant college, CSU had changed its name from Colorado A&M to Colorado State University in 1957. Renowned for its veterinary school and departments of agriculture and animal sciences, it seemed the best place to implement my goal of becoming involved in the science of animal reproduction. I hoped my Harvard background would help me get into graduate school.

Howard H. "Stony" Stonaker was the dean of the animal science department. He was a delightful man, engaging, experienced, and a consummate observer of people. His specialty was beef production with an emphasis on cross-breeding. Record keeping and performance testing of cattle, he believed, were essential for improving a cattleman's ability to market his product. I was impressed by everything I heard and saw when we met, and I was eager to begin work.

But Stony was also a realist. He pointed out that my liberal arts undergraduate education lacked the basic science courses I would need at the graduate level. It would take me a year, he surmised, to fill in the gaps. I was a 32-year-old with a young family. Might it not be wiser, he proffered, to build on my earlier education and my teaching experience by taking advantage of a new master's program in western history being offered by the CSU history department?

The gut check I experienced was palpable. I thought I had put teaching behind me. I wasn't ready to face the possibility of returning to a career in education. John Fox's words haunted me.

Failure and frustration in ranching had made me determined to succeed at what I wanted to do, not what I had been educated to do. But somehow Stony's words sounded reasonable. He wasn't demeaning my goals; he would have accepted me into the graduate program with the understanding that I complete certain pre-requisite courses. But he was a wise man. He had made a comprehensive appraisal of me and what I was best suited for. Rather quickly, I came to believe that if I couldn't ranch in the West, I could teach students about ranching and the other aspects of a region that was filled with such a fascinating history. I made an appointment to meet with Harry Rosenberg, chairman of the CSU history department.

That meeting was a watershed moment. As I write these words, a picture of Harry stares at me on my desk. Like Stonaker, he was a person who fed on optimism and saw extraordinary possibilities in others. He very much wanted the history department's new graduate program to succeed and viewed me as a worthy degree candidate. He looked past the Cs and Ds on my college transcript and saw only a visceral desire to learn. He introduced me to Charles Bayard who would become my mentor and offered me a two-year paid teaching assistantship in European history. I had no reason to refuse. If I couldn't participate physically in western ranching, I could invest intellectually in its history. When I left Harry's office, I felt confident I had turned the corner in a good direction.

Having accepted Harry's offer, my commitment to graduate work became almost obsessive. Although I had experienced spotty success in classes at Harvard and the University of Hawaii, I never thought of myself as a scholar. I needed to prove to myself that I belonged in academia, so I poured all my energy into my studies. My family commitments suffered. In contrast to the balance I had maintained while Jean and I struggled to make a success of ranch life, I became so determined to vindicate Harry's confidence that I neglected Jean and the children. I didn't do it willfully or consciously, but in retrospect, I can see how I began to distance myself from the family.

I took Harry's undergraduate course in medieval Christianity. The paper I wrote for him on Thomas Aquinas, a 13th-century Catholic priest and Dominican friar, produced an unexpected result. I wrote about how the ideas of Aquinas influenced western ethics, morality, and politics. It was a pretty ordinary research paper, but when Harry returned it to me, there was a note suggesting I should consider continuing my studies at the doctoral level. A Ph.D in history had never entered my thinking, but with Harry's encouragement, I now looked at a return to teaching in a far different light. University professor was a new goal to shoot for. It felt good. When I had tried to get into a master's program at Harvard, readers will recall, Dean Bob Watson had written a letter indicating politely that I didn't have the intellectual capacity to pursue graduate work. My father and various teachers had said the same thing at different times and in different ways. Harry's encouragement made me feel reborn. I had a new image of myself and as I came to the end of my two years at CSU, a straight A student, I looked for a mentor to take me on as a Ph.D candidate.

First, I had to research and write a master's thesis. Charlie Bayard and Stony Stonaker urged me to write about Farrington "Ferry" Carpenter. I was delighted with the suggestion. I had come to know Ferry on several occasions when I traveled with Duane Gilfry to the Carpenter Ranch in Hayden, CO, to buy replacement bulls for the Crystal River Ranch. In addition to being a top-rated cattleman and charter member of Performance Registry International, Ferry was the quintessential raconteur. Because of his past history as an Ivy League graduate (Princeton and Harvard), a cowboy, homesteader, director of the United States Grazing Service, attorney, and state politician, he had a lot of stories to tell. Dad thought he was boring, but I thought he was delightful. He didn't take himself too seriously and in 1966 at the age of 80, he was still actively promoting use of growth data that would enable cattlemen to market their product with records, providing them with an edge over the competition. The bull calves he raised, some of which sired Crystal River Ranch cows, carried the genes of stock with proven records of rapid weight gain and well-marbled meat.

I interviewed him on half a dozen occasions. We sat in the living room of his home, one of five homestead cabins that had been joined together. Seated in a rocking chair, he stoked a roaring fire with pieces of local coal while I tinkered with a tape recorder and asked questions about his life. His answers almost always contained a kernel of wisdom. Expressing my disappointment at having to give up on ranching, he told me that whatever career I chose, I would be working to subsidize something else that I really enjoyed. That was just a fact of life. A ranch, or any other goal or vision, could easily become part of my future with a little hard work and persistence. But first I needed a job, an income, and credibility.

The tapes of my conversations with Ferry were used as a basis for my master's thesis, *F.R. Carpenter, Routt County, 1900–1920*. They are now stored in the Steamboat Springs Tread of the Pioneers Museum. When Dorothy Wickenden, senior editor of *The New Yorker*, wrote about her grandmother, Dorothy Woodruff, and a friend, Rosamond Underwood, who came to teach at the Elkhead School in 1916, she consulted these tapes. Ferry had successfully courted Rosamond during her year at the Elkhead School. *Nothing Daunted: The Unexpected Education of Two Society Girls in the*

West is a perceptive description of rural life in Routt County and the role Ferry Carpenter played in establishing a school on Colorado's West Slope. When I interviewed Ferry in 1966, he had been married to Rosamond Underwood for 10 years. His first wife, Eunice Pleasant, died in 1954.

Although I now view my master's thesis as a flawed and incomplete piece of scholarship, I thoroughly enjoyed the research and writing. The whole experience felt creative to me. That I have continued to write after retiring from CSU underscores Ferry Carpenter's wisdom. In order to have the time and skill to write, I needed to be a scholar after all. I needed to improve my oral and verbal abilities at the highest educational level. When Donald C. Cutter, history professor at the University of New Mexico, expressed a willingness to take me on as a Ph.D candidate, Jean and I sold the house trailer and moved to Albuquerque.

University of New Mexico

Cutter was an excellent mentor. I had heard that he encouraged his Ph.D students to complete all the required course work as soon as possible. He had a grant from the Doris Duke Foundation to chronicle the stories of Navajo leaders, which provided his students with expenses and an hourly stipend to conduct interviews. At the age of 34, I was very receptive to the possibility of getting through the doctoral program in three years with a job. Not a few Ph.D mentors placed obstacles in the way of their students. It was part of the graduate school game. Cutter didn't do that. Although his focus on the American Southwest and colonial Latin America would require a reading knowledge of Spanish and an understanding of the role of Spain and Mexico in the Americas, I believed that this focus would serve me well in searching for a teaching position. The Chicano movement had gained momentum at western colleges and universities, and few professors were capable of telling the Chicano story. They didn't read Spanish, nor did they comprehend Chicano history.

To supplement our income and to make it possible for us to live in a real home (1300 Florida St. NE), I accepted a position teaching American history at Albuquerque Academy. I was confident I could take seminars at UNM while teaching at the Academy. Ashby Harper, Academy headmaster, was more interested in my athletic ability than in my classroom talents. The interview with him focused on sports, beginning with a brutal game of squash (he won) and followed by a marathon swimming competition (I almost drowned), proving unequivocally that he, the older man, was better conditioned and more athletic than his potential new hire. Had I beaten him, employment might have been threatened. But knowing that he was the tougher *hombre*, allowed him to offer me a position. A relatively light teaching load reflected his endorsement of my plan to study at the university while teaching at Albuquerque Academy.

As the year progressed, I could see that I was missing out on the camaraderie enjoyed by first-year Ph.D candidates. Cutter's 1967 Ph.D group included Janet Fireman, David Miller, Mike Husband, and Mike Weber, all of whom became my very good friends. We enjoyed each other's company, intellectually and socially and shared information on the best professors, research topics, where to find financial support, and how best to navigate Ph.D requirements. It was a group effort, and I immersed myself in the experience. Albuquerque Academy was an excellent place to work, but it was a distraction. I decided to become a full-time graduate student after only a year at the Academy.

With more time on my hands, I spent weekends and a few afternoons on the Navajo reservation, receiving an hourly stipend from the Doris Duke grant. I interviewed Native Americans about their creation legends, dances, and ceremonies. The tapes I recorded were transcribed and deposited in the University of New Mexico Library. Occasionally, I felt confident that I had unearthed a nugget or two, but those of us who did the interviewing recognized that we were ill-prepared to communicate with the Navajo about their spiritual life. To improve my understanding of Native American culture and mythology, I took a course with New Mexico's reigning ethnologist, Florence Hawley Ellis. She was a transforming instructor, dedicated to high-quality teaching and determined to push students to their limits. Because of her, I revised my course of study to include a minor in ethnology.

Along with seminars, tribal interviews, research, and

occasional conferences, I studied Spanish by reading *The Three Little Pigs* and other children's stories *en español*. For my degree, I was expected to pass a standardized test given twice a year to Ph.D candidates. With seven years of Latin and some French at Brooks School and Colorado State University, I had little trouble translating Spanish into English. But I failed the exam by a few points the first time I took it. I had to wait six months before the test was given again. To improve my chances, I spent July 1969 in Guadalajara taking a course Cutter taught in Spanish at the local university. While in Guadalajara, I saw Neil Armstrong's moonwalk on Mexican television.

By the fall of 1969, I had completed all of my classwork. My dissertation research had begun on the last Mexican governor of New Mexico, Manuel Armijo. Armijo was a shadowy figure. He had kept himself in office with a mixture of political skill and a sly understanding of what central authorities in Mexico City needed to be told so they would think he was doing an adequate job. He was semi-literate, as were most of those who surrounded him, so the difficulty of fleshing out his life with available documents was exacerbated by the paucity of communications (paper was very scarce in Mexican New Mexico) and the ungrammatical and occasionally illegible handwriting of territorial officials. Most of the pertinent records of the Mexican Period (1821–1846) had been collected by the State Archives of New Mexico under the supervision of Dr. Myra Ellen Jenkins. This was the principal resource I used for my dissertation.

Dr. Jenkins was a character. But she was also a good historian and an admirer of Don Cutter. She was suspicious of neophytes like me who were just entering the field of Borderlands history, but she respected hard work and clear thinking. Eventually, I earned her respect, but I spent many hours applying the seat of my pants to a hard chair in the Santa Fe Archives before she took my dissertation interests seriously. For the better part of the late fall and winter of 1969–1970, I traveled daily to Santa Fe, sometimes returning to Albuquerque late at night, exhausted after fighting my way through traffic and bad weather.

By the spring of 1970, I had written a good portion of what came to be *New Mexico in the 1820's: The First Administration of Manuel Armijo*. The shift in focus from biography to a more general analysis of Mexican New Mexico was dictated by the nature of materials with which I worked. Cutter was in Spain, and I needed him to approve my work so I could schedule a defense, graduate, and get a job. I received job offers from the Air Force Academy and Colorado State University. I was tempted by the Academy offer, because I knew the quality and enthusiasm of the students would be high. But I would have had to get back in uniform. My earlier desire to have an Air Force career was tainted by a few bad apples I had encountered, and I had been a civilian long enough to appreciate my freedom. I knew the history department at CSU and was flattered that the selection committee, chaired by my good friend Jim Hansen, would invite me back.[2] However, I needed to finish my dissertation PDQ, in order to qualify for the job.

I decided the mountain should go to Mohammed. I flew to Madrid with a draft of the dissertation in hand. While Cutter critiqued chapters, I re-typed (yes, typewriters!) the draft based on his suggestions. Janet Fireman, who was doing her own research in Madrid, was a great help to me. We managed to complete all the revisions during my short stay, enabling me to present a reasonably complete finished product to the graduate school when I returned. I received my doctoral degree in June.

All in all, the UNM experience was bittersweet. I found a niche that pleased me, and I looked forward to teaching as a professor of history at CSU. But in the nearly three years it took to reach that goal, I had drifted further away from my family. The intensity of the doctoral program and the stress I brought on myself by wanting to prove I could be a scholar combined to narrow my focus and blur my sense of family obligation. I even found time to smoke a little weed with my graduate student colleagues, something that further separated me from my family. Overall, I think Jean, Dan, Nick, and Kit had a good experience in Albuquerque. The schools were good, Jean developed good friendships, and we had a lovely home. But I was leading two separate lives: family life didn't seem to integrate easily with the life of a graduate student. I now realize that such an artificial segmentation was merely a reflection of my own immaturity and insecurity, but at the time, I willingly embraced the separation, allowing too little time and energy for the duties and responsibilities I should have shouldered as husband and father.

We left Albuquerque for Fort Collins in June 1970. My CSU contract specified a salary of $10,000 for nine months of teaching, $3,000 more than I was paid at Albuquerque Academy. We didn't have much money in the bank, but in 1970 we were certain we could get a loan to buy a house, especially if Jean decided to work.

Driving north in a rental truck with Nick and Salty, his half-moon conure parrot, in the front seat, we crossed into Colorado and immediately pulled into a state weigh station. I drove onto the scales, stopped the truck, and rolled down the window so I could communicate with the attendant through a squawk box. Every time the attendant tried to give me instructions, Salty would screech, talking in his own bird language and making such a ruckus, we couldn't make ourselves heard. The attendant was totally confused by the noise. He was located in a small building nearby and could not see into the truck's cab. The more impatient he became and the louder he shouted at us, the more Salty scolded him. Finally, we just drove away, knowing our cargo of house furniture was minimal in weight. I have often wondered what that official wrote in his daily log. "Ryder rental truck entering state with aliens at the wheel. Potentially dangerous occupants and cargo? Be prepared for resistance!"

Family in Albuquerque

Colorado State University 2

In Fort Collins, we rented a small house off Lemay Avenue. The short drive to CSU was across town where ample parking was available near my office in the Clark Building. Soon after I started teaching, Jean studied for her real estate license. With two incomes, we were soon able to purchase a modest home on Green Street, not far from Lesher Junior High School and only a few blocks to the university. As Jean proved herself a very successful realtor, we purchased a bigger home with an indoor swimming pool on Garfield Street. Neighbors Tom and Jean Sutherland became close friends.

Tom Sutherland was born a Scot. He studied agriculture at Glasgow University then attended Iowa State where he received a doctorate in animal science. He accepted a position at CSU in 1957 and taught animal genetics for 26 years. In 1983, he agreed to become dean of the college of agriculture at the American University in Beirut, Lebanon. Two years later he was kidnaped by Islamic Jihad members and held prisoner until 1991. The story of his incarceration is told in <u>At Your Own Risk</u>, co-authored with his wife, Jean. Prior to his departure for Lebanon, Tom frequently shared his mechanical skills with Dan, Nick, and Kit. He was a great role model, a talented scientist, and a perfect neighbor. With drams of Scotch whiskey, he also became a performer, reciting the poetry of his hero, Robert Burns. Tom was an especially good friend. He died in 2016 at the age of 85.

My teaching at CSU went well for the most part: US history survey, a graduate seminar, Southwest/Chicano history, and a huge class (350 students) of Colorado history. My very first class convened in the largest lecture hall of the Clark Building, A-101.

The experience was initially terrifying. Opening the door with a shaky hand, I encountered noisy students, most of whom had heard that Colorado history was an easy way to satisfy a social science credit required of engineering and science majors. I wasn't expecting such a mob. I soon recognized that entertainment would be necessary to hold their attention. As we progressed through the eras of the state's history, I performed as various characters—an itinerant preacher, a cowboy, a mountain man, a 1920s water attorney, and

Itinerant preacher

Cowboy

perhaps my best role, Alferd Packer, the Colorado cannibal. I always felt nervous preparing for these roles, but I continued the acting, because student response was so good. I even did a little singing for effect accompanied by members of the music department, and on one occasion, by my own guitar-playing son, Dan.

Unexpectedly running into several students off the campus one day, I was informed they had taken and enjoyed my Colorado history class. "How did you do?" I asked.

Alferd Packer *Colorado River water lawyer, L. Ward Bannister*

"Not well," they replied. "But we'll never forget Alferd Packer."

The senior secretary at the history department was my makeup artist for many years. She was involved in various theatrical productions and was always willing to meet me at the campus theater to apply makeup. She did her job well. Crossing the campus one day, dressed up as a Spanish missionary to speak with an education class, several students genuflected as they passed by. I must have looked authentic. In addition to frock and sandals, I glued a round piece of a fleshy lady pictured in *Playboy* to the back of my head in order to comply with the friars' commitment to tonsure, a sign of religious devotion and humility. When I played a non-denominational circuit rider who visited mining camps to marry and bury the settlers, one of my graduate students asked me if I would consider marrying him in the nearby mountains, appropriately attired as an itinerant preacher.

"I'll get the license," he told me. "It's perfectly legal for you to do this so long as no other individual better prepared is available. It's like being a ship captain at sea. We will tie the knot in a forest glen, and you just have to bear witness and say something appropriate to the occasion."

"Fine," I said. He was our goalie on a senior men's hockey team, as well as my graduate student, so I was willing to cooperate.

All went well. The bride and her attendants showed up barefoot wearing peasant blouses. The groom and groomsmen arrived with bagpipes wearing Scottish kilts. The groom pulled out a long piece of rope from his kilt and handed it to his bride. The two of them proceeded to tie a knot, which I blessed with funky poetry. The whole experience was quite amusing until my then wife, Silvia, a good Catholic, found out about it. T'was blasphemy in her eyes. I quickly became persona non grata for pretending to make light of a solemn marriage ceremony.

But the standing ovation I occasionally received from the history classes softened the impact of domestic criticism. Any applause on the last day of class always surprised me and confirmed my belief that students were more willing to learn when instructors made a special effort to engage them. History department colleagues viewed my shenanigans as cheap entertainment, but they just had different ways of engaging their students. My chairman seemed to approve and because of the large numbers of students assigned to me every semester, I was given a graduate teaching assistant to help with grading.

In addition to teaching classes, I took over the American West Program. Originating in the late '60s, this summer event began as a series of lectures, art expositions, and performances for the general public, featuring different aspects of western history and culture. In certain ways, it was an attempt to improve town-gown relations. When I arrived in Fort Collins, it was being directed by an engineering professor. The responsibility for such programs fell more logically on those of us who studied the region. When I was asked to take over, I accepted. Colleagues warned me against doing this. Promotion and tenure at any university depend on publications, not service-related activities. Publish or perish! But I was enthusiastic about expanding the American West program. Several other departments in the college were interested in participating, and I foresaw opportunities to integrate unique coursework into the summer schedule. Local artist, Bob Coonts, offered to prepare annual posters, reflecting each summer's chosen theme. Influenced by Juan Miró, Henri Matisse, and Chuck Close, Bob was a talented and internationally recognized graphic artist. His posters always sold out regardless the number we printed. Ten of them are framed and in my possession: 1972, 1973, 1974, 1976, 1977, 1978, 1985, 1988, and 1990.

With a modest budget from the university and with a committee representing faculty, students, and the people of Fort Collins, the American West Program began to offer regular classes, author talks, seminars, art exhibitions, and conferences on an expanded basis. To bring attention to the seedier side of society on the mining frontier, I invited a San Francisco prostitute to speak. Her audience was SRO. On another occasion, I invited Ferry Carpenter to give a keynote address. Two days before he was to arrive on campus, I received a phone call which went roughly as follows:

"Dan, it's Ferry."

"Hi, Ferry! What's up?"

"I'm in the hospital. 'Fraid I can't give the talk."

"That's bad news, Ferry. What happened?"

"My Jeep ran over me."

"What?"

"Yep! I was tightening a bottom wire on the pasture fence. Forgot to set the brake on the Jeep. Plumb ran over me and broke some ribs. But I've got good news."

"Really?"

"Yep! Got T. A. Larson to stand in for me. You don't owe him a cent. He's doing me a favor."

A favor indeed and one for which I was most grateful. I had 250 conferees registered, and lunch with Ferry Carpenter was a big draw. But Larson wasn't far behind as a favorite of western historians. Known as Mr. Wyoming History, he had trained at the University of Illinois as a medieval historian but accepted a job at the University of Wyoming in Laramie with the understanding he would learn and teach Wyoming history. He dedicated himself to the task and eventually published four books on the subject. Like Ferry, he was a raconteur. He gave us an entertaining talk, much of which focused on his 40-year friendship with Ferry.

I truly enjoyed the American West program. It filled my summers with engaging people and a better chance to get to know both CSU and Fort Collins. Mindful of my colleagues' warning about the need to publish, I edited two books related to the conferences we held on campus: *Western American History in the Seventies* (Fort Collins, CO: Robinson Press, 1973) and *Red Men and Hat Wearers: Viewpoints in Indian History* (Boulder, CO: Pruett Press, 1976). Neither one would be considered the kind of scholarly work required for promotion to associate professor, but each represented a milestone in the expansion of the American West program.

My first five years at CSU were enjoyable. I liked the students, my faculty colleagues, and the town. Having originally thought I might want to move up to a "better" university, I found myself completely fulfilled and extremely happy in Fort Collins. Harry Rosenberg was a supportive department chairman who became a good friend and role model. I chaired the university's benefits committee where I learned about IRAs, 401(k)s, defined contribution plans, annuities, and healthcare benefits. I took my graduate students on the university obstacle course, so they would be more tolerant and understanding of each other and would work together with increased trust and respect. For most participants, the experience proved exceptionally powerful, breaking the ice of social interaction that resulted in more animated and respectful discourse in the classroom. It didn't hurt to have me do the course with them.

I also found that classroom behavior was supercharged by taking students on trips to historical sites. Such excursions were difficult with Colorado history students due to the large numbers in each class. But we did make sojourns to mining areas, Native American battlegrounds, and the Carpenter Ranch in Hayden. By far the best trips were those I took with students from my History of the Southwest class. We traveled in CSU vehicles or in our own cars if the group was small. The itinerary varied, but my objective was to immerse the students, most of whom were white and urban, in the Hispanic and Native American cultures of New Mexico.

We normally departed CSU mid-afternoon on a Friday and drove late into the night, camping or finding a motel if the weather was dicey. Because the trips began in the late fall or early spring, we often encountered snow, but the southwestern climate changes fast, and we could alter our destinations according to meteorological circumstances. I tried to arrive near Santa Fe or Taos so students could experience the history of the area, the pueblos, Native American dances, Spanish colonial missions, and other areas where cultural conflict had occurred. The students loved being away from the university routine. They took advantage of the unique foods, sampled more than a little tequila, and stayed out late to experience local nightlife. For the most part, they were cooperative and appreciated my willingness to share my own knowledge of the area with the them.

But there was no shortage of incidents and close calls. On a trip to Acoma Pueblo, we had to transit a small pass west of Española. I was sitting in the back seat of a 12-passenger van, having given the driving responsibilities to a female student. She was a good driver, but she failed to see the ice on the road as we neared the summit. The van skidded, sliding out to the edge of the road. Looking out the window, I saw the van's rear wheels miss going into a deep abyss by a foot or so. Gravel on the roadside arrested our skid. It was a very close call. Our driver was more than willing to return the driving to me. On another occasion, we were returning late one Sunday night to Fort Collins on the highway from Raton, NM. Our five CSU station wagons were traveling in tandem, my vehicle in the lead. Through the rear view mirror, I noticed that one or two vehicles would pull into the passing lane, parallel to each other, and then return to their place in line. As I watched more closely, I realized the students were passing something back and forth. It was a bottle of whiskey. I didn't say anything, hoping that those who were imbibing did not include the student drivers.

When we returned to class, there was a hum in the classroom that hadn't been there before our trip. Students were sharing stories amidst a lot of laughter and friendships were strengthening. A totally new learning environment had been established. They learned so much more from having experienced the human and geographical landscape of the Southwest. They now had more than a textbook image of past events, and they were far more eager to learn more. But I always felt sorry for those who were unable to go, either because of work and family conflicts, or because the money was too tight. For the remainder of the class, they always felt like pariahs.

When we moved from Green Street to Garfield Street in Fort Collins, I purchased a 1970 Alfa Romeo Spider Veloce. In addition to panache, the car had good speed and was very maneuverable. Mystery miles appeared on the odometer once Dan Jr. received his license and when Jean and I absented ourselves from the house for any period of time. During one summer, I took the Alfa to a race in Aspen. I let Dan take the car around the track. He smoked the competition. I squirmed, not because I worried about his safety, but because I knew there would be plenty of repair bills. My worst fears were confirmed. That was an expensive car to keep running, but it was so much fun to drive—as my sons found out.

In the spring of 1975, I was finishing up a lecture in Southwest history, when I noticed Harry Rosenberg standing outside the classroom door. He had a distressed look on his face. As we walked back to the history department, he took my arm.

"I have to inform you," Harry said, "that we will be unable to renew your annual contract for the 1975–76 teaching year. I feel awful about this, but the College of Liberal Arts has budgetary concerns, and the dean has insisted we reduce faculty."

As one of the last members of the department to be hired, Harry had no choice but to let me go. As I found out later, he had fought hard to keep me, but there was little he could do. Promising to help me find another position, he expressed deep personal regrets and embarrassment that at this stage of my career, I would be facing a cataclysmic change. Essentially, I concluded, my CSU career was over.

Alfa Romeo

Mexico

As things turned out, that was not the case. But Jean and I knew I would have to look for another position very soon. Somehow, I learned that the State Department was looking for American history scholars to celebrate the United States bicentennial year in Mexico. The Fulbright exchange program, named in honor of Arkansas Senator J. William Fulbright, was an educational program reflecting the senator's personal commitment to multilateral exchanges of all kinds. Mexico was looking for university-level teachers who could offer courses in American history *in Spanish*.

I was *almost* qualified. I had a Ph.D and university teaching experience. I had a reading knowledge of Spanish and enough Latin and French to provide additional linguistic potential. With a little help from a colleague in CSU's language department, who prostituted her ethical standards by attesting to my linguistic skills, I felt confident the State Department would approve my application to teach American history to graduate students at Mexico City's Universidad Nacional Autónoma de México (UNAM) and at the Jesuit-run Universidad Iberoamericana. Soon after applying, I received a response by phone from the program administrator in Washington, DC. "You're hired," he told me. "Make sure you bring lots of tennis balls. They are expensive here and hard to find."

"What am I teaching?" I inquired.

"Don't worry about it," he replied. "Just bring the tennis balls. I am working with Angela Moyano, a teacher at UNAM, who will help you become acclimated."

In a certain sense, I was delighted at the informality. But I worried about how to prepare. I contacted a Spanish teacher at the

Berlitz Language Center in Denver. We agreed I would arrive on Saturdays with lectures written in Spanish. He would critique my grammar and vocabulary. The Civil War was to be our focus.

I struggled to prepare the lectures, but I liked the plan. Unfortunately, my instructor was more interested in the Civil War than in improving my Spanish. Most of his comments and questions had to do with the details of battles with which he was fascinated. We had dialogs over the course of six weeks, but when the time came to leave for Mexico, my spoken Spanish was still rudimentary, not much better than the broken English of my Mexican students.

The big decision for Jean and me related to the boys. Dan would soon graduate from Fort Collins High School. Nick was a junior. Neither wanted to leave Fort Collins, so Jean found a couple willing to babysit them and the house for a year, while Kit, Jean, and I were in Mexico. I drove the car to Mexico City and met with Angela Moyano, who turned out to be very helpful and who became a good friend. I flew back to Colorado, picked up Jean, Kit, and Muffy (Jean's dog) and flew with them to Mexico City. Poor Muffy almost froze to death on the flight. In those days, dogs were not allowed to fly with passengers. They shared the baggage compartment with the inanimate cargo.

Through Jean's real estate friends, Dan and Sherry Arensmeier, we were introduced to Sonja and Sergio Jinich, Mexico City residents. Sonja helped us find an apartment on the first floor of a house in Polanco, an upscale suburb of Mexico City. It was large enough, with high ceilings, but it was damp and cold, and the appliances were antiquated. Kit attended the American School while Jean sorted out the problems associated with living in the Distrito Federal (DF). I commenced work at the two universities.

By the end of the first semester, we were getting reports from

Dan and Nick that the couple we had hired to care for them and our home in Fort Collins was irresponsible. Jean returned to Fort Collins, shut the house down, found an apartment for Dan, and returned to Mexico City with Nick. It wasn't the best circumstance for any of us, and when my first Fulbright year was over, Jean thought it wise to return home with both boys. I was invited to stay in Mexico for a second year.

During his year in Mexico, Nick played football at the American School and amused himself, and us, with a parrot he named Felonius. The bird was independent and ornery, but he was well suited for the high ceilings of the apartment, roosting day and night on the curtain rods, where he cackled away and pooped at will. Nick was endeared to him and because Jean and I felt guilty about uprooting Nick from Fort Collins, we allowed the bird its freedom. Not until a year later, when I moved out of the apartment, did I realize what a mess he had made out of sight and high enough up in the nooks and crannies of the apartment that cleanup was certain to be accompanied by a severe attack of acrophobia. The landlady was outraged when she saw what had happened, and I had to pay a princely sum before checking out. When I moved out of the apartment to sit a home belonging to American friends who were on leave, Felonius came with me. I did my best to care for him, but one evening, he flew out of his cage and through an open window (no screens on houses in Mexico), landing in a tree about 50 yards from the house. After calling him repeatedly and rattling a seed can from the open window, Felonius tired of his freedom and gnawing hunger. He launched a heroic return flight. Unfortunately, his flying skills and aerodynamic shortcomings combined to cause a disaster. He miscalculated the distance, altitude, and azimuth of his destination, smacking full force into a brick wall and breaking his neck. I was sorry to have to bury him. He was a character, and Nick loved him.

Back in Fort Collins, Nick replaced Felonius with a small macaw, Gordo, who was also a flight risk. He escaped the house one evening and was discovered a day later, angrily screeching from his perch, high up in an elm tree. Because Jean had connections with the local fire department, she was able to get a hook-and-ladder truck on the scene. With seed can in hand, Nick was raised up in the truck's cherry picker and got close enough to Gordo to grab him. Fire department officials made it quite clear, however, that this would be their last bird rescue. Cats were bad enough, they noted, but birds were just not on their rescue list.

In his last year at Fort Collins High School, Dan proved himself to be an excellent competitive swimmer. He was also an excellent skier and was able to hone his skills at a Wyoming race camp during the summer. He worked at Sears in his senior year and enlisted in the Navy after graduation. He had hoped to become a crew member on a nuclear submarine, but because he was partially color blind, he was reassigned to air conditioning and heating duty on an aircraft carrier. Naturally, he was very disappointed, but the Navy experience contributed to his desire to seek further education. After an honorable discharge, he enrolled at Fort Lewis College in Durango.

Looking back at my first year in Mexico, I now understand far better how difficult this move was for the family. I was delighted to be given the chance to improve my Spanish and to immerse myself in the Hispanic culture I studied in graduate school. And, of course, I was delighted to have a job after being forced to leave CSU. But interrupting the boys' lives was asking a lot of them. Jean bore the burden of resolving family issues in both countries. She did not speak Spanish and though she was a trooper in every way, she had to do a lot on her own with minimal assistance from me. I poured myself into the responsibilities and opportunities made available at both universities, determined to make a success of the honor I had received from the Fulbright Commission. As father and husband, I was less engaged.

My class at UNAM met at 4 p.m. Angela Moyano joined us for a few weeks while I got my bearings. Most students at that very large public institution worked full time and were only available for class after *la comida* (lunch) between 2 and 3 p.m. Initially, I was a curiosity for about a dozen graduate students who were profoundly interested in what an American professor might have to say about the *imperialist* United States' involvement in world affairs. They were friendly, but they had already formed negative opinions about the Colossus of the North, and their questions—more like mini lectures — revealed a considered bias against all things *norteamericanas*. Because my Spanish was still rudimentary, I had difficulty jousting with them. Some decided the class wasn't worth their time, but I succeeded in retaining a cadre of students who were willing to work for me and with me to achieve their goals.

One of them was a well-dressed, middle-aged gentleman who spoke excellent English. When he came to class, discussions were more genteel. Students respected him and followed his lead. I soon learned why. Jorge Díaz Serrano was chief of Petróleos Mexicanos (Pemex) in the administrations of two Mexican presidents: Luís Echeverría and José López Portillo. During his tenure at Pemex, he oversaw the expansion of the nation's oil production, making Mexico the 4th largest producer in the world. He had decided to attend my class, because he owned a large collection of American art and was interested in knowing more about the artists and the context in which they painted. Art history was not, by any means, one of my intellectual strengths. But Jorge and I hit it off well and after a few visits to his home to review the many works he had acquired, I began to make reference in class to 18th and 19th century American artists, not only in response to Jorge's interests, but as a way to educate myself about a part of American culture I had neglected in my own preparation. It's truly amazing what you learn about yourself when you step out of your comfort zone and take a look at who you are and where you came from through the lens of citizens from another country. It's also humbling!

The students occasionally invited me for a beer after class. We worked on my Spanish, especially on idioms they often used. I also listened to the radio a lot, especially *fútbol* games, trying to train my ear to the *calo* (slang) used by sports broadcasters. In the evening, I often read myself to sleep with *Excelsior*, the official newspaper of the PRI (Partido Revolucionario Institucional). Within a year or so, I began to dream in Spanish. I also became a reader at the Benjamin Franklin Library where I found books for my classes and a number of individuals—teachers, students, writers—who became close friends. I learned to use public transportation, driving my car only to UNAM or to the Universidad Iberomericana two or three times a week.

On one trip to UNAM, my 1972 BMW 2002 coupe quit running just as I was about to exit the *periférico*, the outer beltway around Mexico City. I had enough speed to navigate the exit, cross a crowded thoroughfare, and enter a local *taller* (workshop) which advertised automobile repair. It all happened quickly and caused no little concern to the mechanics who were resting in various corners of the shop after their *comida*. Miguel, the owner and head mechanic, was fascinated by the BMW and assured me he could fix it, even though his experience, he admitted, was limited to Toyotas and Volkswagens. I wasn't so confident, but his enthusiasm combined with a certain cockiness made me feel that I could safely leave the car with him. The fuel pump had failed, and there was no BMW dealer in Mexico City. A few days later, he called to say the car was working perfectly with a Toyota replacement pump. He charged very little and urged me to stop by again when I was on my way to UNAM. He was delighted to have an American contact who might be willing to transport items from the United States he could not afford to import or didn't want to smuggle. High on his list was an automatic pistol, what any self-respecting Mexican kept in the glove compartment of his car. I disappointed him, but he remained a good friend during my two years in Mexico City.

Beatríz Ruíz Gaytán also proved to be a good friend but on an entirely different level. She was chair of the history department at the Universidad Iberoamericana. Very Spanish, with an accent I found hard to comprehend, Beatríz was a scholar who wanted her graduate students reviewing United States history. Bright, affluent, and well educated, the 4–5 students she assigned to me were enthusiastic about research in original documents. I had brought dozens of microfilm reels of the Mexican Archives of New Mexico with me, so we organized a seminar around Mexican sovereignty of what is now referred to as the Hispanic Southwest of the United States, i.e., Texas, New Mexico, Arizona, California, and parts of Utah and Colorado. The students struggled as much as I did with the writings of these provincial, illiterate Mexican officials. We met at the Benjamin Franklin Library and enjoyed the collegiality of others interested in the 1821–1846 period when Mexico ruled the southwestern part of what is now the United States.

Additionally, Beatríz asked me to present a lecture series on American presidential policy. This was a tough challenge. I had to rely on a paucity of secondary sources available at the Benjamin Franklin library, but because the Iberoamericana promised to publish the lectures in book form, I accepted the invitation. Jorge Díaz Serrano agreed to review what I wrote. The result was *De Truman a Nixon: Uso y Abuso del Poder Presidencial* (Mexico City: Ediciones El Caballito, 1981). In these pages, I tried to trace the growth of an imperial presidency, terminating in Watergate. *Imperialismo* was a subject of much interest to Mexicans, especially to students who had grown up believing that their country was still a pawn in the hands of a much more powerful northern neighbor. They were fascinated by Watergate and the resignation of President Nixon.

Another diversion to my teaching duties came from Colorado State University. The new dean of CSU's College of Liberal Arts, Frank Vattano, called to ask if I might consider acting as liaison between the university and the Mexican Department of Agriculture. Both entities wanted to work together to help Mexico improve its development of certain crops against the mounting threats of drought and insects. I was delighted to offer my services. Frank came to Mexico to discuss my responsibilities. I met him at the airport and drove him to his hotel. I had not realized that in a year's time, my driving techniques had changed, largely for survival. I matched the aggressive behavior of the nation's most macho drivers. "If I am fortunate enough to return home safely," Vattano muttered, "I will be certain to notify my good friend, the chief of police, that you are to be watched closely upon your return." I was pleased on two levels: (1) I had scared the shit out of the dean, proving that I was a good Mexican driver; and (2) the dean had implied I might be re-hired. This was, indeed, a promising scenario.

The only accident I had in Mexico occurred at a *glorieta* (roundabout) when another American objected to the way I was changing lanes. We bumped fenders lightly. There was no damage but on my way to the embassy, I noticed in my rear view mirror, the same vehicle bearing down on me at an increasing rate of speed. At a stop sign, the American rammed me, broke both my taillights, and damaged both our bumpers. I got out to assess the damage only to see the vehicle with its Michigan license plate disappearing down the street. At the embassy, I provided the license number, but I knew nothing would be done. How silly to be smashed up by a road-raged fellow countryman who clearly did not know how to drive in Mexico.

The only other confrontation I had while driving occurred at the same *glorieta*. Forced to go slowly because of heavy traffic, a policeman on foot took advantage of the jam to approach. He commanded me to pull over. He was armed. I stopped. He requested my license. Warned by friends that I should never give up my license to a cop without 50 pesos attached to the back, I was prepared. I handed over the license and money and was given back my credential—*sin dinero*—without further ado. As with other incidents in Mexico, this one reenforced what I was fast learning: While Mexico appears on the surface to be just like the United States in many ways, the culture has its own, very distinct, idiosyncracies. I was both frustrated and enamored by these differences. Once I better understood the culture, my enjoyment and confidence levels increased exponentially, but I never felt comfortable with the privileged groups in Mexico who bullied others to achieve what they took to be their birthright: land, power, patronage.

Officials from the Mexican Department of Agriculture showed me by example how they took advantage of their unique sinecure. I was told to meet them at the airport for a flight to Denver. When I arrived, half a dozen bureaucratic toadies had just usurped seats on an aircraft that had already been oversold. The seats were first class. From takeoff to landing, we enjoyed the best whiskey available on the plane and when we landed in Denver, a limousine was waiting to take us to Fort Collins. All of these expenses, I am certain, were charged to the government.

When we returned to Mexico City, I was invited to a dinner at an upscale hotel. The meal was supposed to begin at 10 p.m. I arrived half an hour early, starving. There were dishes of what appeared to be sliced olives on the table. My hunger gave way to bad manners as I scarfed down a handful of the "olives," becoming aware all too rapidly that I had just inhaled very hot chiles. Water did nothing to allay the burning sensation in my mouth. Just as the dinner guests arrived, all of whom wanted to present themselves to me, I was unable to speak, perspiring profusely, and looking for an escape. I finally made my way to the bathroom where I drank more fluids, washed my tongue with soap and water, and swabbed my sweaty face with a wet towel. I returned to the table, but the pain did not go away quickly. All I could think of was how the guests must have known what I did. The *gringo*, they would have thought, needs more time to acclimate culturally.

I made several trips to CSU with the Mexican contingent, gradually becoming more effective in my role as liaison. I was delighted to have the opportunity to really improve my language skills and to immerse myself more deeply into Mexican culture. From the standpoint of family harmony, however, the decision to remain in Mexico a second year was probably a mistake. I became a husband and father in absentia. Settled into the Garfield Street house in Fort Collins, Jean concluded I was no longer a reliable mate. She filed for divorce. Her attorneys alerted the cultural attaché in Mexico City, who called me with the news. I went to the embassy to call home. Jean and I spoke briefly. My travel visa had expired, but I offered to renew it immediately if Jean thought we might be able to talk things out. She was not encouraging. I do not blame her in any way, but at the time I was disappointed. I called Dad. He was quite emotional and provided advice regarding a good attorney. He had never shown much affection for either Jean or my children, but I felt better having guidance. Jean and I had accumulated few possessions, but we agreed she should have the Garfield Street house and contents. It was a sad time for everyone, and I limped around for several months in Mexico City, trying to focus on accomplishing something there before returning to the US.

Divorce leaves an ugly scar. Dan, Nick, and Kit were deeply affected by what happened. I knew it would take me a long time, if ever, to win back their confidence and trust. Healing occurs with time, but divorce is like a death, and the grieving can last for years.

I moved to a small apartment closer to Mexico City's business and cultural center and played early morning squash regularly with Luís Rubio, a friend of Jorge Díaz Serrano. He had a squash court in his house which was located behind a locked gate and protected by an armed doorman, not something I had ever seen before. Luís belonged to the PRI (Partido Revolucionario Institucional), and he had political aspirations. He was a member of the privileged class, but he was also a lot of fun and a good connection for me while I was trying to come to grips with my new life. "Pinche Gringo," he called me. Not an acceptable moniker in polite company, but one which I accepted, because mostly I beat him when we played. The regular exercise helped assuage the emotional upset of losing my family.

I also spent more time with Jorge Díaz Serrano and his wife, Helvia Martínez Verdayes. Helvia was a talented artist. She had been the model for the statue, La Fuente de la Diana Cazadora, overlooking a *glorieta* on the Paseo de la Reforma. Her face was seen by everyone who traveled that major artery into the heart of Mexico City. She was also known for restoring old Spanish colonial paintings which had been dulled and dirtied over hundreds of years.

Jorge invited me to his 50th birthday party. I arrived fashionably late, as was the custom in Mexico; half the invited guests had yet to arrive. I fetched a drink and took a position along the wall of a large reception room. Each arriving guest shook hands with those already present; another Mexican custom. One arrival caught my eye: Silvia Ruíz Sahagún, Helvia's assistant. I did not know who she was, but I watched her circulate around the room for 10–15 minutes until she came to me. We chatted a bit, had something to eat, and I invited her to dinner. She declined, but agreed to attend the Mexican performance of *Jesus Christ Superstar* with me during the weekend.

Silvia was 31. She lived with her parents and two maids in a modest residence not far from my Polanco apartment. Her work with Helvia involved touching up the paint on old portraits and colonial masterpieces that were disintegrating with the passage of time. She was good at what she did, and she worked well with Helvia who focused more on replacing the backing made of *lleso* (plaster) that had decomposed. They were a good team.

When I met Silvia's parents, Benjamín and Beatríz, for the first time, I received the third degree. Beatríz sat me down in the living room and asked a lot of questions. As a divorced Protestant, I had two strikes against me. My Spanish was decent, but I struggled with the interview. Benjamín stayed out of it. He was more relaxed and informal. He had spent most of his professional life working as a forest management supervisor for the government in the state of Chiapas. He was honest, kind, and caring. In contrast to most government workers, he did not cheat, steal, or take advantage of his position. He had managed to provide for his family, buying jewels from time to time as a financial cushion for later years. I sensed that he was glad to see his daughter dating. Nando, Silvia's older brother, had a college education in finance and was already married with three children. At 31, Silvia was considered to be on the edge of the marriage market. I was something of a curiosity in the Ruíz household, but I was treated with utmost respect, and I enjoyed the time I spent in their home. It felt good to be part of a family again.

After *Jesus Christ Superstar*, Silvia and I took weekend day trips to various historical sites. The maids prepared picnics for us and enjoyed watching our relationship develop. We went out to dinner and to bars to dance. My Spanish had improved, but finding ways to communicate feelings and emotions was difficult. At times, Silvia suggested we try English. I could give a historical lecture in Spanish with relative assurance that the chosen words were more or less correct, but my social Spanish was deplorable. The nuances of Spanish, the ability to understand sarcasm and jokes, were often beyond my grasp.

When the American Embassy invited me to give a lecture on American foreign policy in Puebla, I invited Silvia to come along. The Mexican Secretaría de Educación y Cultura included my presentation in a May 1976 poster that also listed movies, children's programs, lectures, conferences, and many other cultural events. Because of what happened in Puebla, I framed this poster and still have it in my possession.

We were picked up in a black limousine accompanied by a member of the embassy's cultural affairs department. The two-hour drive to Puebla was relaxing and uneventful, but when we arrived at the historic cathedral where I was supposed to speak, we were met by a lone Mexican with a very long face. "There is no audience," he lamented. Apparently, anti-American sentiment extended to anything the U.S. Embassy organized. I had been invited to give my lecture in a large hall with high ceilings and balconies that revealed hundreds of ancient books and manuscripts lining the walls. It was a perfect location, and I was disappointed no one showed up. Our Mexican contact could only shrug his shoulders and invite us to have ice cream.

I have often wondered what Silvia's thoughts were at the time. Perhaps she too was embarrassed. For me, the experience underscored what I had been learning for two years in Mexico: Unexpected outcomes are a frequent part of life in that country. In the United States, we pretty much expect things to go as planned. Silvia's father said to me one time, "*Su país es un país de todo orden.*" Your country is one of order. Unplanned circumstances also occur in the United States, but in Mexico, it's a way of life. While living there, I learned to prepare myself for unexpected adventures. The challenge, which I came to enjoy, was to make the most of the unforeseen, rather than resorting to anger and frustration when plans failed to come to fruition.

As Silvia and I continued to court, marriage became a subject of discussion. I was enchanted with Mexico, Silvia, and the warmth of the Ruíz family. My second year of the Fulbright teaching fellowship would soon come to an end without any hope of renewal. I could see no way to maintain what had become a wonderful relationship other than through marriage. Voices of realism were effectively silenced by emotions, over-confidence, and a grain or two of naivete. I had no idea how cultural differences between Silvia and me might impact marriage and create tensions for us in the United States. I was focused on my feelings, and they were very strong. Marrying Silvia would allow me to nourish the pleasures of what had been an extraordinary experience for me in Mexico.

In retrospect, I regret not taking more time to first work on establishing a solid relationship with Dan, Nick, and Kit. Jumping into a second marriage so quickly was essentially a selfish act. I paid for this judgmental error in many ways and many times over.

Silvia was not particularly sanguine about marriage, but for completely different reasons. She didn't think it would work, because she didn't think I knew her well enough. Her parents had been concerned by certain unorthodox behaviors, she said, and they had sought psychiatric help. I never asked what these behaviors were, but it seemed to me that the very differences which had driven Benjamín and Beatriz to find help for their daughter were for me a part of what I liked about Silvia. She seemed to be respectful but rebellious toward certain out-of-date Mexican customs her parents embraced. I saw no signs of the mental problems to which she alluded and whatever differences her parents found troublesome, they were for me a sign of independence in response to certain traditions and behaviors; somewhat like what I had exercised in the relationship with my own father.

After considerable cajoling, Silvia accepted my invitation to marry. I asked for approval from her father. All he wanted to know was whether or not I could support her. When I assured him I could, the conversation ended. I think both he and Beatríz were pleased that Silvia and I were getting married. They both seemed to like me, and Beatríz saw in me the opportunity to reduce tensions with her daughter.

Shortly after our engagement, I returned to Fort Collins to look for an apartment. On the three-day drive from Mexico City, I went through as many scenarios as possible, trying to honestly assess my decision to marry again. As the miles sped by, I convinced myself that I was capable of resolving any issues that came up, and I knew that if I didn't marry Silvia, I would feel real loss. That feeling trumped what should have been a more powerful loyalty to my three children. But I thought I had learned from my marriage to Jean, and believed the boys and I could reestablish our relationship in time. I felt better prepared, more experienced, hopefully more mature.

I stayed in Fort Collins with a CSU colleague who taught in the language department. Miriam was a good friend—the one who had told the State department that I was fluent in Spanish. But I should have known better than to stay with her while apartment hunting. Innocently, I gave her number to Silvia who called shortly after I arrived. Hearing Miriam's voice on the phone, Silvia became distraught. She assumed Miriam was more than a friend. I should have anticipated such a reaction. We survived the experience, but the incident proved that behavioral expectations in a multi-cultural relationship are driven by and rooted in long-standing assumptions. In Mexico, many wives simply assume that their husbands will have a *chica* or two on the side; even a second family. This first misunderstanding with Silvia was a harbinger of many more to come.

I found a nice apartment for us to rent adjacent to a house belonging to historians Art and Jan Worrall. Art was my colleague at CSU. I then bought an engagement ring and flew back to Mexico. Our wedding took place at the Ruíz home on July 3, 1976.

It has often been said that couples who have a good time at their wedding have long and happy marriages. We certainly had fun, dancing in the Ruíz garage to a live band, until Silvia and I finally departed in her bright-red Volkswagen Beetle. We spent the night in a downtown hotel, both of us pretty blitzed by the time we settled into our room on the top floor. I remember lying down on the bed with my clothes on while Silvia went into the bathroom to bathe. When I smelled smoke, however, I came to in a hurry. Silvia had decided to clean the bathtub with lighter fluid. The plastic tub, which she probably thought was porcelain, caught fire. I barged into the bathroom, poured water on the fire, and succeeded in putting it out. Fortunately for us, there were no sprinklers in the room and because we were on the top floor, we could get rid of the smoke by opening windows. We snuck out of the hotel in the morning, the hotel clerks simply eyeing us knowingly as honeymooners, not arsonists.

For the next few days, we stayed at Luís Rubio's cottage on the outskirts of Mexico City. There was a little golf course nearby and a restaurant. It was a nice way to wind down before beginning our drive to the United States. On that drive, Silvia slept most of the way. When we arrived at the border, we had to open and pour out the contents of several tequila bottles we had brought as gifts. INS (Immigration Service) rules still allow only one free bottle across the border per car.

Wedding: Madeleine, Cua-Cua, Silvia, Min, and Nando, January 3, 1976

Wedding: Silvia, Min, Cua-Cua, and Jorge Díaz Serrano, January 3, 1976

Back in Fort Collins

I had decided to pass through Tucson en route to Fort Collins so Silvia could meet Sass who had been part of our family since the war years, employed as governess for sisters Hope and Meemo. We all loved her. At the time, Sass was living in a small house adjacent to 2146 East 5th Street, Mum and Dad's home. They were not in residence. I already knew that Dad was not especially supportive of my marriage to Silvia, so I wanted feedback from someone who had always been fair and honest in the many years we had known each other. Sass prepared a wonderful fondue and treated Silvia with warmth and a welcoming spirit.

On our way again to Fort Collins, we passed through the Mormon community of Snowflake, AZ. Silvia was asleep as I drove out of town. In the rear and side view mirrors, I could see we were being escorted by two large pickup trucks, each with rifles on a rack in the back window. I pretended not to notice but realized that, because of Silvia's Mexican license plate, a few of Snowflake's anti-Mexican stalwarts had decided to make certain we kept moving. For a few miles things were tense, but Silvia slept through it all. I felt fear and wondered how many additional bigots we might encounter on our trip into Colorado and in the life we had planned for ourselves in Fort Collins.

Our last day on the road was July 31, 1976. As we began the final leg from Denver to Fort Collins, I could see ominous black clouds building in the west over Estes Park. Ten miles from Fort Collins, the rain, thunder, and lightning intensified. We entered our apartment in a downpour. The next day, I learned that 14 inches of rain had fallen over Estes Park in four hours, resulting in a 20-foot wall of water that roared down the Big Thompson River, destroying homes, bridges, irrigation facilities, and killing 143 people. The Big Thompson flood was an epic event that shocked northern Colorado. It was not an auspicious beginning for Silvia and me as we feathered our nest.

A few weeks later, I started classes at CSU. During that time, Jean and the boys came to the apartment to welcome us to Fort

Silvia and Erica "Sass" Habluetzel

Collins. I knew Jean meant well. Her peace offering was genuine. But Silvia viewed the visit as an attempt to interfere with our lives. There was nothing I could say to make her feel differently, and the awkwardness of that brief visit, settling around all of us like a dark cloud, did not bode well for future relationships.

Silvia had additional challenges. Having grown up with domestic help, her knowledge of the culinary arts was limited. When I had evening classes to meet, she felt pressure to prepare a meal in a timely fashion. Unfortunately, I was not much help. Last minute preparation of lectures was my M.O. Although she eventually became a good cook, Silvia was always hard pressed to put meals on the table at a fixed time. She would have preferred cooks and a maid to do the work for her. This was one of many lessons I experienced regarding the subtleties of cultural differences.

The first year for us had other difficult moments. Silvia attended my evening class on the history of Colorado. She worked on her English, met CSU wives from Colombia, Peru, and Venezuela, and gradually developed a routine for domestic chores. She cultivated a friendship with Jan Worrall, living next door, but I sensed she wasn't very happy. She missed the Latino culture: foods, routines, behaviors, festivals, church, her work with Helvia, etc. The move to Fort Collins was proving troublesome. The lesson for me was clear: You can take the Mexican out of Mexico, but you can't take Mexico out of the Mexican.

Especially painful for Silvia was her unwillingness to take communion. The church in Mexico had taught her that marriage to a divorced Protestant was a sin. She felt weighted down by guilt, an emotion which the Catholic Church bestows all too readily on its believers. I introduced her to my good friend Leonard Urban who had been a priest at CSU for Catholic students. We came to know each other at western history conferences I organized. He was politically liberal and an engaging scholar who was appalled by archaic teachings of his faith. Eventually, he left the church and married. But when Silvia needed help, he was still a practicing priest, posted to a church in Mead, CO, about 30 miles south of Fort Collins. I took Silvia to meet with him. It didn't take long for Leonard to persuade Silvia that she had done nothing wrong and that in the eyes of God, she was not a sinner. She resumed taking communion, and the two of us attended a nearby Catholic church.

I did my best to introduce her to my outdoor lifestyle. We took hikes, went fishing, and enjoyed picnics. But Silvia wasn't really interested in outdoor activities. She wanted to be a mother. We agreed to wait until I finished the book I was working on, *The Last Water Hole in the West*, but as the Mexicans say, *"Entre dicho y hecho hay mucho trecho."* There's many a slip twixt cup and lip. Silvia became pregnant in February. Alejandro was born on November 12, 1977.

It wasn't an easy birth. When her water broke, Silvia was sick with a streptococcus infection. I was so stressed by my first live birthing experience that I passed out in the delivery room. Dan, Nick, and Kit had been born without much input from me. In contrast to the detached role I played in their deliveries, fatherhood the second time around found me much more engaged. I had attended numerous preparatory sessions with Silvia prior to the actual event, and I was better prepared, even though a part of me resisted having another baby in the house. We settled on the name Alexander as the official birth certificate name, but he was Alejandro before Silvia left the hospital. I don't know where his middle name Jonathan came from, but by age 16, Alejandro had decided to change his name officially. He no longer wanted to be called Al, AJ, Alex, or Sandy. He liked Alejandro and from that time on, except perhaps for my stubborn father, no one called him Alexander. His mother bestowed on him the nickname, Chivo, goat in Mexican Spanish. *Chivito*, a term of endearment, means little goat. For as long as I can remember, this is what we have both called him.

Alejandro joined us in a new home that Silvia found when it was under construction. Located in southeast Fort Collins, on Stonehenge Drive, it was a strange architectural design: two floors, open ceilings, and a deck on the second floor, off a den which became Silvia's sewing room. I installed passive solar heat in the form of several large black drums filled with water. The south-facing, second-floor den received the warmest sun all year long. In the evening, the warmed up water put out enough heat to keep the second floor toasty well into the night. My office was in the basement. It was a cozy area in which I installed a bathroom with a toilet designed to project waste upwards into the sewer system. It worked … sometimes!

1419 Stonehenge Drive

All in all, our first home was comfortable and well located. A park, two blocks away, had tennis courts and walking paths. An ice skating arena was nearby and across the street, we had good neighbors from Hawaii who also had a newborn. Silvia was sad when they returned to Hawaii, but Wayne and Sue Gutowski replaced them almost immediately with their two children. They too became good friends. I dug up part of the back yard for a garden and planted cherry trees that proved to be very prolific. When Nando mentioned an interest in buying a property nearby so his family could visit us, we found a two-story duplex a quarter mile away. It was rented immediately. Because Silvia's relationship with her sister-in-law continued to deteriorate, for reasons unclear to me, Nando and family never occupied the property. To make matters worse, real estate values plummeted, adding additional angst to the relationship. Nando told us to sell the place, but the market was dead for years. Eventually, I was able to find a buyer, but Nando lost money on his investment.

Silvia and I spoke only Spanish when we were together. We even argued in Spanish. For me, this was a very demanding and stressful experience. There were no rules. Typical of second children like me, I am a peace maker, not an agitator or arguer. My passive-aggressive side sometimes emerges, because I don't like to engage in verbal duels over seemingly unworthy minutiae. Silvia, the quintessential Latina, preferred a more theatrical and dramatic approach to expressing anger, disappointment, and frustration. But she was a superb mother, and Alejandro benefited from growing up in a home where all he heard and spoke was Spanish. He now speaks the language very well, even teaching Spanish at Arapahoe High School when the designated teacher was unable to return for spring semester. And I have to say that arguing with Silvia, as much as I disliked the experience, improved my own speaking ability. Of course, I could never really keep up with her for a sustained period. Her staccato, stiletto approach to controversy usually left me shaking my head, wounded and angry. But there were times I held my own. The level of Spanish I can still speak on occasion is a direct result of many such encounters as well as the experience of speaking only Spanish at home for more than 20 years.

In the summer of 1979, I received an inquiry from the Fulbright Association regarding my possible interest in teaching at the Universidad Nacional de Cuyo in Mendoza, Argentina. They were looking for an American history professor to teach graduate students. Mendoza is located in the heart of Argentine wine country (Malbec varietals) about 130 miles from the Chilean border. Having been recently promoted to associate professor, I was eligible for a sabbatical leave. It seemed that a semester in Argentina would be a great experience for Silvia and me: a Hispanic culture, opportunities for travel, and something unique for my résumé. Little did I know that Mexicans feel hostility toward the Argentines because of their arrogance. *"Se sienten el umblígo del mundo,"* Silvia used to say. They think of themselves as the belly button of the world.

We invited an Argentine graduate student to our home for a steak dinner in order to learn more about his country. The visit did not go well. The young man proceeded to reinforce Silvia's bias by criticizing the steak we fed him, comparing it negatively to Argentine beef. As things turned out, his comparison was quite accurate, but his rudeness strengthened Silvia's hostility toward Argentina.

We flew to Buenos Aires by way of New York. Because he was less than two years old, Alejandro was not required to have his own seat. He slept on our laps the entire flight. I was in the middle seat. Next to me, on the aisle, was a very large Argentine lady whose own lap was piled high with gifts purchased in New York. For six hours, I was unable to move, resulting in pains I had not ever before experienced. Fortunately, we landed in Río de Janeiro to refuel, so I got a break.

In Buenos Aires, we met with Fulbright staff and university people, spending the night at a hotel where my *gringo* sense of trust resulted in our losing an entire piece of luggage and its contents. I gave a talk to a small group about the Mormon experience in the United States. The next day, we flew across the pampa to Mendoza where we were greeted warmly by our hosts from the university.

Argentina was experiencing almost 100% annual inflation. I was told by the embassy to cash my checks and spend the money immediately on food and rent. I was not supposed to open a savings account, but the banks were offering nearly 60% interest. We saw no other way to maintain liquidity over the course of an entire month. Argentina was still reeling under the impact of Isabel Perón's removal from power in 1976. An armed struggle was under way between government loyalists and Marxist-Leninist revolutionaries to replace her. Soldiers representing the Argentine army patrolled the streets of Mendoza. Suspicious of leftists at the university, they made themselves visible in the surrounding area. I felt extremely uncomfortable the first times I walked to my classroom. Armed soldiers were everywhere, and I was a strange looking foreigner.

Finding a place to live was difficult. Realtors, as such, were few and far between. We were shown several places we could afford, none of them being very satisfactory to Silvia. We finally settled on a one-room apartment situated on the second floor, above a very noisy family below. Silvia had to wash diapers and other laundry in the kitchen sink. There was no washing machine or dryer. Clothes had to be hung on the roof to dry. Alone this would have been enough to upset Silvia, but when a passing bird dropped a fecal bomb on her eye one day, the resulting furor almost caused a premature return home.

But we managed to get through it. My contacts at the university proved to be wonderful people. Students had fun correcting my Mexican Spanish, and my colleagues provided access to clay tennis courts, where I was invited to enjoy friendly competition and good exercise. On weekends, we rode the bus downtown and ate at sidewalk cafés, savoring Malbec wine, Argentine beef, and locally baked breads. Diesel-powered busses spewed exhaust on our clothes and tableware, but we learned to focus on the wonderful food. Friends occasionally took us on outings, one of which ended up at the Chilean border where we got a glimpse of Aconcagua and other mountains in the incredibly beautiful Andes. We didn't cross over into Chile for fear that Silvia might have problems returning to Argentina with her Mexican passport.

Before the semester ended, one of my graduate students had decided she wanted to complete her studies at CSU. She was not a historian, but she was admitted to the university, eventually marrying an American student. Another Argentine student, who had stayed in Argentina to complete her B.A., came to CSU where she earned a doctorate in sociology. Neither of these students would have had a chance to study in the United States without the Fulbright scholarship program.

Our departure from the Mendoza airport when the semester ended remains a poignant memory. Saying goodbye to everyone who came to see us off was bittersweet. Silvia was very glad to be going home. I was sorry to leave such good friends. My six months in

Mendoza were far more pleasant than what Silvia had experienced in a very small apartment, without a car, and with a two-year-old to care for. My Spanish had improved, and my perspective on American history was tweaked by the experience of having to once again view the Colossus of the North through the eyes of our Latino neighbors.

Not long after we returned to Fort Collins, I offered to teach a class on American history in Spanish. Most students who signed up were language majors, but that did not matter to me. I taught the class in our living room one night a week. Silvia participated. It wasn't a big success, but it provided a new experience for me that would not have been possible had I not immersed myself in Mexican and Argentine cultures.

In comparison to the dry winters we now experience, the fall and winter of 1979 were very snowy. Before we left Fort Collins, in late November, a large snowfall had covered our driveway. I shoveled one side to extricate our car and to open a path for a bachelor who would rent the house in our absence. He made no effort to clear the other side during the entire winter. I was shocked to see snow and ice still there when we returned in April. It was a good winter to be in the southern hemisphere.

Settling back into our routines that spring, it became evident that Silvia wanted another child. Her Latina friends were encouraging her and cajoling me. I countered with my argument that four children were more than enough. But Silvia was determined. She became pregnant in July 1981 while we were on vacation in Vail during our timeshare week at Sandstone Creek Club. I had purchased that particular week so we would always have a family vacation in the summer. To sweeten the pot, the Club gave us an extra week in April. It is the 16th week of the year, which almost always includes the final days of Vail's ski season. It also includes April 17, the day Cristina Erica Tyler was born. Cristina is now the owner of this timeshare.

Looking back on Silvia's second pregnancy, I was not very pleased. I felt used. In her defense, Silvia was taking a considerable risk. She knew I didn't want another child, but if she could produce a girl, she was confident we would all be happy. She gambled. At supper one evening, a day or so after a scheduled checkup with her doctor, the phone rang. She answered it and immediately retreated to the bathroom and closed the door. Obviously, this was a private conversation. When she returned to the kitchen, she had a changed demeanor. An ultrasound test had shown her wish had come true. She was going to give birth to a girl.

I was delighted, but I remained entrenched in bitterness at the thought of yet another baby. I did not provide Silvia the support she deserved during the remainder of her pregnancy. I even went to New Mexico to a conference during the last weeks of her term. Cristina Eleffson, a longtime Mexican friend who had also married a gringo, flew in from Mexico City to be with Silvia while I was away. It was a terrible time for Cristina: her son had recently drowned in their swimming pool. But she was a great help to Silvia in my absence. She called me in Santa Fe when the baby was born. I rushed home. Under the circumstances, it seemed appropriate to name our daughter Cristina. Her middle name, Erica, is a tip of the cap to Erica "Sass" Habluetzel, who was always a rock of support for me when I was having problems with Dad.

It took a while, but Cristina's presence in our home became a joy that increased exponentially with the passage of time. As with all my children, I love her dearly, and I'm ashamed that I was less than jubilant when Silvia became pregnant against my wishes. It's now water over the dam, but knowing how it has all turned out, how Cristina has enriched my life, I feel especially remorseful and wish I had done better by her mother when she was pregnant.

At CSU, my career took a new turn. Since employment in 1970— with the exception of two years in Mexico—I had spent summers as director of the American West Program, organizing the lectures, art shows, classes, films, and field trips dealing with varied aspects of the trans-Mississippi West. I volunteered my time, because the area of focus was consistent with my research interests, and because the programs we developed were coordinated and implemented with the input and assistance of local citizens. It was a good way for town and gown to intersect, and I enjoyed the experience.

Colleagues warned me that I might never make full professor if I didn't do more original research, and writing. Most of us had little time to crank out books and articles during nine months of teaching. Summers were for travel, research and writing. But I enjoyed the American West Program: Native Americans shared their point of view about White man's history; miners and ranchers told their stories; and successful authors, like Frank Waters and Jack Schaefer, spoke to us about their works.[3] I did not want to abandon something that gave me enormous satisfaction.

In the summer of 1984, I received a call from G. Emlen Hall who was then working for the State Engineer of New Mexico. He invited me to participate in a water rights case involving federal, state, and local entities. Because the State of New Mexico was planning to build water projects that would ultimately impact streams flowing into the Rio Grande (much of the Rio Grande's water was already promised to Texas and Mexico by covenant and treaty), it was necessary to adjudicate tributary water rights of Indian and non-Indian inhabitants of the Pojoaque and Nambe drainages. Under the 1846 Treaty of Guadalupe-Hidalgo ending the Mexican War, Spanish and Mexican water laws were to be honored under United States sovereignty. The teaching and research I had done in Mexico and Argentina, along with a book published by the Museum of New Mexico Press, appeared to qualify me as a witness for the segment of the trial that was about to focus on Spanish and Mexican customs and laws.[4]

Em's invitation was an opportunity to capitalize on past experience and stake out a historical specialty of my own. I certainly was no water expert at the time, but I could read Spanish documents. I could also speak the language, and I had been trained at the University of New Mexico to work with primary sources that defined the laws of both countries. I accepted the invitation, knowing full well it would take my career in a different direction. The American West Program would have to be directed by someone else.

New Mexico v. *R. Lee Aamodt* was my first experience in court. My assignment was to write up a historical overview of Hispanic water law, how it applied to North America and how, specifically, it was interpreted and implemented by New Mexican officials over 200 years of Spanish rule and the 25 years of Mexican sovereignty. This was a tall order with which I struggled mightily. Much of what I wrote was generic. When it came time for me to be deposed by attorneys representing the pueblos of Nambe and Pojoaque, I was a nervous wreck. I didn't do very well, and it showed. But my foot was in the door. I recognized what I needed to do to get up to speed. By the trial date several months later, I was in much better shape.

Scheduled in the U.S. District Court for New Mexico in Santa Fe, the case involved the indigenous rights of Native

Americans against those of Hispanic and Anglo-American settlers who had been farming side by side with shared water since the first quarter of the 17th century. Being so distant from centers of jurisprudence in Mexico City, local communities in New Mexico gave considerable weight to mutually agreed upon practices which were relied on by actual water users in the Rio Grande Valley. Consequently, in 1984, I paid close attention to what was happening in New Mexico on the ground and compared what I found to what was actually written in archaic laws forged hundreds of years earlier on the Iberian Peninsula. The outcome occasionally turned into a chaotic mix of myth and reality. As expert witness, my job was to represent to the court, what the law actually dictated and what customs and precedents had developed over more than three centuries.

On the witness stand, I managed to hold my own, largely because the Darth Vader-like attorney for the Native Americans had to rely on his toadies to translate the same documents with which I was quite familiar. My best moment occurred when Darth tried to prove that I had misunderstood the meaning of certain documents related to irrigation rights. I had stated that for most non-Indian farmers, water used on farmland following a harvest was at least as important as that used during the growing season.

"That is an incorrect reading of local agreements," the attorney stated. "I would like to have you translate for us the following documents that will prove you are in error." Immediately, one of his toadies slapped a well-magnified copy of a Spanish law on the witness table. Darth sat back smugly and waited for me to cave. Judge and courtroom became very still. I began to sweat. My own attorney came over to discuss the matter. As I looked at the document, however, it was clear that what I was being shown had been taken from a source that did not relate in any way to the issues being litigated. Someone without much experience had misread both the dates and the source of information. After waiting an appropriate amount of time to allow the courtroom to think I had been conquered, I pointed out the attorney's error. He was quite embarrassed, his only comment: "No further questions, Your Honor."

A small victory, but an important one. It proved to me that an attorney, no matter how sharp and experienced, was only as good as the information provided him by clerks and paid experts. I had spent so many hours at the Archives of New Mexico, struggling with the cryptic handwriting in Spanish and Mexican documents, that I had become, in fact, something of an expert. When the trial ended, I celebrated by buying a radio for my Volvo 242. That might sound like a small celebration, but on a professor's salary with two small children at home, it was a glorious luxury.

After *Aamodt*, I was asked to participate in additional water litigation. Although I only went to court 50% of the time, I was usually called in when a lawsuit was filed and either the plaintiffs or defendants wanted a chronological and historical explanation dealing with the Hispanic background of the conflict. A few of my reports were published in history and law journals, and one study on the Pueblo Rights Doctrine was turned into a book by Texas Western Press.[5] I met pretty much the same people in every case. There were not a lot of us doing this kind of work. The extra money was welcome, but there were times when the work was unpleasant.

One of those moments occurred in Alamosa, CO. Denver had been making noise about tapping into the water that drained off the Sangre de Cristo Mountains into the aquifers of the San Luis Valley. These aquifers were relatively shallow and were used by farmers to supplement stream water. Denver was concerned about growth. The city felt the need to provide additional water for an expanding population, and the Denver Water Board was weary of doing battle with the West Slope for water that naturally flowed into the Colorado River. The possibility of tapping underground reserves in the San Luis Valley was appealing, but to locals in the area, it felt like rape. Denver, the big and powerful city, was always seen as a bully.

I was asked to give my opinion regarding how Spanish and Mexican laws would have applied to Denver's contemplated water grab had the San Luis Valley still been under Mexican sovereignty, as it was before 1846. My research made clear that there was no law prohibiting removal of water to another river basin, provided existing users were not harmed. Denver was planning on drawing water from the sub-aquifers, not from the shallow pools used by valley irrigators. While I did not declare support for Denver's plans, the essence of my report found no conflict between Hispanic law and Denver's long straw. I delivered my conclusions to a standing-room-only auditorium full of farmers and local officials, some of whom were packing heat.

At the end of my presentation, during a Q & A, I was all but pilloried. To that audience, it made no difference what my research had concluded. For them, the bottom line was that the water beneath their farms belonged to them and would stay in their valley. This emotionally charged view, so easy to embrace, is also inconsistent with the Colorado Constitution. Article 16, section 5 states that the waters of Colorado belong to ALL of the people of the state and that domestic uses have priority over agriculture and manufacturing. Denver's desires were based on the need for drinking water. But the people of the valley totally disregarded the facts and were more than willing to take the law into their own hands. Very directly, they told me and Denver, to stay the hell away. The local judge who was supposed to hear the case resigned after a number of death threats. I exited Alamosa on my own, but I felt as if I had been ridden out of town on a rail.

Following the Alamosa experience, I accepted invitations to participate in litigated water conflicts, mostly in New Mexico and Colorado where Spanish and Mexican settlement had established the rules and customs associated with Hispanic law. I also introduced the history of water law and western water development into my classes at CSU. One of my graduate students, Brian Werner, was employed by the Northern Colorado Water Conservancy District (NCWCD) in Loveland. I invited his boss, Larry Simpson, manager of the NCWCD to speak to my Colorado history class about water issues. With Brian's encouragement, Larry invited me to write a 50-year history of the Colorado-Big Thompson Project (C-BT). The NCWCD, was the organizational and administrative entity created in 1937 to oversee construction of the C-BT which, when completed, would deliver Colorado River water under the Continental Divide to farms and cities on the Front Range. The growth, energy, and prosperity of the largest trans-mountain water diversion project in the world made it a fitting subject for a historical study.

I was delighted to have this opportunity. I asked for and was granted a one-year sabbatical leave to focus on research. Most documents, correspondence and newspaper clippings were located in a storage room in the basement of NCWCD's headquarters in Loveland. Surrounded by archival boxes reaching from floor to ceiling, breathing the dank and chilly air in a storage vault containing decades of historical materials, I gradually pieced together the story of an incredible trans-mountain water diversion project that enabled Colorado's Front Range communities to support its postwar population boom.

As Brian Werner will attest, the five years I worked on *The*

Last Water Hole in the West were filled with unexpected surprises. I interviewed people who had been involved in construction. They told stories about engineering mistakes, accidents, and bureaucratic foolishness by the Bureau of Reclamation. A few of the men I spoke to were hostile; others were more than happy to tell their side of things. I never knew quite what to expect. I traveled from the headwaters of the Colorado River to the towns of Sterling and Julesburg, looking for anyone who had been involved with the C-BT in its early years. During one of those trips, I committed an egregious mistake when I placed a valuable scrapbook on the top of my car, got distracted, and drove a mile before realizing what I had done. Silvia, bless her heart, spent weeks piecing together the torn articles that had blown away during my short drive.

After finishing each chapter, I would stop off at Brian Werner's home to deliver the draft. He was a good editor. His girls, however, tended to be rambunctious. One evening, when I arrived to make a delivery, his oldest opened the door and greeted me with a well-aimed punch in the crotch. I survived, but I made subsequent deliveries to Brian's office in Loveland.

Silvia designed the book cover. She followed my instructions and delivered a product reflecting her artistic interpretation of what I had asked for. It was not an immediate hit with the linear thinking water community, but they came to accept it in due course. Having spent so much time in isolation working on the book, I wanted Silvia to have a connection to my *magnum opus*.

Now, 30 years after publication, it's easy to see that I could have written a shorter version of the C-BT's 50-year history. At the time, I wanted to include all the detail related to engineering challenges and the social, political and economic conflicts inherent in East Slope-West Slope water struggles. How all the players finally came to an understanding regarding construction and financing is a remarkable story. The C-BT's importance to northern Colorado is undeniable, and engineers from all over the world have come to marvel at the completed project. I don't think *The Last Water Hole in the West* is a great book by any means, but as a resource for understanding the complexity of moving large quantities of water to population, farming, and industrial centers, I believe it is useful. One reviewer who basically agreed, also noted that the excessive detail was a distraction. As an example, she pointed out, I might have considered editing out an unnecessary description of T-33s flying over the ceremony that celebrated completion of the last phase of the project. Yes, but those were my airplanes. Give me a break!

Alejandro and Cristina were 15 and 10 respectively when *The Last Water Hole* was published in 1992. By then, we had moved into a home Silvia designed on 913 Sandy Cove Lane in the southeast part of Fort Collins. The house was about a mile east of College Avenue, a block or two west of Lemay Avenue, and a block north of Harmony Road. That neighborhood was basically trailer parks when I first arrived in 1965, and Harmony Road, which had become a major, four-lane artery between College Avenue and I-25, was a two-lane farm road with little traffic. Indeed, the City of Fort Collins had grown threefold in 30 years.

Our ranch-style home had a formal greeting room in which I frequently entertained graduate students. It also had a wood-burning fireplace and an open deck surrounded by the master bedroom and living room. In the southeast corner of the lot, I dug a deep pit for a round trampoline which received almost daily use. Alejandro and Cristina had their own bedrooms downstairs, on either side of a large playroom where I eventually installed a pool table.

Alejandro was a good student, urged along by his mother

who insisted that he read more books than anyone in his class. He had little interest in competitive sports, but he was musical with laudable skills on the violin and a killer voice. So good, in fact, he was invited to sing "God Bless America" at the Washington Monument during a Veterans Day celebration. His mother and I appreciated the tenor and range of his voice, but we didn't realize how extraordinary it was until we heard him perform the lead at Fountain Valley School in *Joseph and the Amazing Technicolor Dreamcoat*.

Alejandro was very close to his mother, and it wasn't until I was engaged in giving talks about *The Last Water Hole in the West* that we developed a special bond. He traveled with me, managed the slide projector, and developed as a young man interested in spending more time away from home. We both agreed he should do the last two years of high school at Fountain Valley School in Colorado Springs. He left home in the fall of 1994.

Cristina was quite different. She loved sports and wanted a horse. For her sixteenth birthday, I found her a small, black gelding, Ebon, trailered him to our neighborhood, and walked him right to the front door. The surprise was complete in more ways than one. Ebon proved difficult to manage; a real disappointment to Cristina who was taking dressage lessons and beginning to show competitively. Eventually, I bought a heavy western saddle and tried to pound some sense into Ebon, but he was stubborn. We eventually gave him to Fountain Valley School, where he enhanced his reputation as an incorrigible equine. There were other horses along the way, but none ever good enough to beat the high-priced full bloods against whom Cristina competed.

Cristina also played soccer. She was a good player but lacked a bit of confidence and tended not to be as aggressive as her competitors, until her previously mentioned experience at a game in Monument. She is a lovely, gentle lady and naturally expects others to be the same way, but on that day, she dug deep into her competitive nature and gave as good as she got. At Poudre High School in Fort Collins, she too was a good student and was accepted at the University of San Diego. During her last year of high school, her mother and I had a falling out over the rules of the house as applied to our teenage daughter. Because it was just one battle too many and because I was trying to finish up *The Last Water Hole in the West* at the time, I decided to move out to a nearby apartment where I could get relief from the arguments and finish my writing. The move was hard on Silvia. Cristina had started dating and because her bedroom was in the basement with window wells that allowed for easy egress, she occasionally met boyfriends in their cars, at night. I returned to the house to help Silvia with the crisis. We went to group counseling in Boulder to mend tears in our marriage, and I think we actually made progress. I hated going, because the meetings were after supper and lasted several hours. We returned home late, and I usually had to teach the next day. But we were unified in our determination to provide Cristina with better parenting and although there continued to be occasional late-night sorties, the rules of the house loosened a bit, and tensions diminished all around.

During her final year at Poudre High School, I gave Cristina a bright red, two-door Subaru Impreza. A little hot rod! It was as big a surprise as was Ebon, but the car proved almost as pugnacious as the horse. It was a stick shift, Cristina's first experience with a clutch. I tried every tactic I could think of to help her master those gears. We drove on side streets, alleys, and parking lots. We drove fast and very slow. I spoke softly, screamed on occasion, and tried to make her laugh, all to no avail. She just couldn't work right foot, left foot, and right hand at the same time. She wanted so badly to succeed, that she put too much pressure on herself. She became a wreck. We had plenty of tears. I finally just quit. When Silvia replaced me in the passenger seat a day or two later, everything improved with less pressure. Within days, Cristina was driving herself to school in a car that was the envy of her classmates. The experience reminded me of what could have been my last check ride in a T-33: realizing the instructor that day was hung over and possibly incapable of flying, I became proficient out of necessity. I proved my competence and got my wings; Cristina proved she could drive and got her car.

Life With Two Families

Looking back at the '80s and '90s, I recall the discomfort of trying to be a father to two sets of children. Silvia seemed to prefer keeping Dan, Nick, and Kit at a distance. I tried on occasion to bring us all together, but such attempts were awkward and unpleasant. Because these circumstances permeated most of the years Silvia and I were together, I am unable to reflect on this part of my life without mentioning the stress I experienced. I felt the "loss" of my first three sons very deeply.

Thoughts of ending the marriage crossed my mind, but I was fearful of the emotional consequences which divorce would have on me as well as on Alejandro and Cristina. One divorce was hard enough! Silvia and I saw marriage counselors; over the course of 10 years, I think we went to seven different individuals, plus a monthly group counseling session. The latter gave us moments of surcease as we drove to and from Boulder. But I came to realize that Silvia really wanted the counseling to go on indefinitely. The suggestions counselors made to us were not viewed by her as a road to marital harmony and although I am certain she wanted improvement as much as I did, what she really hoped for was a regular venue at which she could articulate feelings partly rooted in a time long before we met. Right or wrong, I felt frustrated by what seemed like a circular, never ending pattern of complaints. There appeared to be no end to the litany of criticism. Consequently, our relationship actually worsened. I found myself living with a person who had a lot of anger, and I didn't know how to diffuse it. It beat me up.

I did my best to stay in touch with the older boys. Not very successfully, I might add, but anyone in my shoes will understand that it is almost impossible to maintain a close relationship with family members if one's spouse stands in opposition.

Dan Jr.'s situation was especially challenging. After his discharge from the Navy, he attended Fort Lewis College in Durango. He had financial help from the GI Bill and succeeded in getting occasional assistance from the college, but he struggled to make ends meet. I had difficulty helping him. We were on a fairly tight budget ourselves and when I spoke to Silvia about providing monetary support, she became angry. When Dan found himself in a jam, needing to hire an attorney, I sent him money. Silvia disapproved. I was unable to persuade her that in the long run, Dan would do us all proud. In fact, Dan graduated from Fort Lewis, earned a master's degree at San Jose State University and a doctorate at Oregon State University, all of which more than justifying the small amount of assistance I provided. But Silvia remained hostile, convinced that Dan was a grown-up and should be self-sufficient. And he was a male. Silvia resented the first-class treatment her brother had received and had little sympathy for the needs of my three older boys.

Nick took a different route during those years. His directional compass moved considerably after graduation from high school, but when he secured a job hanging drywall in Anaheim, he found an interest in the construction business that would eventually become a career. Looking for a bachelor's degree in construction management, Nick returned to Fort Collins and enrolled at CSU. He found small remodel jobs to help pay for tuition and met his future wife, Suzi, whose mother, a realtor, had worked with us to purchase the Stonehenge Drive home. Suzi and Nick both took my very large Colorado history class. Nick's 89.3% final grade average netted him a B+, about which he gave me a hard time for many years. Deservedly! I buckled 21 years later, changing the grade officially to an A on his 50th birthday.

I had to enjoy Nick's success in private. Silvia wanted nothing to do with him or with Suzi. We were invited to their wedding reception in August 1987. On our way, Silvia was so unpleasant that I turned the car around and took her home. By then it had become clear that any connection I wanted with my older sons would have to be experienced in isolation from my wife. The stress this added to my life was enormous. When Nick needed me years later to help him move from Maryland to California, I disappointed him. A new semester was about to commence at CSU, but the real reason I had to withhold my assistance was that I was feeling too bruised and battered to tell Silvia that I would be gone for a few days to help my own son. In retrospect, that was a bad decision. I should have been tougher.

Nick and I did manage a powerful reconnection of sorts while he was in Fort Collins. We were/are both fans of *MASH* (Richard Hooker, *MASH*, New York: William Morrow, 1968). One of the surgeons in that book and TV series was Hawkeye Pierce, an irreverent party animal who drank a lot. On a trip to Japan during the Korean War, Pierce visited a friend who worked at Dr. Yamamoto's Finest Kind Pediatric Hospital and Whore House. On his return to MASH Unit 4077 in Korea, Pierce's vocabulary was infused with the phrase "Finest Kind." It was his answer or comment on just about anything.

I was playing on a men's hockey team when Nick was trying to promote his home remodeling skills. Our team and Nick's business needed a name. We decided on Finest Kind, but when the hockey jerseys came back to us from the printer, the lettering was slightly off. Instead of "Finest Kind" the shirts read "Finestkind." We spent a lot of hours explaining this to curious observers.

Of the three boys, Kit probably had the best relationship with

Silvia. I think she identified with his struggle to make something of himself after a few years of uncertainty. Successfully completing his high school equivalency degree, Kit took on the difficult challenge of aviation mechanics. He had an innate ability to understand things mechanical, and he did well, graduating from a Denver school with a license as an A & P Mechanic. He was married when he took jobs in Hawaii and Fresno, CA, but it was in Durango and Grand Junction where he and Laurie had their two children: Cody and Jesse. I visited as often as I could, but it was never enough, and I always struggled when I wanted to get away for a visit.

In spite of these pressures, there were many things that happened in the '80s and '90s that still provide good memories. Several books I had been working on were published, and my career as a water historian took off. I had a slight setback medically when a troublesome gallbladder shut down, and I had to have it removed surgically. This operation has triggered certain digestive inconveniences over the past 30 years. But at the time, major surgery was the only medical option. Mum and Dad were visiting Fort Collins when the gallbladder stopped working. We all ate out one night and finished off a great meal with crème brûlée. I awoke in the middle of the night with tremendous pain. Surgery followed a few days later. Arthroscopic techniques were not yet an option, so I have a five-inch scar across my gut.

Except for dietary restrictions, loss of my gallbladder didn't really slow me down. When Dan Jr. suggested a seven-day hiking trip in the San Juan Mountains in July 1993, I agreed to join him. After years of irregular contact, the prospect of companionship with Dan in an environment he loves was really welcome. I was also enthusiastic about the route he had chosen to Durango from the Rio Grande Reservoir. It would take us to an area called the Window on the Continental Divide. For years I had been talking about a lost Spanish gold mine to my Colorado history class. With considerable evidence that such a mine had existed while Spaniards occupied what is now New Mexico, I had used the story to generate historical excitement among students who were, as a group, somewhat bored by the past. A few students—I later learned by way of postcards they sent me—took a leave of absence from the university to look for the mine. I was eager to have a chance to see for myself where this supposed mining had taken place. According to stories I had heard, Spaniards found gold in the vicinity of La Ventana on the Continental Divide. While hauling it to Santa Fe, they were attacked by Utes. The survivors managed to return to the mine and hide the evidence of their excavations. Years later, when the threat of Indian attack had diminished, they were unable to find the mine. That gold has yet to be found.

I was somewhat wary of hiking at altitude. In retrospect, it seems silly that at age 60 I was worried about the ill-effects of carrying a backpack over 12,000 feet. One of Dan's friends planned to bring a pack animal, and Dan indicated that my load could be lightened. I brought along an oxygen bottle and was a tad ashamed when it had to be carried by Buford, the pony.

The expedition launched on Sunday, July 18, at 30 Mile Campground near the Rio Grande Reservoir. Because of a late start, we struggled with flies, heat, and dust as we launched our climb up the Weminuche Trail. The next day we made it to the base of the Window on the Continental Divide, camping at 12,000 feet. The stars were incredible that night. Above most of the bugs and dust, we enjoyed a clear sky with little wind and no light pollution, except the embers of a dying fire. It was surreal; life imitating art. The broad sweep of heavenly bodies made me feel insignificant but fortunate to be part of a panorama that few get the chance to see. It was easy to sleep that night.

After climbing a second pass (Columbine), we landed in Chicago Basin. Signs of overuse of this Wilderness abounded. Lots of trash and more tourists as we headed down Cascade Creek to the Purgatory ski area where we were picked up and taken into Durango. We had been in the Weminuche Wilderness for a week, and we had bonded as a group. While extended Wilderness trips impact people differently, we all felt a level of renewal; a spiritual renaissance. It was hard to say goodbye. Dan was clearly in his element, and I was grateful to have shared in the joy he felt and the leadership he exerted. I also recognized how badly I had needed my batteries re-charged and how satisfying it was to have that experience with my oldest son.

Perhaps I should have known how much I needed a week in the Weminuche. A month earlier, in June, Mum had passed away. Her death occurred while I was doing research at the Herbert Hoover Library in West Branch, IA. Silvia alerted me after one of my siblings called the house to advise us about funeral arrangements. I decided not to attend. Three months earlier, I had made a trip to Tucson when Mum called from Tucson Medical Center to say she had been diagnosed with ovarian cancer. I flew to Tucson and went straight to TMC where I spent a lovely afternoon with her. She was upbeat and full of life; just as I will always remember her. She refused to dwell on her cancer and introduced me to the doctors, nurses, and residents whom she had befriended. I knew her condition was serious, but she did not want our time together to be marred by maudlin conversation.

I left the hospital in the late evening and went to 2146 East Fifth Street, the winter home she and Dad had owned since 1946. By the time I arrived, Dad was in bed. Meemo greeted me. I was in deep doo-doo, she reported. Dad was furious that I had come to Tucson without first asking his permission. In addition to his concerns about Mum's health, he remained profoundly jealous of the closeness Mum and I had enjoyed for a long time. I think I reminded him of the Harper side of the family. Whatever the reason, his grief over Mum's condition was exacerbated by what he viewed as disrespect from me. As the family patriarch, he felt dishonored that I had come to see her without asking for his blessing. In the morning, he left the house for breakfast, unwilling to associate with me at all. We did exchange a few words when he returned, but the extent of his rage was all consuming. I took my leave and returned to Colorado. When Mum died, I decided that Dad would be better able to deal with his emotions if I wasn't present. This was not an easy decision, but in retrospect, I think it was the right one. Without actually mouthing the words, Mum and I had said goodbye at TMC.

Mum with Tally, 1960

Dad had a hard time with Mum gone. He was 86 with significant health problems. The loss of his partner of 63 years was a devastating blow. She had spent most of her life at his side, fielding his bad humors, acting often as his foil, preparing his meals, keeping a home for him, and frequently serving as a punching bag when he was angry with one (or more) of his children and grandchildren—which was often. When she died, he floundered and lost a sense of purpose. Even though he completed the third and final volume of *A Joyful Odyssey*, which Mum had urged him to do, the will to live gradually faded. He died three months later, in September 1993. The note Mum wrote to him reveals the love and respect she had for Dad: "Live on, dear Dad, and finish your book. It has already touched and gladdened many of us, and it will also touch so many more in the future. It is your gift, your legacy, your love for all who come after you."

I did attend his funeral. Dad had scoffed at formal religion and clergy most of his life, but prior to death, he had arranged for a service in a nearby Episcopal church, selecting very traditional hymns and readings. We scattered his ashes, supposedly near the site where Mum's ashes were scattered, in one of Mt. Lemon's many canyons. No one was too sure of the location, and it didn't really matter anyway. Rob made the toss, and Dad came right back to him on the wind. Had I made the toss, the wind would surely have shifted.

Losing both parents in such a short span of time is difficult, no matter the past history. Death severs the umbilical cord with finality. Mum's passing made me feel disconnected and sad. I had lost someone with whom I could almost always share feelings, a real emotional crutch when times were tough. When Dad died, I found myself on a roller coaster of emotions, most of which were connected to feelings of regret. I had always wanted my father to be more of a friend and less of a judge. From the athletic fields of Fountain Valley School to my life as a professor at Colorado State University, I never really experienced much fatherly support. When I expressed these feelings to Mum, she said that Dad was jealous. I never understood that; jealous of what? But perhaps she was onto something. I remember Dad telling me once that he envied my ability to enjoy outdoor and athletic activities with my children, experiences he felt deprived of because of his bad eyesight. Maybe so. But in later years, we clashed more frequently over what he viewed as my ongoing lack of deference. His death heightened feelings of remorse; of what could have been. No one made him laugh more, he once said; and no one made him angrier. As far as our history as father and son is concerned, that's probably a good epitaph. I just wish there could have been more laughter.

Months after Dad's death, Sid urged me to participate in dividing up the contents of the Tucson house. In their wills, Mum and Dad had instructed us to go through the house and tag items of interest with pieces of yarn. Each of the five of us was to use a different color. If possessions ended up with more than one yarn color, we were requested to act like gentlemen and ladies to negotiate a solution: you take this, but give me that!

Silvia and I flew down to take part in the distribution. She had an interest in a few of Mum's finer pieces of clothing, chinaware, and jewelry. Unfortunately, one of my siblings was offended by the thought of Silvia owning any of Mum's personal possessions. I was astounded. I didn't know if the reason for this proprietary behavior had to do with the fact that Silvia was my second wife or that she was Mexican; maybe both. In any event, when confronted with this opposition, I determined that Silvia and I would have to leave. The hostility was palpable.

Parked at the front of the house was Dad's red Datsun pickup. There were no strings of yarn on it. I told Silvia we would be driving home. We got into the pickup and headed for Colorado, leaving behind my colored pieces of yarn on a few paintings, an old refrigerator, and an 18th century chair Mum had inherited with Gorham Bacon's initials on the bottom.[6] Those items were delivered relatively quickly to Fort Collins. Taming the bad feelings regarding my sibling took a lot longer.

By the mid-90s, I was beginning to consider retirement. Dan, Nick, Kit, Alejandro, and Cristina all seemed to be settled comfortably in various stages of life, and I sensed I could be a better two-family dad if I had a second home in the mountains where we could enjoy ourselves without worrying about Silvia's disapproval. Dan had begun work on a Ph.D in meteorology at Oregon State University, Corvallis, OR. In addition to being a full-time student, he was actively engaged in hang gliding, a hobby in which he tried to interest me. But when I was invited to go tandem with him, my knees buckled. As he correctly reported to his mother, I chickened out. Ultimately, we enjoyed another adventure together on bicycles which turned out splendidly.

In 1996, Nick and Suzi left Maryland and headed for Sunnyvale, CA. Nick had been working his first job after graduating summa cum laude from CSU in 1989. He was hired by Thompkins Builders, a large construction firm operating in the Washington, D.C., area. Nick's mom, Jean, had married George Lamphere, one of the company's top executives. This relationship added pressure to what Nick felt in a very competitive and stressful work environment. He and Suzi stuck with their respective jobs in the Baltimore-D.C. area for almost seven years, the highlight of which was the birth of my first grandson, in 1991.

Philip was born with cystic fibrosis. Both parents must have the CF gene if a child is to inherit this disease. To this day, I do not know if his mother or I passed the gene to Nick. Whatever the transmission route, the news was devastating. Nick and Suzi dedicated themselves to unselfish and determined care for Philip, instilling in him a belief he could achieve anything if he established a lifestyle based on healthy choices. The move to California was designed to get Philip closer to the doctors who specialized in CF. But it was the daily, persistent, and loving care for Philip by his parents that enabled him to mature, socialize, and graduate from high school with honors. His acceptance at prestigious Cal Poly in San Luis Obispo, made possible the pursuit of a degree in computer engineering. Additionally, he became a talented drummer with his own band, Louder Space, which has played before noisy throngs from San Luis Obispo to Kailua. Philip is now organizing fundraisers for CF. I asked him to serve on the board of the Daniel Tyler Health and Education Foundation, so he could direct additional funds to researchers working on CF. He did a great job, providing extra cash for those doing pioneering research. Ultimately, he helped me close out the foundation. About the same time, Nick and Suzi sold their Sunnyvale house and moved to Austin, TX.

Kit and Laurie had married in the late '80s. They tried a year at Fort Lewis College, but the timing wasn't good. When Kit received his A&P certificate, they started looking for work. His first job was with Mid Pacific Airlines in Hawaii. Working conditions in Honolulu favored *Kama'ainas* who tended to make life difficult for mainland *Haoles*. After a year, Kit and Laurie returned to the mainland. Kit took a job with United Express in Fresno, CA. He and Laurie stayed in Fresno for three years before moving to Durango, CO, where Kit began employment with Mesa Airlines based in

Farmington, NM. His round-trip commute of 100 miles a day created stress and prompted another move, this time to Grand Junction. By then, Cody was part of the family. He was born in Durango in 1992. Jesse arrived the following year. By the end of the decade, they were settled in Colorado Springs where Kit had been hired as the personal mechanic of a businessman who flew around the country in a Beechcraft King Air. It was a good job; fewer bosses and corporate regulations, his own hanger, and the opportunity to learn business from a very successful entrepreneur.

About the same time, Alejandro left home to attend Fountain Valley School in 1994. The school was a good fit for him. Although he had to be reminded occasionally that he wasn't working to capacity, his development as a thespian under the guidance of Chris Lowell was a joy to watch. Mainly as a result of his talent as a vocalist, he was recognized at FVS graduation. At Johns Hopkins, where he earned his undergraduate degree, he became part of the Mental Notes, an a capella group that competed with other colleges in the region. It was that organization which brought him and his future wife, Kim Minh Nguyen, together.

Cristina was a sophomore at Poudre High School in Fort Collins when Alejandro graduated from FVS in 1996. She was a good student, a flautist in the school orchestra, and a member of a competitive Arsenal soccer team. With little free time, she still managed to take dressage lessons on low-cost horses I bought for her. She did well, but it was tough to go up against the high-end horses and private trainers who knew the tricks of the trade and had unlimited budgets.

By 1998, I had the feeling that if I was going to see Dan, Nick, and Kit with any regularity, I would have to do so outside of Fort Collins. I made short trips into the foothills to see what I could find in the way of an acreage where I might run horses and cattle. The longing for a way of life reminiscent of the Crystal River Ranch had never gone away. But most of the small ranches I looked at were run down and unattractive.

Craig Harrison, a creative businessman whom I came to know because of his interest in water, owned a cattle ranch in North Park near the town of Walden. He was selling 40-acre lots in timbered areas on his land where there was little grass for grazing and no chance of crop cultivation. Lot purchasers would have a three-acre envelope on their 40 acres where they could build a home. Views of the Rawah and Medicine Bow mountains were exquisite, and the town of Walden, 20 miles away, had ample supplies of necessities.

It seemed to me that a 40-acre lot on a working cattle ranch was close to perfect as a getaway for me and a place to spend time with friends and family. Only two hours by car from Fort Collins, the ranch location would allow me to experience the mountains without being too distant from home. I gave Craig a $5,000 deposit on a $200,000 lot. I had 30 days to change my mind.

I wanted another opinion, so I invited Dan Jr. to take a look at the property. We walked all over the ranch, discussing pros and cons. Dan liked the location, but he wondered what people would do when they visited? Women would want a nice place to dine out, shops to browse, and other amenities one would expect in a mountain town. Walden is pretty basic; essentially a supply town for North Park ranchers. We could have horses, but the winters are severe in North Park. What would we do with animals when the snows came? Dan was thinking broadly. He was also concerned about the apparent absence of hang gliders anywhere in the valley. I came to the conclusion we should look elsewhere. I asked for my money back and decided to go farther west to Steamboat Springs where we had all enjoyed good skiing in a resort town that offered a great deal more than Walden.

Thanks to an ongoing friendship with Liz Lockwood, a Fort Collins realtor with whom Jean had worked, I was introduced to Kris McGee, a Steamboat realtor. Kris had attended Punahou for his high school education, and his uncle was a class behind me at Fountain Valley. We had a lot in common. He showed me properties all over the Yampa River Valley. The one which most excited my imagination was located about five miles south of the town in the foothills. It was on a slope at the end of a two-mile road that served a residential community called Country Green. Views of the Haymaker Golf Course, Mt. Werner, the ski mountain, and Rabbit Ears Pass were awesome. Located at the end of the road, the lot was exposed to minimal traffic and nearby homes were mostly out of sight on their own three-acre lots. I envisioned building a two-level house with a deck wrapping around three sides, a hot tub on the deck that overlooked the valley, and five-minute drives to town, to Mt. Werner, and to the golf course. An excavator I brought up to the lot confirmed that the kind of house I had in mind could be built without violating Country Green HOA rules. The neighbor (owner of the local liquor store) across the street would have to be able to see over my roof if he lay prone on his living room floor. This meant we would have to drop the house lower on the hill than I had wanted, doubling excavation expenses. But the views would still be unobstructed, and I remained committed to purchase.

The owner of the lot was in financial difficulty. He was asking $140,000. I paid it. Kris and I determined that 10 years earlier, he might have paid $40,000. He was getting a good return on his investment, but because of Dad's death six years earlier, I had inherited assets that could be tapped for this project. Still, I was nervous about committing so much money to a piece of raw land, knowing that a lot more money would be required to build a house.

I included Silvia in everything I was doing. She didn't object, thinking, I suspect, that a Steamboat home would turn out to be something like the Acapulco homes upper class Mexico City residents owned and used when they wanted to get away from the city. I had no interest in shutting her out of the process. I believed that she would come to Steamboat from time to time, but that I could use the place by myself to recreate with my older boys, all of whom enjoyed the skiing, fishing, and hiking Steamboat offered.

I needed a builder. A good friend who worked out at the same Fort Collins gym expressed interest. His company built homes in Wyoming and Colorado and was interested in testing the Steamboat market. To save money for his clients, he used CSU construction students to draw up architectural plans. After a few meetings in Steamboat and Fort Collins to make sure the house I had in mind could be built on the lot, we had a set of operational plans to review. The first dirt was moved in the spring of 1999 with the goal of completing the home before the snow arrived in November.

The spring of 1999 was my last semester at CSU. In addition to my teaching, I made many trips to Steamboat to witness the construction process. For the most part, the house went up as scheduled, but we had a decision to make regarding a water supply. There was no city water in Country Green; all my neighbors had drilled wells, some sunk more than 500 feet into the bedrock sandstone to find small amounts of water—one to two gallons per minute. I asked a professor at Colorado Mountain College to give me a sense of where and how deep a productive well could be driven on my property. He was an experienced geologist and dowser: a water witcher. Using a stick as a divining rod (and a whole lot of intuition), he found the best spot for drilling. He estimated that we would find water at 300 feet and a deeper pool at 400 to 500 feet. At that time, drillers were asking $25 per cased foot to drill a well. I was nervous about spending another $12,000 to $15,000 for a well that might only produce a trickle and whose pump could break down entirely, causing additional expenses down the road. I decided instead to have my water hauled to the property from town. I contracted with a company to install four 1,000-gallon concrete tanks on the uphill side of the house next to the garage. With flow-through valves in each tank, I would have about 3,500 gallons of usable water. A buzzer wired into the house would go off when the tanks dropped below 50% capacity. In contrast to the unknown quality of well water, I would have water that had already been tested and purified, and I could call for a truck with a 2,000-gallon capacity to bring water within 24 hours of the buzzer going off. For delivery service, I would pay $160. If I used one load a month, I would have eight years before expending a total of $15,000, and I would not have any worries about water quality or troublesome pumps.

Kris McGee warned me that this system might be a short-term solution financially, but in the long run, he cautioned, I might be creating a problem. Selling the house down the road to someone who needed a bank loan could negate the chance for a fast sale; banks wanted proof that a home had a reliable water supply. Hauling water was dependent on having a provider with good water rights and the necessary equipment. If the company went out of business, or the river got too low to honor the provider's priority, the occupants of such a home would be out of luck.

I understood the argument, but I was willing to take a chance on a delivery system that would obviate the expense and maintenance of a well. I calculated that most visitors would understand the need to conserve: short showers, no irrigation of plants, and toilet flushes according to need: "When it's yellow, let it mellow; when it's brown, flush it down." Sixteen years later, during the process of selling the house, I was fortunate to find a buyer who was perfectly fine with the system we had installed and because he paid cash, we did not have to involve a lender. I was lucky. Now that I am living in Denver, I don't fret over a running faucet as I did in Steamboat. But as Cristina and my grandchildren know all too well, when they visited me in Steamboat, and I heard the downstairs shower running more than 2–3 minutes, they could count on a visit and a gentle reminder of the importance of conservation: "If you want to soak in hot water, we have a hot tub. Use it!"

We never ran out of water, but I was always mindful of the level in the tanks. When the buzzer stopped working about five years after installation, I used an eight-foot stick with marks on it to determine how much water remained in the tanks. In winter, especially after I had been away from the house for a while, I had to shovel great quantities of snow in order to get to the tank lids, which were often frozen to the tanks. When the water truck arrived, the task of getting a hose from the truck to each tank proved enormously challenging.

But we survived and when I sold the house in 2015, the tanks were still clean, and the system was working. In my 16 years living there, only one mouse got into the water through a hole caused by a broken piece of concrete. I flushed the tanks then, but that was the only time I had to deal with contamination. In many ways, that water system defined living at 34630 Country Green Lane. Visitors participated in conservation willingly, for the most part, although some, especially the ladies, tended to view me as an unreasonable nag.

Silvia and I furnished the house at American Warehouse. The first night we stayed there as a family, we had her mother with us. It was a cold and snowy December day, around 15 degrees, as I recall. Fortunately, all the systems worked well, and I was able to take my first morning dip with coffee in hand in the hot tub, a daily routine that has stuck with me ever since. Because the excavators had not left us with much room to park cars, aside from the two-car garage, I asked Dan Jr. to help me build additional space with railroad ties. When the entire area was blacktopped, we had ample space for several additional vehicles.

I loved that house, and I loved living in Steamboat. I would still be there had not life's exigencies required a move. The fond memories of 16 years in the Yampa Valley will never fade away.

In May 1999, while the finishing touches were being put on the house, I taught my last class at CSU. I had asked the history department to let me teach a class on The American Cowboy. It was in that class that I gave my last lecture and when the period ended, I gathered my notes and retreated to my office on the third floor of the Clark Building. The bittersweet feelings of pending retirement washed over me as I contemplated a teaching career of over 30 years in that institution. A knock on the door turned out to be one of my older students from the "Cowboy" class who had surmised that my teaching days were over. I had not given any thought to celebration, but Monica persuaded me to go for a drink.

We ended up in a downtown restaurant sipping martinis. And not just one. I have a limited tolerance for alcohol. One martini is plenty for me. We each had two. And they were huge. By the time we left, I was barely ambulatory. Monica decided we should go play pool. I didn't think I would be able to stand up long enough to hit a ball with a cue, but we ended up at a pool hall playing at a table in

Life With Two Families | 191

Steamboat house in winter

Steamboat house

192 | *Looking Back At Ninety*

Steamboat hot tub with Betty

the middle of a room, surrounded by other people drinking and socializing. Although I had brought a pool table to Steamboat, I didn't use it much, preferring to let my guests have fun while I relaxed upstairs. I did play billiards at Harvard, but my aim and game were only so-so. That night in Fort Collins, however, I couldn't miss. I ran the table, not once but twice. The young people sitting around the room applauded, and the louder they cheered, the better I got. Who would have imagined such an outcome from someone as blitzed as I was? Thanks to Monica, that was a truly memorable night, one that I will always recall, however, with very mixed emotions. A few days later, I received a phone call from her saying that on the way home that night, she had veered off the road and struck a tree. Her ten-year-old son, Ezra, who had been riding shotgun without a seat belt, went through the windshield and was pronounced dead at the scene. I never got over that. How could such kindness on her part be rewarded with such cruelty? I will never understand.

I left CSU without fanfare. I didn't want a party, having attended a few of my colleagues' celebrations. They were awkward, mostly because of the conflicting emotions associated with a long tenure at a large institution, where relationships ebb and flow and petty conflicts among faculty tend to linger far too long. The hardest part of leaving was deciding what do with my files of speeches, lecture notes, books, and research materials. Unable to make decisions, I boxed up way too much and carried it all home. Over time, I have been able to sort out things of value, now carefully preserved at the CSU Archives. But even as I write, there are boxes in my garage which will be of interest to no one but which I do not have the heart or courage to throw out. I even have the costume I wore for my Colorado history class when I presented as Alferd Packer, the Colorado cannibal.

Almost 66 years old, I felt extraordinarily healthy and lucky to have had such an enjoyable career at a wonderful university. The friendships with students and faculty continue to brighten my life. And I chuckle when I recall that when I accepted an assistant professorship at CSU in 1970, it was with the thought that I might stay a few years and then move on to a liberal arts institution. But as I walked away from my office for the last time, I realized how fortunate I was to be able to work at a place where I was so free to follow my own instincts as a teacher and writer. Partly as a payback, I started the Gateway to Graduation Scholarship in 2008, when many students were having trouble remaining in school long enough to graduate. Since then, I have established several other scholarships at CSU. It has been rewarding for me to make a difference in the lives of students who need help.

Early Retirement Years

Alejandro graduated from Johns Hopkins in the spring of 2000. Silvia and I attended his graduation. We were proud that he earned a degree in international relations, although it wasn't until the last year and a half of his education that he discovered and minored in his real love: psychology. Cristina did not make the trip with us. She was preparing for her own graduation from Poudre High School, which we also attended. Her joy was enhanced by having a letter of acceptance from the University of San Diego.

By this time, Alejandro and Kim Nguyen were more than friends. After a vacation trip to Florida, they departed Baltimore in Alejandro's Ford Contour, which I had purchased in Fort Collins as a surprise and driven to Baltimore. Houston was their destination, Kim's family home. There were raised parental eyebrows in Houston, but Kim had been admitted to the University of Texas Medical School in Houston, and her family was very proud of that achievement. Alejandro had no job and no place to live, but he had already visited Austin for a job interview and thought he could find work there. With Kim's assistance, he learned that the department of mechanical engineering was looking for someone to counsel students and keep them on track during their four-year undergraduate program. When he interviewed for the job, he became the front runner. As a male with a degree from JHU, he had the upper hand. The department was top heavy with female assistants, and his interviewer was delighted to receive his application. He found a small apartment before taking Kim to Houston. The 165 miles between them would prove vexing over the next two years.

In July 2000, the extended Tyler family celebrated a reunion in Estes Park. The gathering of more than 75 people was attended by families representing the three children of my grandparents George Frederick Tyler and Stella Elkins Tyler: Sidney F. Tyler, George F. Tyler, Jr., and Molly Tyler West. By the year 2000, many of us had separated from our Philadelphia roots, residing in Colorado, California, Montana, and other states west of Pennsylvania. Ironically, the western location and much of the organization of the reunion were promoted and organized by the East Coast Tylers. They did a great job. The lodge was suitably western, the activities were varied and appealing to all ages, and the weather was perfect for three days. We drank a lot of beer, learned much about our relatives, and swore that we would repeat the experience in a few years. Unfortunately, we have not followed through on that commitment. We made several attempts during the COVID-19 years, but failed due to travel restrictions and the fears related to an unpredictable virus.

Silvia did not attend the reunion. I am unable to recall exactly why she chose not to come but by 2000, I spent more time in Steamboat, and I probably didn't make much of an effort to persuade her to join us. I knew the accommodations would be rustic and probably not clean enough for her standards. But I also remember just wanting to be free to enjoy my family. I had been to several of her family reunions in Mexico and had a very good time. We didn't do well at similar functions in the US.

In addition to settling the house in Steamboat and getting to know the local community, I was working on a biography of Delphus E. Carpenter, Colorado's interstate streams commissioner in the 1920s. Of the books I have written, *Silver Fox of the Rockies* (University of Oklahoma Press, 2003) is most likely my best effort. It deals with Carpenter's determination to settle water rights issues on the Colorado River by means of negotiations among the seven interested states. He developed a plan based on the compact clause of the Constitution. It was interpreted as a way to keep the federal government from claiming the undivided waters of the Colorado River, avoiding litigation, and securing distribution of water for the future with a covenant approved by Congress. The 1922 Colorado River Compact, for which Carpenter is mostly responsible, became the standard format for all but three interstate river agreements in the American West between 1922 and 1971. Unfortunately, the Compact was based on exaggerated flow data and instead of being worded in percentages of flow, it specifies the Upper Basin's obligation to deliver 7.5 million acre-feet to the Lower Basin before taking its allocation. At this writing, the Colorado River does not produce enough water for the cities, agriculture, and hydro-electric power needs, and the two main reservoirs have almost reached dead pool levels.

Although the research and writing of this book took up a lot of my time, I was enthusiastic about Dan Jr.'s suggestion in the late spring of 2001 that I join him on the 500-mile Cycle Oregon tour. I wasn't much of a bike rider when he threw this idea at me, but it sounded like a fun adventure, and I needed a break from research and writing. I also wanted to spend more quality time with him, enjoying something he was good at. Somewhat fearful that a standard bike might compromise my back over the course of seven 60 to 100-mile days, I decided to invest in a recumbent. I found one in Denver with a wind screen on it and rode 15–25 miles several times a week in the Fort Collins area to build up my tolerance for fatigue and pain. Recumbents are very comfortable; you have a back rest, and your feet are pedaling in front of you. But you have absolutely no leverage when you are going uphill, so you have to gear way down. With a long wheelbase, the bike tends to be very slow and wobbly going uphill.

Cody riding the recumbent in Steamboat Springs, 2007

Early in September 2001, I loaded the recumbent on a trailer which I attached to my 1999 Subaru Outback. My immediate destination was Baker City, OR, where my sister Hope and her husband Buck Buckner live on a small ranch. I had never visited them. Their place is located only 65 miles from Prairie City where Cycle Oregon would begin. We had a short visit, but I used the time to get my camping gear organized and stowed in a large duffle bag which would be carried in a van by tour staff from point to point during the seven-day tour.

On September 7, I met Dan and his wife Cherrie, in Prairie City. Finding them was not easy. We didn't have cell phones, and there were 2,000 participants, all squeezed into a large field where we camped the first night. Eventually, we connected, had an evening meal, listened to instructions from organizers, and settled into a restless sleep in our respective tents. The tour set about early the next morning.

It was quite an experience. We received daily maps showing mileage, elevation gains and losses, water and meal stations, along with camping sites at our daily destinations. Along with the main route, there was usually an optional route that added miles and challenged the younger, more athletic riders. At 68, I was one of the older participants, but the average age was 43, and the oldest rider was 82. We represented 42 states and six different countries. With the preparation of 46,000 meals, distribution of 45,500 gallons of water, 14,750 bagels, and 18,000 Clif bars available as snacks, along with 66 volunteers who cared for us day and night, we were like a mobile army moving through the high desert of SE Oregon.

Massages were available in the evening for those with sore backs and legs, but at the end of each day, I was just fatigued, hungry, and ready to hit the sack. That recumbent was easy on my body, although I really struggled to get up a few of the passes. Friendly riders often rode alongside me on the uphill legs. I would have to tell them to get ahead or behind me due to my wobbly, unstable progress. Every day, at about the halfway point, Dan and Cherrie would come zooming by. While I was one of the first out in the morning, they slept late. Dan occasionally complained that Cherrie wasn't providing enough pedal power, but they were like rockets on wheels when they passed me. When they arrived at the campsite, they would grab my duffle from the truck and reserve a space for me, next to their tent. A huge favor which I appreciated.

On the morning of September 11, I was heading back to pack up my camping gear after eating breakfast when I noticed a commotion around a pickup truck. Although we were in a very rural area without much communication to the outside world, the truck had a radio which had picked up news about an attack on the Twin Towers in New York. We had no TV, so we learned only very basic details and weren't sure what to believe. It was very eery departing the campsite that morning. The route was enshrouded in fog, and the shock we felt about the recent news made everyone nervous. I remember riding alone, hearing only an occasional bird call, and wondering if the world might be coming to an end. That night at our campsite, *The Oregonian*, a Cycle Oregon sponsor, brought in several dozen newspapers. They were grabbed eagerly and passed around very slowly. I never got one, but from those who read the abbreviated description of events, I learned more about the attack and the casualties that followed.

A pall descended over our group. We were unable to contact family members, and we had very little information to digest. With the rumor mill working overtime, we were trying to process what appeared to be a national disaster. The tour had scheduled a down day which fell on September 12. Dan and I cycled into French Glen where we found a TV at the local hotel. The images we saw made clear the extent of the attack. We had no choice but to continue the tour, but not a day passed without extensive speculation on what the attacks would mean for the future of our country.

We arrived back in Prairie City on September 14. I picked up my duffle, located the Subaru, strapped down the recumbent in the trailer, said a hurried goodbye to Dan and Cherrie, and took off for Boise, ID. I called Silvia that night. She expressed empathy for what had happened in New York. I was grateful. TV stations were still replaying images of the tumbling towers. I found it very hard to watch. The drive back home, which should have been a joyous and relaxing two days, was dominated by a heavy heart. As with the JFK assassination on November 22, 1963, I will always remember where I was and what I was doing on September 11, 2001.

With winter came snow, lots of it. I skied more regularly and with the aid of clinics and more experienced friends, I improved my technique. I was never much of a bumps skier, but as I became more familiar with the terrain on Mt. Werner, I sought out bump runs and tree runs and looked forward to the dumps of 6–12 inches which made everything softer and more fun. Family visits made the house a happy place, and Christmas became very special in that world of white.

But the winter drags on in Steamboat. When March and April come along, residents are ready for daffodils and leaves on the trees. The mud season, which I enjoyed because the town was far less crowded, was also a time when shops and restaurants closed so merchants could get a break from the winter craziness. Many left the town for warmer climes.

Fortunately, a big family event, not unexpected, gave me the excuse I needed to follow suit. On April 20, 2002, Kim accepted a marriage proposal from Alejandro. He had left Austin, was living in Houston, and had been accepted into a Ph.D program in industrial psychology at the University of Houston. An engagement party was soon scheduled.

Silvia and I picked out a lovely, hand-carved, wooden box as a gift and had the Vietnamese, Mexican, and American flags painted on the top. Fortunately, I checked the accuracy of the flags before wrapping the gift. The artist had selected the flag of Communist North Vietnam from which Alejandro's future father-in-law had fled at the age of 16. Oops! I got that changed in a hurry.

It was my first trip to Houston. We arrived on a 90-degree day in 90% humidity. The air conditioning was blasting away everywhere we went. I don't like A/C, so I determined to bring fresh air into our hotel room. When I managed to open a window, the inrush of a fetid, wet air mass almost bowled me over. It became very clear that survival meant living with air conditioning. The Nguyens had it going full bore at their home, and it contributed to a very pleasant first meeting of our families. What I remember feeling, however, was a joy for Alejandro and Kim that I was unable to fully experience because of the powerful and ever-present emotions related to my failing marriage. Silvia and I had lost the ability to communicate in any meaningful way, so it was very difficult for us to share the warmth and tenderness of what was transpiring with our son. I don't know how much the Nguyens sensed this chasm between us, but I felt awkward and embarrassed.

Partly to celebrate Alejandro and Kim's engagement, and still hopeful that things might change between Silvia and me, I organized a July trip to Maui for all of us. We did the touristy things—beach time, luaus, parachute sailing, snorkeling—and for the most part, we had a good time. But I will never forget being challenged by Cristina when she raised her voice (very unusual) at her mother and me and said, very firmly, "Would you please stop the infernal bickering?" It was then I realized what an awful example we were setting and what a hole we had dug ourselves. When we arrived home, I went up to Steamboat to take care of a few things. On my way back, after several days, I picked up flowers for Silvia. The arrangement included the lovely orange and blue Hawaiian birds of paradise. After parking the car in the garage, I entered the house where Silvia was cleaning the front hall. I handed her the flowers. She put down the cleaning equipment, took off the rubber gloves she was wearing, and marched out the same door I had entered so she could dump the flowers into the trash bin. Within minutes, the front door bell rang. I opened it and was handed a subpoena by a process server. Silvia had filed for divorce, knew when I would be returning from Steamboat, and arranged to have me served the moment I arrived.

Looking back on that moment, I can say that I was feeling a plethora of emotions: relief, sorrow, regret, shame, and anger. I grabbed more clothes, personal possessions, and documents, and headed to a motel where I called my good friend Jim Hansen. He agreed to come over to help me load a U-Haul with what I wanted to take to Steamboat. Cristina and I met for lunch. I think she was sad. I know I was, but I also think she felt comfort, knowing that the tension between her parents would end. She was about to be a junior at the University of San Diego, and she had other things on her mind.

I don't remember a conversation with Alejandro. I'm sure we talked, but he was increasingly occupied with concerns about the faculty at the University of Houston. He had plenty on his mind as he and Kim planned and discussed careers and their forthcoming January 2004 marriage. I do remember that he told me he stood behind me and that I had his support. He wasn't choosing sides; he was just telling me he loved me. It meant a lot.

Hansen showed up at the house as planned. We loaded clothing, furniture, mostly stuff from my office and the garage, things that Silvia did not want or need. I left all the kitchen and dining room items, including the nice silverware and dishes that came from my parents. I knew they would eventually come into the hands of Alejandro and Cristina. When we finished loading the truck late in the afternoon, I took one last look at the home Silvia had designed, and headed out the door en route to Steamboat. Just before the sun set, I arrived on the east side of Rabbit Ears Pass. I remember feeling a huge sense of liberation as that U-Haul and I growled our way up the steep slope. I knew there would be lots of tough times ahead with lawyers and fights over a final settlement. But that awful feeling of living in an unhappy home was gone, and I was optimistic that things might work out better for everyone in the family, including Silvia.

I unloaded the U-Haul by myself. Quite a feat, given the size of the pieces Hansen and I had loaded. Months later, Silvia came to Steamboat to see what she might want to take back to Fort Collins. Her selection of the living room furniture—all of it—puzzled me. She had no place to put it, and we had both selected the sofas and chairs specifically for the Steamboat house. My attorney and I objected to this demand, and she backed off. There were other disagreements and lots of trips to Denver and Fort Collins to participate in discussions about financial matters. But I think in the long run, the settlement was equitable. I wanted Silvia to have sufficient assets so she could make a life for herself, and I am convinced that's what she got. It wasn't until November 2003 that the dissolution of marriage was finally filed in court. In broader terms, however, our marriage had ended years before, so when the dust settled, I looked for another companion who would share the wonders of Steamboat with me. I needed one.

Betty

I didn't wait long to throw out a net. After a couple of months in Steamboat, I felt fairly settled. I had met Renny Daly and Jain Himot through the Over the Hill Gang skier group. We joined forces when the Gang asked members to spend a day picking up trash on Rabbit Ears Pass. We also played golf together and attended concerts put on by Strings in the Mountains, Steamboat's summer music festival. As my social activities picked up, I felt a growing need to find a partner with whom to enjoy my new community.

I placed an ad in the Crimson Classified section of the *Harvard Alumni Bulletin*. Most entries I had seen in the Crimson Classified were by women seeking men. Those women made themselves appear to be smart, successful, well-heeled, and beautiful. Only a few ads were from people who resided west of the Mississippi, so I figured that a western male might attract attention. At $5/letter, I decided that my offering should be relatively short, to wit: "Hopeful: Harvard A.B. retired university professor (history), sixtyish, looking for kind, optimistic, upbeat, generous woman to share outdoor interests (skiing, hiking, biking, golf, etc.) in Colorado Rockies. Divorced with five grown children, happy with self, good health, athletic, lover of the mountains where I live, but enjoy some travel. Much more. Contact rockydan@aol.com." Within days, I received the following email: "I don't exactly know why I am writing, as I clipped out your 'personal' for a friend who lives both in Denver and SF. As I reread it, I thought why don't I write, as I think of myself as 'optimistic, upbeat, and generous with outdoor interests'?" This response from bettcin@aol.com continued on for another 1,000 words. I assumed it was from a Betty. As Betty

Henshaw later explained to me, because her late husband was also a Harvard graduate who received the Bulletin, she had been glancing over Crimson Classified ads for some time since his death. She had never replied to an ad, but when she saw my entry, she decided to take the leap, describing at length whom she thought she was and making reference to the interests and activities which related to my inquiry. It was a bold step for her and caused alarm from protective friends and family members. I loved her email. The obvious thought and care she put into it and the complete honesty with which it was composed were refreshing. I did have other responses, but none had such a ring of authenticity. I wrote Betty the following day and promised her I would send a reciprocal bio. "My hope," I said, was "to find a companion who is gentle, intelligent, loves to laugh, and has interests of her own I can support." I stated that I had been divorced twice, "but I'm not beating myself up over the failures," I noted. "I still think, as my children tell me, that I have a lot to offer." For the next month, we communicated through cyberspace. We got the big issues out of the way early: sex, politics, religion. Betty spoke of the sometimes disappointing relationship she had with a travel partner, Robert—ironically, someone who had an obsession with cleaning and germs—and expressed a desire for something more meaningful. "I am not sure why I answered your email," she noted, "but you sounded nice, and I felt an urge to push on with my life." Along with the emails, we shared pictures, but it wasn't until October that we spoke on the phone.

I flew to Cincinnati in December. We both had a few days before Christmas without obligations, so we decided it was time to bite the bullet and meet face to face. Although there were nerves associated with the meeting, because of the relatively long exploration of each other via email, we both had a pretty good idea what we were getting into. Betty was living on the top floor of the Highland Towers apartment building with a magnificent view, close to the banks of the Ohio River. I was impressed. But what I remember most about that apartment is an unexpected encounter I had with a picture of her late oncologist husband, Ed. Betty was not with me when I saw that black and white photo. She still has no idea how it impacted me. But I remember now, 20 years later, that something in me triggered a vow, articulated silently and sincerely, to make certain that Betty would be cared for from then on no matter what happened to us. There had been no exchanges between us about a committed relationship or marriage; we really didn't even know each other. I was just overcome at that moment by a very emotional feeling of commitment based largely on the joy I felt about having met someone who made me feel content and fulfilled. I even called my good friend, Hermann Bleibtreu, in Arizona, to express my feelings. Herm was delighted.

From Betty's apartment, we traveled 25 miles northwest to Shandon, OH, where the Henshaws had a farm. When Ed died, Betty left Rochester, NY, and came to Cincinnati to care for her 90-year-old mother-in-law. Dottie was hard to deal with, but Betty did her best and when the old gal died, Betty inherited one half of the farm; her brother-in-law, Stan Henshaw, inherited the other half.

Betty loved the place. She brought in an original 1850s homestead cabin and hired a Kentucky woodsman to rebuild it. She had parties there as well as in the old barn which she cleaned out. Square dances, birthdays, 4th of July celebrations, and other festivities were held there. Having grown up on a 160-acre farm in southeast Nebraska, Betty felt very much at home on the Henshaw property. Me too! It was fun to see her so happy there. Over the next 10 years, we spent as much time in Shandon as in Cincinnati.

Betty's rental cottage on the beach in Kailua

Shortly after our first meeting, Betty invited me to visit her in Hawaii. Her only son, Dr. Dan Henshaw, was chief radiologist at Kaiser Permanente in Honolulu. He and wife Patty had two children: Sawyer, who was about 8, and Tommy, who was about 2 and had been adopted as a baby from Japan. Since Dan and Patty took up residence in Hawaii shortly after Ed's death in 1993, Betty had been spending winters in Kailua, Oahu, where she rented a three-bedroom house on Lanikai Beach, not more than half a mile from Dan and Patty's home.

I jumped at the chance to return to Hawaii. I had not been back since leaving Punahou in 1963, but one of my best friends, Bob Torrey, who also arrived at Punahou School in the summer of 1958, was still hanging around. He was retired from teaching, but he had remarried and was volunteering at Punahou on a regular basis. Dan and Patty were planning to send Sawyer to Punahou. She was already attending the feeder school, Hanahauoli, located close by.

The Kailua side of Oahu was not as familiar to me as the Honolulu side. Punahou is located in Manoa Valley, in the hills above Honolulu. When I lived there, our house was just a few miles into the valley, past Punahou. But the school has a vacation cottage on Kailua Beach which was made available to faculty. Jean and I spent at least two long weekends there with the boys, but otherwise that area of the island was not well known to us.

Betty's house on Lanikai Beach was wonderful. From the back door to the ocean was no more than 50 yards. Because of a large reef offshore, waves were minimal and the water good for swimming, so long as the tide was in. Getting up at dawn and walking the beach with a cup of coffee in hand was an amazing experience. Electrical and mechanical systems in the house worked most of the time, but one of the perks of renting there was a caretaker who was generally willing to help get things repaired when there was a malfunction.

That visit in February 2003 was the first of 12 straight years wintering in the Islands. Beginning with a fortnight, my stays continued to lengthen until I was spending 6 to 7 weeks on the beach. We entertained a lot of friends and family who came to Hawaii for short periods, but we also enjoyed having the house to ourselves. Luana Hills Golf Course, now the Royal Hawaiian, a beautiful public/private course carved out of the jungle, was minutes away. Betty loved accompanying me when I played. She is such an aficionado of nature that our outings gave her enormous pleasure, even while I grumbled about bad shots and lost balls. We took trips to the North Shore, to the *USS Arizona* at Pearl Harbor, and to the other islands for brief changes of scenery. And we made a pilgrimage to Punahou School within weeks of my first visit.

Not much had changed on the campus. A few new buildings

had been squeezed into the existing property. Night blooming cereus still decorated the lava rock boundary walls of the school's property. Students of many ethnicities were prowling the campus when we arrived, and a deep baritone voice, echoing years of pedagogy and punctuated by frequent and familiar chuckles, caught my ear. It was Bob Torrey holding forth, surrounded by a group of adoring students. I made my way through the bodies and interrupted: "Hi, Bob! Do you recognize me?"

With Bob Torrey, 2003

"No," he replied, "but I'll bet I should."

"Yes, you should," I said. "We prepared lesson plans together for five years beginning in 1958, and you and I started Punahou's first soccer team."

Not often at a loss for words, Bob Torrey was speechless. Of course we had both aged, but my appearance was so out of context for that time and place that he was totally taken by surprise. Good friend, godfather to Kit, and someone who had traveled all the way from Hawaii to Fort Collins to attend my 40th birthday party, Bob made up for a momentary lapse with a warm *abrazo*. It was a nice moment, and we continued to see each other every year I returned. Betty and I even took a trip to Alaska with Bob and Joyce several years later. I count him as one of the special people in my life.

My first meeting with Dan and Patty Henshaw was a little different. Dan had been concerned about his mother dating someone she met through a personals ad, but he was accepting and uncritical by the time I arrived in Hawaii. Patty, not so much. Betty had warned me that the relationship she had with her daughter-in-law had been edgy from the get-go. Apparently, Patty had been concerned that a mother of an only child would insist on interfering in her son's life even after marriage. Consequently, she was polite but kept Betty at arm's length. This was hard on Betty, especially when grandchildren arrived. Her naturally generous and uncritical personality had little room for such behavior. And these tensions had been exacerbated by Betty's travel companion, Robert, who had come to visit the previous year. So, when I was introduced to the mix, there were a few awkward moments. Patty's hesitance made things difficult, but I think she became more accepting as she came to recognize that her husband would be far less the target of Betty's time and attention than the new guy from Colorado. Furthermore, her son Tommy and I got along very well. I took him on the golf course; we built things together; and when Dan and Patty wanted a vacation in Mexico, I invited him to stay in Steamboat.

Interestingly, the biggest challenge for both Betty and me came from a mysterious and secretive source. As our relationship became more committed, Betty decided she would like to keep a Jeep in Steamboat. We looked for suitable vehicles. Betty stated in an email to one of her friends that she was going to buy a Jeep to keep in Steamboat. Shortly thereafter, she received the following anonymous email from Severalfriends@yahoo.com: "Our long time friend, Betty: Do you really think you should be buying a car to keep in Colorado? Doesn't this lock you in a bit too much? We don't want you to give up your home in Cincinnati and friends around the country." Continuing on, Severalfriends described me as "a very smooth character" and noted that they had done an investigation. "We know you may feel lonesome for male company, but there can be a very high price to pay. . . . Be very, very careful. . . . Just have a good time and don't get too committed. Play the field. We don't want to see you hurt, and we can see how he slyly pushes you into things. We'd rather you spent more time with us than see you in a questionable situation." Within minutes of receiving this email, Betty replied that she would appreciate knowing who Severalfriends were. "We prefer not to in case you don't heed our advice. It may take years for these attributes to show up in your relationship and until they do, you would be upset with us for saying anything and we want to continue our wonderful friendship with you until we can say 'We told you so.' Just know that we discovered some things that made us very concerned. Money talks." Betty thanked them for being concerned about her well-being and happiness. She asked for more information and advice, but the senders refused to cooperate, saying only that "Ed had a great concern about your vulnerability, and one of us is concerned about a commitment to him on your behalf. Ed felt that it would be so easy to be mislead when one was so pure of heart. We love you. . . . Just be careful." Betty thought the emails were coming from a jealous Robert. She wrote to him at the Severalfriends yahoo address and wished him well. Severalfriends responded immediately, stating that Robert was in no way involved.

We were stuck. Yahoo wouldn't give out the name associated with the account, so we concluded that further investigation was a waste of time. Betty did not buy the Jeep; probably a wise decision. But we both felt that the whistleblowers had acted cowardly by refusing to identify themselves. And as I write these lines, I wonder if any one of them might have anything to say now regarding the years I stood by her, cared for her, and protected her from occasional rash decisions by her own family? As best I could, I have honored the vow I made to Ed Henshaw on my first visit to Betty's apartment in the fall of 2002.

Hoping to bring my three older boys closer to me and to each other, I invited Dan, Nick, Kit, and their children to join Betty and me for Thanksgiving in Hawaii. We rented a special Kailua beach house for the occasion. It started off well, with a climb to the pillbox, a tour of the *USS Arizona,* and a visit to Waikiki. But the tension between Dan Jr. and Suzi exploded one night after Betty and I had gone to bed. I was awoken by a rising crescendo of angry voices. I grabbed a towel to wrap around me and headed out to find Nick and Dan about ready to fight and Kit in the middle trying to calm things down. Eventually, the tension was defused. Dan and Cherrie left the next day, while I did my best to remain cheerful on the exterior even though I was crushed by my sons' bad behavior. I don't want to place blame. Animosity between the brothers had been simmering, and it bubbled to the surface in Hawaii. It was inappropriate, immature, disrespectful, unproductive—all those things. But I had no control over what happened. I regret not being able to head off the encounter. Knowing how much the altercation had upset me, Betty suggested we spend a week on Lanai following the boys' departure.

This was a good decision. Not many people visit that tiny island. One time headquarters for Dole Pineapple, it is rustic, backward, and quaint. Roads are mostly unpaved; Lanai City has a population of 3,000, one third of which are foreign born, mostly Filipinos who worked the pineapple fields. There is one hotel in Lanai City and a fancier Lodge at Ko'ele. Two golf courses, casually maintained, were attractions for me. But we had the most fun renting

Jeep on Lanai

a Jeep and four-wheeling down to Polihua Beach. On another day, we kayaked the coast from Manale Bay. Betty paired up with our guide in a kayak. I followed in my own kayak, on the lookout for the huge, green sea turtles. At one point, I felt the upward shove of a large wave about to break beneath my kayak. Only a furious amount of paddling prevented me from being tumbled on shore with a broken kayak and most likely, a broken body.

In January 2004, Alejandro and Kim Nguyen celebrated their marriage in Houston. Silvia and I had driven to Houston for the engagement party, but this time we flew separately. The emotions of a conflicted relationship were still in the air at the wedding and although everything went smoothly, Alejandro made a point of standing between us during tense moments. I felt badly about this, and the memory still makes me squirm. How nice it would have been to enjoy the occasion, especially now that I know what a strong marriage Kim and Alejandro have built over the course of almost 20 years.

A few months later, in March 2004, Betty and I were enjoying a warm spring day on Mt. Werner. She had been taking ski lessons and reached a level that made it possible for us to ski blues together. We chose a run called One O'Clock for our descent and had stopped about half way down when we heard a shout up above. When I turned to look uphill, I saw a ski bearing down on my head, I crouched and turned downhill and as I did so, Betty's legs got caught up in mine. She lost her balance, and one of her skis ended up in a twisted heap. The dreaded toboggan ride followed, along with X-rays, crutches, and an early end to skiing. The fall resulted in a torn ACL and a bucket handle tear of her right knee meniscus. We were hopeful the injury could be repaired, but when Betty went for

Kim and Alejandro wedding

Kim and Alejandro

surgery, the doctor declined to operate. Betty's heart was in atrial fibrillation, and she would have to take a blood thinner to reduce the possibility of stroke. When Dr. Milan DiGiulio—niece Stephanie Henshaw's husband—suggested that Betty's knee would most likely heal by itself in time, we gave up the thought of surgery and focused on the importance of a healthy heart. She has been on a blood thinner ever since, and she continued to walk better and farther than most anyone her age. But her skiing days had ended.

Meanwhile, Cristina was still working her way through the University of San Diego. She had decided to specialize in the science and politics of environmental issues. Her academic focus included a semester of study in Queensland, Australia.

I decided to join her in Australia when she came out of the bush. I flew to Los Angeles prior to boarding a plane for Sidney. During that 24-hour layover, I had the opportunity to attend a Pasadena City Council meeting. Brother Sid had been a member of the Council for several years. He was much respected, especially because of the business acumen he was able to utilize in his role as councilman. The evening meeting involved a discussion of Segway scooters and whether or not Pasadena should allow them on its sidewalks. I was invited to try one before the council convened. I concluded they would be great fun and a good way to get around the city. My brother, however, decided they could be a considerable nuisance, especially for older people with limited agility who might not be able to get out of their way. Much to my chagrin, he voted against the Segways. He knew where he stood with his constituency. They re-elected him several times.

After arriving in Sidney, I had a day to wait before Cristina arrived from Brisbane. Suspecting that she would probably appreciate a cleanup after three months of camping, I made a hair appointment for her. That was a smart move. She deplaned in a somewhat ragged condition but in good spirits. It took a while for her to catch up on sleep and feel refreshed, but we had several days in Sidney to enjoy the sights before heading home via Auckland, New Zealand. We spent a night there and ran into a Steamboat Springs couple in a restaurant. Small world!

Cristina graduated from USD in December 2004. Over her four plus years of college, we had driven back and forth between Colorado and California several times. During these enjoyable trips, we both became aware that a Starbucks Grande really loosened my tongue. This was good. There was a lot she didn't know about me, and I had too few opportunities to tell her things about myself. For most of my life, I was not a coffee drinker; I was a morning person with energy to burn. But when I started writing books, I found that coffee really stimulated the brain synapses and allowed thoughts and words to flow more freely. The quality of my writing after five cups of coffee wasn't necessarily any better; sometimes, in fact, it was awful. But as Cristina discovered, I am quite sensitive to caffeine and even now, when I enjoy a cup of Joe during my early morning hot tub soaks, I can still feel my senses waking up and my thoughts taking verbal shape. It's a great way to plow through the fog of sleep and plan for the day. It's also a mid-morning stimulus when I need the get-up-and-go that now seems to have gotten-up-and-went. Fortunately, the latest medical conclusions support caffeine as beneficial for the geriatric population, so I am consuming coffee unapologetically.

After graduation, Cristina decided to live in Steamboat. Things with Mom weren't great, and they didn't improve much when she decided to stay with me for a while. But the post-college Steamboat interlude provided opportunities and experiences neither one of us would have had if she had returned to Fort Collins.

We enjoyed sharing my house and spent time skiing on Mount Werner when the snow was good. Over the course of several years, Cristina worked as a house cleaner, a nanny, a dental office manager, and a Starbucks trainee. Eventually, she rented her own apartment which she occupied with Addison "Snort", the canine love of her life. Snort was a mix of several breeds, ferocious looking, and not very fond of men. He had been tied up as a puppy and left tethered to a rope for days at a time. When he finally broke away, he was taken to the Steamboat dog pound where Cristina and I found him in April 2005.

When they made eye contact, Cristina and Addie knew in their separate ways that they were made for each other. I was concerned that such a big dog would be hard to manage with Cristina working long hours, so I had to give one of those tired lectures about responsibility and consideration. I remember the two of us sitting on the deck discussing the pros and cons of dog ownership, and I also remember feeling that whatever logic I dredged up against owning a big dog was essentially dead on arrival. The emotional bond already established was far greater than any of my so-called common sense.

Cristina brought Addie home the day after they met. When she was at work, he stayed in her small bedroom. Occasionally, I took him for walks, but neither of us was good on a leash. When Cristina moved into her own apartment, I was relieved. I also sensed that the two of them would probably develop an even closer relationship when she had a place of her own. In retrospect, I am so glad I followed my instincts. When I sold the Steamboat house in 2015, a reminder of Addie's brief stay with us was still quite evident on the carpet. How hard Cristina worked to get out that stain I will never know, but to the discerning eye, a shadow on the carpet remained, a memento of what turned into a love affair between my daughter and a Red Husky-Akita mix. Snort died in 2021 when Cristina was living in Seattle. His death was traumatic, but his replacement, Cashew "Cash," has proven to be a blessing for our entire family.

Because Betty and I went back and forth between Steamboat and Cincinnati, I was not in residence the entire time Cristina stayed there. This was probably a good thing. Betty and I really enjoyed the time in both states, especially when we had been apart for a while. She and I also did some traveling in 2005, first to Pittsburgh for a wedding, then to Cambridge for my 50th Harvard reunion.

The Pittsburgh event enabled us to make a few side trips. Since reading David McCullough's *The Johnstown Flood*, I had been eager to see the site of the 1889 dam collapse that resulted in over 2,200 deaths, $17 million of property damage, and four square miles of total devastation in Johnstown itself; all because the executives at Carnegie Steel and their coal and railroad cronies wanted to have a private fishing lake. Unwilling to repair spillways or reenforce a dam that had been constructed 40 years earlier to provide water for the Pennsylvania Main Line Canal, the bigwigs who bought the lake from the Commonwealth of Pennsylvania were unable to deal with excess water build-up when torrential rains fell in the spring of 1889. Because the high, steep hills of the Allegheny Mountains were always prone to flooding, the homes of German and Welsh steel workers built on the edge of the Conemaugh River were especially vulnerable when the South Fork earthen dam broke, and a flood wave 60 feet high roared down the valley. Within 45 minutes, the lake was totally drained, and the town of Johnstown, 14 miles downstream, populated mostly by steel workers, was all but eliminated.

I was interested in this event as a historian and also because of my experience with dams in the West. I also wanted to know more about the social and legal impact of this incredible example of Robber Baron irresponsibility. At first, Andrew Carnegie and Henry

Clay Frick used the law to claim they were not personally responsible, but in time, a public outcry over the company's refusal to accept responsibility and pay damages changed the American legal system. Today, tort law holds companies responsible for defective reservoirs and ensures that damages caused by shoddy maintenance are included in owner liability.

After visiting Johnstown, we drove 30 miles southeast to the site of the September 11, 2001, crash of United Flight 93. We were unable to visit the actual crash site, but the story of bravery on that San Francisco-bound aircraft was well documented at a nearby memorial. According to the 9/11 Commission 2004 staff report, four al Qaeda hijackers boarded the plane in Newark. At 35,000 feet over central Pennsylvania, these men forced their way into the cockpit, killing the pilots who had just sent out a mayday call. By then, two other commercial flights had been flown into the Twin Towers in Manhattan, so when Flight 93 descended abruptly 700 feet and changed course, the FAA and Air Traffic Control knew that a third flight had been commandeered by terrorists. What they didn't know was that the hijackers were planning to fly the plane into the Pentagon.

Passengers on board were able to contact family members using the plane's airphone. From them they learned of the two other hijackings. They decided to fight back, arming themselves as best they could with blunt weapons and marching down the aisle toward the cockpit. Two of the hijackers were killed, but those who were at the controls tried to throw the attackers off balance through violent flight maneuvers. Eventually, the passengers reached the cockpit where struggles for control of the aircraft resulted in Flight 93 turning upside down and nose diving into an empty field near Shanksville, PA. Everyone on board was killed.

I was deeply impacted by this visit; more so than by the trip I made years later to the Twin Towers memorial site. On that hazy spring afternoon, in the middle of nondescript Pennsylvania farmland, I was reminded that it is never too late to evaluate the information you have at hand, the knowledge that something wrong or unjust is happening, or is about to happen, and to take action then and there to change the outcome—even if said outcome only makes a small difference. The passengers on Flight 93 chose not to succumb to the diabolical plans of the hijackers. They believed they had a chance to take back control of their lives. They showed enormous courage by their actions and while they became martyrs in the process, they saved the lives of many who would have been killed if the aircraft had reached its intended target. Their behavior was heroic.

Before returning to Steamboat, Betty and I headed to Cambridge where I joined Harvard classmates celebrating our 50th reunion. I felt so old, but as I write this, I am hoping to have a chance to attend my 75th reunion in 2025. The reunion was fine but nowhere near as much fun as the 25th; lots of friends missing and others with debilities of one sort or another. We stayed in one of the college dorms—Leverett or Lowell if memory serves. It was hot and humid, and the beds were uncomfortable. But it was fun to march in the graduation procession, the class of 2005 applauding our every step. And we weren't too far from the procession leaders, members of the 1930 classes, who were well into their 80s and 90s. In retrospect, one of the best things that happened in Cambridge was our discovery of Peet's Coffee. I have been a devotee of Major Dickason's Blend ever since. Something about the smell of that coffee when you open a fresh package is addicting.

I returned to Steamboat just before the vintage cars of The Great Race came through town. These vehicles were involved in a rally race organized in 1983 by Texans who wanted to emulate (sort of) a 1965 movie by the same name, starring Tony Curtis, Jack Lemmon, and Natalie Wood. That movie, in turn, was an attempt to recreate (sort of) the first transcontinental race between two seven-horsepower Olds Runabouts which started in New York in 1905, hoping to reach Portland, OR, in a month. Their route followed the historic ruts of the Oregon Trail, 60 years after the first prairie schooners lumbered across the West, and though the country was reasonably civilized by then, the cars and their drivers faced bad weather, numerous breakdowns, wild animals, thirst, accidents, and sickness. Cars and drivers arrived in Portland battered, bruised, and three weeks past the estimated time allotted for the trip.

The Great Race, which passed through Steamboat in 2005, crossed the country from east to west in stages over a 14-day period. The route was planned so as to avoid major cities and highways, following two-lane roads at various speeds, hardly ever exceeding 45 mph. Automobiles had to be at least 45 years old, street legal, with only factory parts. Each car had a driver and navigator whose job was to follow a prescribed course at a predetermined pace. It was not a speed race. Points were awarded on the basis of how punctually vehicles arrived at check stations based on a specific start time. The oldest vehicles were given a handicap. Modern navigational aids were forbidden, and GPS assistance resulted in disqualification.

Nick owned a 1957 Triumph TR3 at the time. It occurred to me that the two of us might have fun entering his car in the 2006 race, which was scheduled to depart from Philadelphia and end 14 days later in San Rafael, CA. I was naive about the cost of such a venture and how much work Nick would require of himself to ready the Triumph for a 4,000-mile rally race. But we decided to do it. Nick worked weekends and nights for months, and I wrote seemingly endless checks. While he was doing all the real work, I was putting my creative energy into a manuscript that would ultimately become *Love in an Envelope: A Courtship in the American West* (Albuquerque: University of New Mexico Press, 2008).

I had come across the courtship letters of Delph Carpenter's parents while writing *Silver Fox of the Rockies: Delphus E. Carpenter and Western Water Compacts* (Norman, University of Oklahoma Press, 2003). Leroy Carpenter and Martha Bennett had met in 1871 at the Methodist Church in Tipton, IA, scarcely a month before Leroy's father decided to move the family to the Union Colony of Greeley, CO, where prime farming land and water were available for enterprising farmers who were literate, had high moral standards, and followed the tenets of the Temperance Movement. Leroy, 27, carried with him to Colorado an image of 17-year-old Martha Bennett. He wrote her. She wrote back. Over the course of 14 months, they decided to get married. What they discussed in letters preserved in a small, wooden box by generations of the Carpenter family was the focus of work Betty and I shared for almost two years. We transcribed the handwritten epistles and provided context for the issues Martha and Leroy deliberated. The contrast between their courtship by mail, often waiting two weeks or more for answers to critical questions, and our instantaneous email courtship was not lost upon us. Nor was the fact that in both cases, the participants fell in love.

As was now becoming our routine, Betty and I returned to Kailua for the winter. We arrived in January 2006, a little early for me, but Betty wanted to celebrate her 70th on January 11 in Hawaii, with friends and family. She rented Moana Lani, a large house on Lanikai Beach, not far from the house we stayed in every year, and she invited a dozen friends from Ohio, Texas, and Massachusetts. It was a very festive occasion with professional hula dancers, Hawaiian chefs preparing luau, and endless Piña Coladas; a memorable

Betty's 70th birthday, January 11, 2006

Hula pretenders at Betty's birthday party

moment for all of us. We enjoyed each other's company, the beautiful house, the beach, and several excursions. Betty was at her best; perhaps the best she would ever be before being gradually victimized by the impairments of dementia.

After returning to Colorado, Nick reported that there was a rally race in Texas which might give me experience as a navigator. It lasted only three days, and we would be able to enter with a rental car. I called Herm Bleibtreu to see if he would join me as driver. He agreed. We sent in our entry for the Great Race, San Marcos, TX.

Undoubtedly, the San Marcos event helped me get a better handle on my role as navigator. Herm loved to drive, and even though we didn't have a very accurate speedometer, we managed to follow the route without getting lost. When the final day's ceremony took place, we were surprised to receive a 4th place award out of a dozen or more rookie entries.

Herm enjoyed himself and agreed to join our team for the Philadelphia to San Rafael run with his sister, Hilde, accompanying Betty in a Dodge Caravan. This would be our sag wagon, holding spare parts and emergency equipment that might be needed as the Triumph proceeded westward toward the Pacific Ocean. Because support vehicles were required to follow different routes to daily destinations, Herm and the ladies took it upon themselves to make certain Nick and I had accommodations and meals awaiting us when we arrived. The assistance they provided meant a great deal to us after a long day of occasional stressful driving.

Nick shipped the Triumph to Philadelphia from Sunnyvale. After unloading, he and I took it to race headquarters for technical inspection. Everything checked out perfectly, but the cynicism of the inspector to whom British cars were a joke, ramped up Nick's competitive juices during the inspection. "The only thing missing in my view," the inspector joked, "is a net to catch the parts when they fall off the car." We would have the last laugh, but at the time, when we were nervous novices, that cutting remark stung.

Inspection of Pontiac Grand Prix, San Marcos

Parking sign for #13, San Marcos

Race inspection, Society Hill Hotel, Philadelphia

Ready to rumble

After a few meetings, a trial run through Philadelphia traffic, rally school, and registration, we were ready to rock and roll. Around 1 p.m. on Saturday, June 24, lined up in front of the Philadelphia Museum of Art on the Benjamin Franklin Parkway, Nick's Triumph, "Victoria," with a black and yellow 13 on both sides, embarked toward the first night's destination: York, PA.

From then on, the routine was consistent. We would arrive in a designated city around 5:30 p.m. for a Parc Fermé (closed park for public viewing of cars); around 7:30 p.m. we would drive to our hotel, find food, shine up the car, do minor repairs and adjustments, and crash into bed. Up at 6:00 a.m. the next morning, we would breakfast and be ready to receive the day's rally book by 7:30 a.m. Sometimes, Nick and I would go over the more complicated directions in the rally book, but as the days passed, it was all we could do to make our start time after a brief perusal of speeds and directions. We did learn early on, however, that it was important for the navigator to know what was about to happen on the next page of the book so that we wouldn't inadvertently pass up a critical turn. We learned the hard way.

From York, we executed daily runs to Washington, PA, Dublin, OH, Indianapolis, IN, and St. Louis, MO. I will never forget crossing the Mississippi River and passing through that day's finish line to be announced by Motor Mouth, the official Great Race spokesperson, as having only a 19-second discrepancy from the perfect rally time. I think we finished in second place that day. It felt really good, because the first few days we didn't do very well and my Steamboat friends were sending me e-mails in which they gave me a lot of grief for such poor daily performances.

We crossed Missouri and Kansas and entered Colorado in pretty good shape. The Triumph was running like a champ, and Nick

Over the Mississippi River into St. Louis

and I were gradually developing some teamwork. Granted, I really sucked at calculating how to make up time when we got stuck behind a truck. And there were times I had to rely on my own knowledge of the western landscape when I didn't understand the written rally instructions. But through it all, we really did pretty well. And we made up for quite a few years of inadequate father-son communication. When we arrived in California where Motor Mouth publicly announced No. 13 as "Best prepared British car to ever run the race," Nick and I shared a mental victory lap that was far more meaningful than any prize could have been. We ended up 7th in Rookie Class out of 25 entries. As Nick wrote to me after he sold Victoria: "She was built for a purpose, and she performed like a real trooper…. She will remain in my heart as the best sports car I ever had the privilege to own."

"Was it fun?" we were asked. Well, not exactly. It was stressful, and it was hard work. But it was worth the money, worth the energy expended, and more than anything, worth having my son do such a great job with me as a partner. It was a long time before I actually got out of bed in the morning without thinking first about The Great Race. And it was even longer before either Betty or I initiated conversations without describing some aspect of those 14 days.

A few other 2006 events merit mention. Betty and I attended the Kentucky Derby with her in-laws, Stan and Charlotte Henshaw, plus their two children, Emily and Stephanie with spouses, respectively Matt Hunt and Milan DiGiulio. Betty was able to get tickets through the North Side Bank in Cincinatti. She is the largest shareholder in that bank after the owners, so it wasn't surprising that she was able to score six tickets at a reasonable price, at a time when most people wouldn't think about paying sky high prices. The bonus for Betty was being able to bring Emily and Stephanie. Her two

Reading the rules following penalty for having stopwatch

Crossing the finish line in San Rafael

nieces have always been special. Betty was unable to have more than one child, so she took a very keen interest in brother-in-law Stan's children. After graduation from college, Betty took each one on a trip to a place of their choice. Steph opted for a trip to Italy. She and Betty explored Venice, Rome, Florence, and Parma for two weeks and through several unexpected circumstances, she met Milan DiGiulio, her future husband and father of her three children. Emily chose Peru by way of the Amazon River. They walked the canopy of the rainforest, fished for piranha, and traveled to Machu Picchu. The relationship between Betty and her nieces has remained strong through the years. As hard as it was on both of them, they were each able to visit Betty at Cherry Hills Assisted Living in Denver, and they stayed in touch through cards, letters, and pictures of their growing families. I have often sought their counsel through the many phases of Betty's illness, and they have been consistently kind, concerned, and helpful.

For the Derby, we all dressed up, drove to Louisville, and fought the traffic and the mobs of people into Churchill Downs. Everyone bet a little money and lost most of it, but the mint juleps and camaraderie were memorable. When we returned to Betty's farm, we prepared for one of Betty's famous parties. Friends and family came from all over to celebrate the Derby weekend. No one ate until *My Olde Kentucky Home* had been sung.

From Ohio, we drove to Squam Lake, NH, to witness the marriage of Steamboat friends, Renny Daly and Jain Himot. As previously stated, I had met this couple early on when I arrived in Steamboat. During our time together, I learned that Renny is a 1966 Yale graduate and Jain is connected to the New England Agassiz family, which is also part of my heritage. George Russell Agassiz married a Simpkins, and Mabel Simpkins Bacon married my

Kentucky Derby style

grandfather, Richard March Hoe Harper.[7] Renny and Jain have proved to be very good friends. Their wedding occurred on their boat dock at Squam Lake. Our ongoing friendship has been reenforced many times since with all kinds of golfing adventures, trips to Hawaii, Christmas Day brunches, and lots of wine and good conversation.

Before returning to Steamboat, Betty and I made a trip to Columbus, OH. Knowing that I had developed an interest in British sports cars, Nick had found MGs for sale in Ohio. The first one we checked out was a 1952 TD. It looked to be well cared for, but it wouldn't start. The second one was a white 1956 MGA. Bob Johnson had bought it for his wife, Rae, but he was spending so much time keeping it running that he decided to sell. I bought "Albert" from him and arranged to have it shipped to Cincinnati where Betty's friend, Tom Stegman, owned a stable of very valuable antique sports cars which were cared for by a talented, full-time mechanic. As a result of his mechanic's expertise, the engine and drivetrain were overhauled. I then put Albert on a truck heading to Denver. It was delivered to Sports Car Craftsmen in Arvada where I requested a carburetor adjustment to reflect the altitude change. Paul Dierschow, the owner of Sports Car Craftsmen, expressed surprise at how well the SUs were already tuned. A few minor adjustments, and Albert was ready for the 5,500-foot climb to the Eisenhower Tunnel at 11,000 feet. With Betty following in her 2007 Lexus RX350, we embarked for Steamboat early on a warm August morning.

The drive was pretty easy, but Albert warmed up more than expected. By the time I got to the east end of the tunnel, the temperature gauge was reading well over 200 degrees. It soared again when we drove over Rabbit Ears Pass, but the engine didn't miss a beat and with enough downhill runs to cool off, we arrived in

Steamboat in pretty good shape.

For the next 10 years, I drove Albert around Steamboat, occasionally out to Craig for golf, once or twice to pick up Jesse at Poulter Camp, and a few runs to Kremmling. I am by no means an automobile mechanic, but I found a friend in Steamboat who let me work with him when we addressed minor mechanical and electrical issues. It was enough hands-on work for me to feel that the car and I had developed a relationship. When I had to sell the Steamboat house, I decided to give the car to Philip. I wanted it to stay in the family.

His dad and I developed a sneaky plan. Because the LA air is notoriously bad for anyone with lung issues, Nick and I hoped that by trailering the MG to Austin, where it would be maintained in Nick's garage, Philip might be persuaded to leave LA behind and resettle in the better Austin air. The three of us packed up the car on a U-Haul trailer hitched to Nick's pickup. Two days later, we were in Austin. Philip was happy to have the car, but our plan didn't work.

The MGA stayed in Austin until the fall of 2019 when Nick brought it to me in Denver where I had been living since 2016. Because it was awkward for Philip to own such a fun toy while he and girlfriend, Tara, were committed to jobs in Los Angeles, I bought it back from him. A monogamous Triumph man until very recently (MG Midget purchased in February 2023), Nick was happy to remove the MGA from his garage while he worked on his latest acquisition: a Triumph GT. I am glad to have Albert back home, now much improved with a five-speed transmission.

If the reader will allow a small backtrack, I would like to mention the eight years of service I gave to Fountain Valley School as a member of the Board of Trustees. I don't recall the events leading up to my selection, but I had maintained a loose connection to the school over the years, and I had visibility there when Alejandro arrived in 1995, the same year a new headmaster, Jack Creeden, took over. I got along with Jack very well. When I was asked to serve on the board, Alejandro told me that my first responsibility should be to improve the food in the cafeteria.

We always ate well when there was a board meeting, so I didn't pay much attention to Alejandro's complaint. He maintained that the food did get better during Creeden's tenure. Mostly, I helped FVS raise a lot of money. The school needed new dorms, a better athletic facility, and a number of additional capital improvements. I became the chairman of a $30 million capital campaign. As with quite a few other challenges in my life, I learned on the job. I learned how to make asks, how to thank people who donated, and how to report results to the board. We did extremely well in the beginning, getting to $15 million in a few months, but we really struggled after that and had to shut down the campaign short of the goal. The dorms got built, but the athletic facility had to wait another 10 years.

The collegiality of board members made the quarterly meetings enjoyable. We ate out a lot, enjoyed golf outings, spent a few nights at the Mountain Campus near the base of Mt. Princeton, and occasionally dressed up for a fancy dinner at the Broadmoor Hotel. My eight years on the board were enhanced by having my old college roommate and FVS alumnus, Herm Bleibtreu, serving at the same time. On graduation day in 2011, the school honored me with a Distinguished Alumnus award. Betty, Cristina, and Alejandro's family joined me for what was a very humbling experience.

In October 2006, Betty and I joined a group of Harvard alums on a tour of Benjamin Franklin's Paris. I had not been to Paris since my grandmother Tyler (Granny) and her butler, Frederick Banks, escorted my brother Sid, cousins Molly and Winky West, and me on a first-class trip to Europe in 1950.

I was a better prepared tourist in 2006. For one thing, I had spent six weeks prior to departure boning up on my French. I took French at Brooks School and at FVS, but it had receded considerably due to the 26 years speaking Spanish with Silvia. I thought I had made progress studying on my own prior to arriving at Charles de Gaulle Airport, until we hailed a taxi. The driver asked where we were going; I answered in Spanish. But we arrived safely at the Hôtel du Louvre where our accommodations were small but elegant. In the following days, we visited places related to Ben Franklin's diplomatic years in Paris up to and including the signing of the 1783 Treaty of Paris ending the American Revolutionary War.

Franklin was seen as a man of the world, unburdened by national or cultural prejudices. He was also viewed as an extraordinary man of feeling, nice, charming, polite, and social with new ideas. In the Age of Enlightenment, he appeared to be a representative of the openness that older nations of Europe were striving to achieve. From our tours of the Louvre, Versailles, the National Library, and the many homes and restaurants frequented by Franklin, Jefferson, and the Bourbon monarchs, we were able to get a real sense of Paris in the 18th century.

Unfortunately, I got whacked by a bronchial virus on our fifth day. Betty went on the remaining tours by herself, and I stayed in the room to rest and read. My reverie was disturbed on several occasions by French women coming in to change sheets, clean, and do inventory. At one point, I found myself in the puzzling position of holding the end of a tape measure so one of the maids could size the bed. I wasn't sure whether she was planning an attack on me or had orders to determine the dimensions of the bed for new sheets. I thought of asking her if she would like to try it out in its present condition, but fortunately for both of us my French wasn't that good.

Nor was my health. Whatever the bug, it had entered my chest. While Betty was touring Lafayette's home, I was visiting the *pharmacie* in search of a curative medicine. All they offered, however, were homeopathic lozenges which I bought before returning to bed, thinking that I would eventually need a doctor. That night, after taking several of the lozenges, I was awakened by a shudder through my back muscles which I had never experienced. Thirty minutes later, I was asleep and breathing normally. Who knows what chemical miracle had occurred? It didn't matter. I had become an instant Francophile.

We returned to Cincinnati for a couple of months before heading down to Houston to be present for a C-section which Kim had scheduled for December 28. But at the last minute, the baby turned, and Kim decided to let nature take its course. With reservations for Hawaii, we were unable to stay past the 31st, so we missed Ainsley's birth on January 4, 2007. My fourth grandchild; first girl! What a delight!

We were back at Lanikai Beach well before Christmas. I golfed at various courses where greens fees ranged from $10 to $250. The former, Kahuku Golf Course, is a nine-hole links course near a retirement community. No pro shop, no restaurant, no carts, no tee times. Course maintenance was hit and miss. Once you deposited your money in a container and the first tee box was clear, you were on your own. The up and back layout of the holes was perpendicular to the offshore breeze which often blew with considerable force. But the walk was always enjoyable; the ocean views unbeatable. Nearby Turtle Bay Golf Course had two 18-hole courses, one designed by Arnold Palmer, the other by George Fazio. Both were PGA-approved championship courses, and they were fun to play. Just very expensive. We got more bang for the buck at Kahuku, but we loved having lunch at the seaside grill at Turtle Bay.

Kit and Trina came to Kailua for five days that winter. It was a meaningful visit. Kit and his godfather, Bob Torrey, had a chance to fill in the 44 years since they had last seen each other. We enjoyed hikes to the Pill Box, kayaking to the Mokuluas, and eating at our favorite restaurants: Buzz's Steakhouse in Kailua and La Mariposa in Neiman Marcus at the Ala Moana shopping center, close to Waikiki Beach.

When they returned to the mainland, Betty and I drove across Oahu to Dillingham Airfield where I used to practice landings while flying L-19 Bird Dogs for the Hawaii National Guard. The strip had been taken over by a sailplane club, and Betty had been gifted a dual ride for her 70th birthday. Tow planes were the same L-19 aircraft I flew in the Hawaii Army National Guard.

Betty and I squeezed into the back seat of a glider and strapped into tight quarters under a plexiglass canopy that came down on the top of our heads, while a powerful sun heated up the cockpit very fast. But good ventilation made the 30-minute flight enjoyable. We flew out to sea to catch a glimpse of humpback whales before turning toward Ka'ena Point, the westernmost part of the island. There, the winds blew from every direction, causing an abundance of uplifting thermals that allowed us to gain altitude. After a few 360s and historical commentary from our pilot regarding NASA's satellite tracking stations below, we returned to Dillingham for a smooth landing.

Back in Colorado for spring and summer, we fell into what

had become a comfortable routine. Betty enjoyed creating delightful combinations of blooming flowers in pots and railing boxes on the deck of the Steamboat house. We attended Strings in the Mountains concerts, took short trips to the Great Sand Dunes National Monument, the San Luis Valley, Creede, and Silverthorne so I could play golf at The Raven. Rob and daughter Katherine came for a visit in September, and we all got in a good hike up Fish Creek Falls. Before snow arrived, I took the MGA down to Colorado Springs where Kit was maintaining a Beechcraft King Air. The hangar was big enough to hold plane and car with room to spare. I was happy to leave Albert in a warm and protected environment for the winter. Before the year was out, Betty and I made a trip to Carnegie Hall to see the award-winning Homestead High School Orchestra perform. Philip was a member of this group and was also part of the school's marching band. His musical talents as drummer, guitarist, and vocalist have since expanded and improved. He has organized two bands and cut several CDs. He is a remarkable young man who has achieved greatly. To me, he is the embodiment of real courage. I would like to think that his drive to succeed and overcome results in part from the Tyler genes, but whatever fortitude there may be in the Tyler family, Philip has taken it to new heights. He is a champ now in his own right.

Betty and I decided to celebrate Christmas 2007 in Hawaii. It wasn't my first choice, because I prefer snow at Christmas time. But it was fine. We were able to see more of the Henshaws because of the holidays—no school, less work. Dan Henshaw and I teamed up in a kayak one day with son Tommy (age 7 or 8) following in his own kayak. We were hoping to snorkel around the coral heads. An offshore breeze was blowing when Dan dove down to anchor us about a mile offshore. It took him several attempts to place the anchor. Meanwhile, Tommy was blowing out to sea. I mentioned this to Dan when he came up for air. "He'll be alright," Dan responded as he worked on securing us to the coral. By then, Tommy was almost out of shouting distance. He weighed so little that the wind was carrying him toward big breakers at flank speed. The last words I heard from him before Dan panicked and pulled up the anchor were, "You guys don't care if I die." We got to him just before he collided with the waves. Even with a tow rope attached to his kayak, Tommy whimpered nonstop all the way home.

As a Christmas present, Betty gave us a four-day holiday at a condo on Molokai. It was situated on the Kaluakai Golf Course, and we could hear the waves pounding at night. The course was rustic but fun to play, and the peaceful evenings made for a relaxing change of scenery. We toured the island's picturesque spots but passed up the 150-year-old leper colony located on the north side of the island beneath 2,000-foot cliffs. The only way down is by a narrow path that has 26 switchbacks. You can walk or ride a mule, but you have to have a permit, so we chose to visit other parts of the island. On our flight back to Oahu, we were accompanied on the six-place, single-engine aircraft by one of the few remaining lepers who was en route to Honolulu for treatment. Eight thousand patients once lived in the colony; only a few remain and thanks to new drugs, they aren't contagious. When the last ones die, the Hawaiian government plans to open the 10,000 acres to tourism.

We returned to Steamboat in January for six weeks of great skiing. 2008 was one of those 400-inch-plus snowfall years and while the skiing was superlative, the snow buildup on my roof was especially worrisome. Even though the roof was metal and would generally allow snow to slide, the front door faced north. With heat from the house, snow froze early on, and the ice was held in place by counterposing sheets of metal that restricted any possibility of an easy slide. Eventually, seams expanded as the buildup of snow reached four feet in height. I hired individuals to clear the roof from time to time, but the ice remained in place well into spring. After almost 10 years of heavy snow, a leak appeared over the main door. Sections of the roof had to be replaced, but the faulty design was never changed. The present owners fight the same battle, but they have installed an electric roof and gutter heating system that prevents ice dams.

It was fun to live in such a snowy winter land, but maintaining access down 100 yards of driveway to the garage required 45 minutes of snowblowing. Another half hour was required to shovel a path to the hot tub; and if I needed to check the water level in my four 1,000-gallon water tanks, I needed a half day to shovel my way in so I could measure with a stick. I also had to blow snow off the deck. Sometimes, after being in Hawaii for 3–4 weeks, the snow accumulation was over three feet on the deck, most of it having slid nicely off the roof as the sun heated up the metal panels. The resulting pile of solid ice was impossible to move. And then there was the propane tank. Located on the north side of the driveway, the tank was buried in the hillside. I tried to have it filled before the autumn snow falls, but some years, the combination of visitors and cold temperatures consumed more gas than anticipated, requiring a fill under the worst possible conditions. Before the gas truck arrived, I had to guess where the tank was located. The plows, snow blowing, and heavy snowfalls caused the disappearance of marker poles which I had placed in the ground by the intake valve. Guessing where the steps to the tank might be, I would just dig a path in the general direction hoping for the best. It was quite a job, especially when my aim was off, which was most of the time. I

Front door ice

Snowblowing

never ran out of propane, but I sure ran out of gas removing snow when we had the big winters. Sometimes, there was nothing left in me for skiing.

Winter guests came to ski. Jack Weizeorich from Chicago arrived every year until 2014. With 11 children, he almost always had someone joining him at his rented condo for a week or so. We took local clinics, when they were offered, and explored lesser-known trails through the trees with different instructors. I. J. Fischer was our favorite. He took us into wild places and allowed each one of us to lead from time to time. Even in my seventies, I felt as if I improved each year. Jack had knee problems. Whiskey and ice only went so far; he also carried a bit of extra weight. But he was a trooper, often in pain when we skied, and a really good friend. I reflect on the many years we skied together with great pleasure and affection.

In May 2008, I made a trip to Oregon to catch up with Dan Jr. I brought him my 1950s Gibson guitar, which he generously passed on to Philip. I hadn't played it since Hawaii, and it had become something of a collector's item. We met in Corvallis and headed north to Dog Mountain, Dan's favorite hang gliding site overlooking Lake Bonneville, WA. We ate and slept in Dan's Classic Cruiser camper by the lake and enjoyed a few days together while Dan honed his flying skills. I pleaded guilty. Somehow, I just didn't have an appetite for that particular thrill. In retrospect, I suppose I should have.

Back in Steamboat that summer, I celebrated my 75th birthday. Dinner at Café Diva turned out to be the most expensive meal I had ever bought at $518 for six of us: Cristina and Patrick Grinage, Peter and Jeanne Parsons, Betty and me. It was a fun evening and a good meal, but that record amount was significantly eclipsed a few years later when Alejandro, Cristina, and I celebrated

Dan Jr. preparing for flight

Dan Jr. flying solo

Cristina's graduation from a master's program at Columbia University at La Grenouille, a French restaurant in New York. Beginning with a champagne favored by Winston Churchill according to our waiter, we enjoyed the most delicious sole, followed by a chocolate soufflé that came to our table right out of the oven. When our waiter stopped by toward the end of the meal to see how we were doing, I told him it was one of the best meals I had ever enjoyed. In broken English, he responded, "Oui, monsieur, but you would have enjoyed it much more had you not eaten so fast." Then he handed me a bill for more than $600. What an experience!

That summer, I was working on a biography of W.D. Farr. *Cowboy in the Boardroom*, published by the University of Oklahoma Press in 2011, was for me a combination of personal and professional interests. W.D. Farr had sold the Crystal River Ranch to Grampy in 1946. He was also one of several people I looked up to as a wise and knowledgeable water guru. His son, Bill Farr, called to ask if I would write the biography. I agreed—for a price! I don't have any regrets about taking the money, but reviewers have argued that impartiality disappears when authors are paid for their work. I don't know of anything I would have changed had I done the research and writing pro bono. W.D. was a fine leader who was respected by almost everyone who had dealings with him. The last and perhaps best chapter in the book is about leadership. I think it came out well.

I do like to write, but the long hours of archival research have lost their appeal. *Cowboy* was my last scholarly endeavor. When Kim sent me pictures of my grandson Andon dancing at a wedding, it occurred to me that I might be able to write a children's book based on my his athletic gyrations. The result was *The Little Dancin' Boy* which I self-published in 2015. I found a very talented

Steamboat Springs artist to do drawings based on the actual photos, and I worked with several bilingual scholars to include a version in Spanish under the same cover: *El Pequeño Bailarín*. The book came out well, but the publishers neglected to print the title and my last name on the spine, so it never got the circulation in libraries and bookstores I had hoped for. Nevertheless, I had fun writing it, and Andon will have a lifelong memento to enjoy once he gets over the embarrassment. In 2020, I bought a YouTube promotional package with a very British voice over.[8]

Betty and I continued to make excursions hither and yon. In Nebraska we settled down in camouflaged bunkers to watch sandhill cranes gather for the night in the middle of the Platte River. We traveled to the hot springs in Saratoga, WY, to Montana to visit Sandy Pew (Pew Charitable Trust), and to the Broadmoor Hotel to take in the US Senior Open, thanks to a gift from Kit and Trina. But our biggest annual adventure was always Hawaii, where we were regularly joined by a variety of friends and family.

In the winter of 2009, Hermann Bleibtreu and his wife, Kathy Wreden, a former graduate student of his at the University of Arizona, came to visit. I have mentioned Herm several times previously. He has been a good friend through high school and college, and we have maintained our friendship for close to 70 years. Herm had two children with his first wife, Carol. His daughter died from an overdose, and his son recently took his own life. Herm now has a form of dementia that will worsen with time, but he is far and away the most delightful and generous person I have known in my life. At one point, he was pulled from the Department of Anthropology at the University of Arizona to take on the responsibility of dean of the college of liberal arts. His scholarship, leadership, and gentle manner set him apart from the more selfish and cynical professors in academia. Very much like W.D. Farr, Herm knows how to bring people together.

He and Kathy were wonderful guests in Hawaii. They enjoyed touring Oahu and spending time at the island's cultural sites. They came to Hawaii twice. I wish they could have returned again, but Herm experienced additional symptoms of dementia and felt more confident remaining in his home in Sonoita, AZ. Emma, his dog of many years has passed away, but with Kathy's weekend visits, he has been able to live alone happily and safely.

It is hard to watch anyone suffering from dementia, especially a devoted friend or family member. I have experienced years of dealing with this loss. Betty has Alzheimer's disease. It is a terrible affliction; "the long goodbye."[9] But I have learned that the essence of someone afflicted with dementia never totally disappears, although there is no one way to tap into this visceral quality with all sufferers. Emotions tend to be more on the surface as we age. They are further exaggerated in dementia sufferers as they gradually lose control of their lives. Herm and I still talk on the phone and as I write this in 2023, I plan to visit him soon in Sonoita. We will renew a bond of long standing, and we will massage that aspect of our mutual humanity which is so important to a fulfilling life: caring deeply for one another.

Betty's dementia has required discipline from me, a great deal of patience, and a regularly renewed commitment to honor the vow I made to her late husband, Ed. I don't know exactly when I first recognized that something was wrong, but around 2011 or 2012, I became aware that Betty was manifesting mental anomalies which significantly changed her behavior. She seemed less willing to make decisions and although she knew how much I enjoyed going back and forth between Cincinnati and Steamboat with her, she talked about leaving Ohio entirely for an apartment in Denver.

I was surprised. All her friends were in Ohio and New England. Except for me and a few of my friends and family, she knew only one other person in Colorado, with whom she was not especially close.

But she was politely adamant. She wanted to sell her half of the Henshaw farm to her brother-in-law, Stanley Henshaw, who owned the other half. Stan was delighted. He always felt it a bit awkward to own the farm with Betty, and he wanted his daughters, Stephanie and Emily, to be able to use and eventually inherit the farm. With the money she received, Betty bought a condo in Denver.

The farm sale happened quickly and by December 2012, we were in Denver looking for her condo. We probably visited five or six units in the downtown area, but the one which really caught Betty's eye was on the 36th floor of The Spire, a relatively new building, across from the Convention Center. The Spire had several units for sale. The one Betty bought was located on the 36th floor of the southwest corner of the building. It had an impressive view of the mountains from Long's Peak to Pike's Peak, with floor to ceiling windows that aggravated my acrophobia when the blinds were raised. I got used to it, but Betty had no acrophobia. The view, the downtown location, and the prospect of having almost unlimited sunshine won her over. She was totally at ease taking visitors out on a narrow balcony that looked down on 14th Street. The 1,760 square feet of living area with two bedrooms and two baths were, indeed, very comfortable. The building had four elevators, a spacious workout room, two hot tubs and grilling facilities on the 9th floor, as well as a special gathering place on the 42nd floor for people who were residents of the upper stories. An excellent staff of managers and maintenance people were dedicated and efficient. For Betty, The Spire was a great choice and an excellent investment.

But furnishing the condo gave me further insight into Betty's declining cognitive state. When we moved her out of Highland Tower Apartments in Cincinnati, we dedicated a space in the living room for collecting the things she would bring to Colorado. I rented the largest U-Haul I could find and bolted a hitch onto the rear of Betty's Lexus. We were planning to load the antiques she wanted to keep along with other personal possessions in the U-Haul. But as the living room pile grew, we ended up having to contract a moving company. When her possessions were delivered to a storage unit in Denver, we went out to buy beds, desks, living room furniture, TVs, rugs, etc. The task required lots of choices and decisions. Betty couldn't do it. She liked the shopping, but she had lost confidence in herself and was unable to imagine how various furnishings would fit in the new space. I had planned to accompany her on buying trips to provide opinions, if she needed them. I ended up making all the decisions.

When furnished, the apartment looked very nice. I invested in cousin Linda Lowry's *Morning Dip,* a 3' x 5' oil painting of her semi-nude yoga instructor throwing water on her face while sitting in Boulder Creek. $6,000! But I loved it, and we hung it over the TV in the living room for all to see.

We also hung a lot of Betty's art on the walls. With all the daytime sunshine, great views day and night, and interesting art, the apartment gave off energy and happy vibes. We liked spending time there when we came out of the mountains. The Denver Center for the Performing Arts was a block away on 14th Street; the 16th Street Mall was two blocks east; Pizza Republica was directly below Betty's windows; the Tattered Cover Bookstore was a five-minute ride north on the 16th Street Mall shuttle; and the Convention Center was across the street. We had two indoor parking spaces on the 4th floor just steps away from the elevator. Going from The Spire to I-70, when we returned to the mountains, was a five- to ten-minute drive.

The only real issue for me was street noise. I like to sleep with the windows open, but the bedroom faced Stout Street which was frequently used for drag racing after midnight. Additionally, the fire and police departments repeatedly traveled Stout with sirens blaring. This was more than the white noise associated with city living and because I wasn't sleeping as well as I used to, the nightly disturbance became unpleasant. Betty had lost quite a bit of hearing, so she had no sympathy for my grumbling.

In May 2011, we traveled to Colorado Springs for Cody's graduation from Fountain Valley School. FVS had also decided to reward my work on the Board of Trustees with a distinguished alumni award. I was very humbled to be on the stage during graduation ceremonies and to share in Cody's accomplishments. I was able to present him his diploma. He had grown up and proved himself at FVS. He had done the hard work to pass tough classes. He had earned the respect of his teachers and made lasting friends in the three years of matriculation. I have always been proud of Cody, but he faced an uphill battle when he entered FVS as a boarding student in 2008. The Pueblo public schools had done him no favors, and he was challenged to catch up to his grade level. But the small class environment at FVS and the quality of his teachers gave him the confidence to challenge himself. His graduation and acceptance at CSU was a resounding affirmation of his accomplishments. Watching him smoke the ceremonial cigar following graduation ceremonies was, for me, pure joy.

Cody had repeated a grade, so Jesse was just one year behind him. More interested in football, which FVS had abandoned, he played for the Widefield Gladiators and eventually brought Cody with him. But Jesse really wanted to play at the collegiate level. He

Cody, middle, at FVS graduation

Jesse, left, at Cody's graduation

was a tough lineman but a shade on the small side for Division I football. Nevertheless, he was a great ambassador for FVS and when he too applied to CSU, acceptance was in no small part a result of his diversified activities and excellent academic record. The awarding of his diploma in 2012 occurred 64 years after brother Sid and I first set foot on FVS ground. I was extremely proud at that moment!

After Cody's graduation, Betty and I decided to explore the Inland Passage to Glacier Bay. Bob and Joyce Torrey met us in Seattle for a short flight to Juneau where we boarded the *National Geographic Sea Lion*. With 60 passengers on board, a skilled crew, and a draft of only six feet, this vessel was able to maneuver into shallow coves where wildlife and glaciers were close at hand. Every morning and afternoon, we took advantage of excursions in the ship's zodiacs. Some days we hiked; some days we chased after sea lions and fur seals. And few days went by without humpback whale sightings. We witnessed glaciers calving, grizzlies mating, eagles in such quantities we stopped counting and vistas of the mountains, forests and inlets that were breathtaking. Everyone who has traveled the Inland Passage will say the same thing: an awesome experience! When I read Kristin Hannah's *The Great Alone* a few years later, the images of small Alaskan fishing villages, the heavy mists, jagged, snow-capped mountains, and the biting cold were still in my memory bank.

Having done something special with Dan (Cycle Oregon) and Nick (The Great Race), I wanted to find something special to do with Kit. Betty and I discussed options related to fishing. I knew he wanted to catch a big fish, so I was thinking in terms of steelhead trout in Canada. W.D. Farr had taken his boys to the Fraser River for several years, and they told tales of monster fish and lengthy battles to bring them in.

Zodiac time with Betty

Kayak time with Bob and Joyce Torrey

But my focus shifted. As a result of Betty's open and pleasant personality, I ended up organizing a trip to Central America. Betty's seat companion on a flight from Denver to Cincinnati had connections among marlin fishermen in the Caribbean. She returned with the contacts I needed and pretty soon, I had organized a week's expedition to Quepos, Costa Rica. Kit was thrilled with the possibility of landing a marlin.

We departed January 7, 2012. Kit drove up with Trina from Colorado Springs. The weather was awful, so I drove south from Betty's downtown condo to a Starbucks north of Castle Rock where we joined forces. We made our flight to San José with plenty of time to spare, landing early the next morning. A short hop over the mountains in a small plane ended on a very narrow runway carved out of a forest of African palm oil trees. After getting our fishing licenses, we retired to the Mariposa Hotel where we had a great room with a balcony overlooking the Pacific Ocean.

We went fishing the next day. Our crew of two was courteous and capable. We went out 10 to 20 miles from shore, set about six lines in the water, and began trolling. It wasn't long before we hooked a sailfish; then another and another. Three fish the first day, but no marlin.

The next day, our luck wasn't as good, but the third day, we struck gold. While Kit and I were resting in the stern, not paying much attention to anything, the captain let out a shout. I looked aft to where our lines were trailing and saw a monster marlin break water, traveling perpendicular to the boat's direction. The captain pushed the throttles full forward, expecting to set the hooks, but the combination of the marlin's leap and the boat's opposing force resulted in the line snapping. Our dream of a record fish disappeared.

Kit with fish on the line

First sailfish

For the next few hours, the crew grumbled about having lost such a large trophy. I don't know what we would have done with that fish had we caught it. Estimated at 450 to 500 pounds, a marlin of that size would not have fit in the boat. It was a discouraging time, but the lines were still out, and there was always a chance for hooking another blue. With a pod of dolphins surrounding our boat, it appeared we were in the middle of schools of small fish. A feeding ground. Sure enough, we hooked another marlin, and Kit brought it in. Probably under 200 pounds, but it was a nice fish, and I felt good that we had accomplished the objective we came for. It was a fun trip.

In the summer of 2012, I attended Cristina's graduation from the University of Denver. An M.A. in environmental policy fit with her B.A. from the University of San Diego, reflecting her passion for a sustainable earth. She found a job in Denver working with the Department of Energy as an environmental specialist, making certain that companies were in compliance with government regulations. Unfortunately, the office was poorly staffed and beset with personnel problems. She worked there for two years before deciding to pursue another degree which she hoped would challenge her talents and provide personal satisfaction.

Following Cristina's graduation from USD, I decided to travel to California and Oregon to see Philip at California Poly and Dan at his home in Corvallis. Philip and I had a short visit, but we got in a good hike up Bishop Peak and toured the local establishments in San Luis Obispo, some of which he and his band, Louder Space, frequented for occasional performances.

In Oregon, I stayed with Dan and his new wife Karie. Dan had received his doctorate at Oregon State University in meteorology and was continuing to work with his mentor on various aspects of Mars weather. He and Karie had a nice home, not far from the Willamette Valley where we traveled to do wine tasting. I fell in love with their Pinot Noir and purchased a case for Steamboat. Dan and I also took a short flight in his Cessna 172, an aircraft he has maintained and upgraded over the years. He is an excellent pilot, having further developed the instincts and skills he nurtured as a hang glider pilot.

Betty and I enjoyed a picturesque fall in both the Yampa Valley and in Cincinnati where she hosted a reunion of the American Ladies, so named because they had gathered annually in the spring for almost 20 years to hike part of the British Isles. Their British tour guides, the same ones each year, referred to them as "The American Ladies."

The gathering at the Henshaw farm was a lovely occasion. Betty, as always, a genial and organized hostess, welcomed more than a dozen of those who had hiked with her in many places from Scotland to the Channel Islands. I am convinced that because of these annual excursions, Betty, born in 1936, retained the mobility that many in her age group have lost. The size of the group remained about the same every year, because daughters began to attend even as older ladies retired.

One family, the Avrils from Dallas, came to Betty's party that fall. Betty Avril brought her gorgeous twin daughters, each of whom had joined the walking tours at different times. They were ardent Romney fans in a year that Barack Obama was seeking reelection. We laughed a lot, drank a lot, and teased each other about our opposing political views. I even agreed to wear a Romney pin for most of the weekend. But I soon got rid of it when the gathering ended. Unfortunately! In January 2020, I would have worn that pin proudly when Romney cast the only Senate Republican vote to impeach Trump!

Back in Steamboat I organized a ukulele group. I have always desired to play an instrument well, but I either lacked the discipline or found myself too busy to pursue the goal. I took piano lessons as a child in Pennsylvania, but disliked practicing. My musical ear was/is so sensitive that it got in the way of learning to read sheet music. And I was a poor student, yearning to be outside playing sports, when I should have been practicing scales. But I learned just enough to be able to play simple songs on the piano in the key of C and as the years rolled by, I tried to master the guitar with a year of lessons with Richard Choy in Hawaii and the banjo with a year of lessons in Fort Collins.

When Betty and I began spending 4–6 weeks in Hawaii, I decided to take up the ukulele. I could strum it and sing, which gave me pleasure. My voice is nothing like Alejandro's, but it's decent, and I have such a keen musical ear that I sing mostly on key. I had no desire to pick the four strings and play melody (tuff uke) like Jake Shimabukuro, so I organized a small group of Steamboat folks who just wanted to play chords and sing in harmony.

It was quite an experience. We started out with about 10 people. Some just wanted to talk about their musical knowledge; others couldn't get past two or three basic chords. We ended up with a core that met regularly once a week, after business hours, in a real estate office. We had the usual disagreements on what music to play, everyone bringing in a favorite which was usually too difficult or not appropriate to the uke.

Betty and I attended one of the first concerts of Denver's Ukulele Orchestra, the creation of Gary Jugert. I met him backstage prior to the first performance at Christmas. Even though his players were mostly mediocre, Gary had an energy and sense of humor that I admired. I invited him to Steamboat to give a clinic to my group. He and his wife, Donna Bright, stayed with us while Gary organized and led a two-day clinic. Twenty-five people showed up, and I thought our little no-name group would be swamped with new members. But such was not the case. As life gets in the way for most folks with musical intentions, so too did the well-intentioned participants lose enthusiasm for practice, discipline, and constancy. For the next few years, although we attended functions in Denver to learn more and get better, our group remained small. We never performed!

Gary's Denver Ukulele Orchestra, however, got bigger and bigger, and the quality of music improved significantly. By the time Betty and I moved out of Steamboat to Denver, his orchestra was playing both popular and classical music and the group size was pushing 100. I played with them for over a year, mostly baritone ukulele, until Gary decided to organize the Denver Guitar Orchestra. In April 2017, I joined the DGO, abandoning the ukulele. I have not looked back. Gary is a good musician, and he is a people's director, not a demanding perfectionist. He wants everyone to have a shot at playing music and while this means that some members of his orchestra are tone deaf, unable to practice, and musically challenged, he believes that the joy of participating in a musical group will suffice to encourage the effort necessary to improve. That style of leadership worked for me, while the discipline of playing in an orchestra served as a wonderful distraction from the pain of watching Betty's dementia worsen.

In addition to the Steamboat ukulele group, I spent a lot of time during the winter of 2012–2013 shoveling snow. We had several winters in a row of over 400 inches which made for great skiing, but it got to a point that I would wake up and say to myself,

"Oh, no, not another powder day!" I had purchased an old Toyota pickup with a plow on it which I backed into the garage so I could make a clearing run up the driveway. As long as the plow worked, my life was easy, but good friend and neighbor, Peter Parsons, liked to borrow it. He often returned the unit with something broken, so I ended up using my snowblower. During the snowy months of 2012–2013, there was also the problem of where to put the snow when the banks got really high. Winters in Steamboat were often spectacular, but snow removal turned into a real chore and although there is probably little connection, I blamed fatigue from too many days of shoveling for a bad fall I took on the slopes, resulting in a shoulder separation. By summer, the shoulder was just creaky, and the trees I had planted around the house in very poor soil were beginning to show appreciation for all the moisture.

Toyota pickup snowplow

Kim shoveling snow

August 2013 was my 80th birthday. Nick and Suzie suggested a celebratory gathering at the elegant Tickle Pink Resort in Carmel. Betty and I joined them, along with their friends David and Carie Boesch, Sid and Betsey, and Toby and JoAnn. We played golf at Laguna Seca. Sid, the tennis player, even took lessons prior to the gathering. We ate fabulous meals at the resort restaurant and consumed lots of alcohol. It was a really fun party, at a very special place. I will never forget Sid's toast which was an adaptation of the Beatles' hit "When I'm 64." The number he used for me, 104, made us all laugh, but as I write this, I am a few months shy of 90. Who knows what may happen?

A month later, Alejandro and I were in New York attending Cristina's graduation from Columbia University. I had been aware that the DOE job was frustrating her, so when I saw Columbia's advertisement in *The New Yorker* for an M.A. in environmental

Alejandro, Cristina, and Snort at the Columbia Lion

sustainability, I suggested she look into it. She did! She was accepted, spent a year living in the Big Apple, and graduated with a focus on the financial aspects of sustainability in the corporate world.

This was a watershed moment in her life. Patrick, the boyfriend, whom she had met in Steamboat, was living in Denver. He had lost both his dog and his dad, and he wanted Cristina to marry him. Although he understood her desire for additional education (and even helped her move to New York), discord was inevitable. Cristina poured herself into the Columbia program 100%, while Patrick became increasingly impatient. Eventually, he gave up and found another woman. This was very hard on her, but she stayed the course at Columbia. Alejandro and I shared in the celebration of her successful accomplishment.

After our $600 dinner at La Grenouille, which I mentioned previously, the three of us took the train to Philadelphia. I wanted to show Alejandro and Cristina the Tyler family roots. We toured Neshaminy Farms, my grandparents' estate in Bucks County, Elkins Park, where my father was born, and the Tyler Art School at Temple University. We did a little historical sightseeing in Philadelphia, before returning to New York. Alejandro and I flew back to Denver, and Cristina started looking for a job.

It took a while, but ultimately, she was hired by Framework, LLC out of Stamford, CT. Framework is an advisory and analytics firm which helps companies create value, minimize risk, and build trust through sustainable business practices. It was then owned by two women who practice what they preach. Although Cristina ascended quickly as an up-and-coming consultant, the commute to Stamford—two hours each way by subway and train—proved exhausting. When an opportunity arose to transfer to the Seattle office, she grabbed it. For a few years, things worked out well; she bought her first home, was able to work there most of the time, and enjoyed the companionship of a very loyal dog. Who knows how things would have turned out had she not experienced a serious ankle break while walking her new puppy, Cash, in a nearby park?

Back in Colorado, I celebrated the publication of *Mum* (Denver: E&R Publications, 2013), a biography of Gandy, my mother. I had spent the previous two years researching her life. She and I were always close, not unexpectedly because of the tension between my father and me. But I had felt she got short shrift in my father's memoir (*A Joyful Odyssey*, 3 vols) and because I felt myself more Harper than Tyler, I decided to research and write the story of her life.

It was an enjoyable journey. Betty and I pursued her roots by investigating her early growing up, her education, and other foot prints from Milton to Cape Cod, MA. We stayed in the Harper home in Yarmouth Port, now the Inn on Main, a bed and breakfast, and we fleshed out her connection to the ancestral Bacon, Simpkins, and Agassiz families. I also explored her year in Florence, Italy, through contacts with historians and archivists, concluding with a description of her life as wife, mother, and grandmother up to her death in 1993. It was a true labor of love.

The winter of 2013–2014 followed the same pattern of skiing at Steamboat until mid-February, then joining Betty in Kailua. But this vacation had upsets along with a really enjoyable visit from Philip and his Louder Space band: Clay on guitar, Oren on bass guitar, Chris doing vocals, and Philip providing rhythm, guitar, and occasional vocal assistance.

Soon after the band arrived, I received a phone call from my nephew, Toby, saying that his dad had been in a bicycle accident returning home from a visit to his cardiologist. He said that the preliminary reports indicated Sid would recover. But that was not to be. Even though he arrived relatively soon at an ICU nearby, Sid suffered from severe head trauma and never fully regained consciousness. I was sitting on the beach when a second call arrived with the news that he had died on March 27, 2014. At that moment a huge anvil-shaped cloud was rising over Kaneohe Bay. I took a picture of it. It is still in my cell phone. To me, at that moment, the cloud was a symbol of my brother's passage from one world to another and even though its beauty and power were awesome, it did little to assuage my grief.

Philip and his buddies had been playing music on the beach and at several places in Kailua. They also put together a gig for the Henshaw family and friends, and they invited me to sing "Hallelujah" with them while I played the ukulele. It was an emotional moment. I had trouble getting through the song, but Louder Space held it together.

The next day, Dan Henshaw took them on a hike. It was a pretty rugged up and down trek through a lot of mud and tropical growth. When I picked them up at the designated arrival spot, they were whipped. I had brought juice and snacks which they were almost too tired to consume. Dan Henshaw has a reputation of taking guests and family members on outings that are somewhat dangerous. He almost lost Betty's best friend, Joan Smith, on a kayak trip around the Mokuluas. And I have already mentioned the casual way he allowed Tommy to float out to sea. The four young men were tired that evening, and Louder Space was quiet.

After the guys returned to the mainland, I took Betty to see a neurologist in Honolulu. Following quite a few requests on my part, Dan Henshaw was finally persuaded that the changes we were seeing in his mom were more than just the gradual decline of a woman in her late seventies. The doctor ordered a CT scan. Images showed significant retrenchment of the frontal lobes. Probably Alzheimer's, the doctor concluded.

I remember sitting in the car with Betty in the clinic parking lot after the diagnosis. I felt vindicated by the diagnosis, but I also

Louder Space on Lanikai Beach

Louder Space playing on the beach

felt emotionally drained. In many ways, I had already anticipated the deterioration of what had been a lovely, mutually supportive relationship. It was depressing, but I turned to Betty before starting the car, and I told her we would fight this together. At the same time, she would have to do everything in her power to retain positive brain activity. I know she heard me; I know she understood. She had that deer-in-the-headlights look, but I could tell she was processing what I was saying and how I was saying it. If memory serves, I think that's about when she decided to put a lot of energy into crossword puzzles. For the next seven years, 2014–2022, Betty entertained herself with all kinds of puzzles as the dementia slowly worsened.

Winding Down

By the late spring of 2014, my goals and priorities had changed significantly. I refocused. Because of Betty's dementia, most of my planning and thinking revolved around the goal of keeping her healthy and active. When Betsey Tyler asked if I would speak at Sid's celebration of life in Pasadena, I happily agreed. But I also knew that the emotional impact of the experience would require someone to assist Betty, as I struggled with the powerful feelings associated with losing my brother. Fortunately, Carol Tyler arrived from Philadelphia to fill that role. She had lost her husband, my first cousin Pete Tyler, several years earlier. She understood what I was going through and what Betty would require. She was an angel.

Sid's service took place at All Saints Episcopal Church on April 12, 2014. More than a thousand people attended. Sid was admired by many because of his 12-year role (1997–2009) as a Pasadena city council member. His talent with budgets and fiscal matters combined with a passion to protect Pasadena's urban forest and other environmental areas at risk. He was reelected six times.

I found it difficult to express my own feelings at the service. Barely a year apart in age, Sid and I had been very close growing up and even though our paths after college took us in different directions with different experiences, that bond was always strong. I miss him today. He was a good family leader after Grampy died. The silver lining, I suppose, is that I have come to know and admire his oldest son, my godson, Toby. Along with Rob's son, Harper, Toby has taken over responsibilities related to the family trusts. Toby spoke before me at the church service. He had a tough time, but he did admirably. The loss he still feels is incalculable.

Tickle Pink Inn, Carmel Highlands

Toby and I saw each other under better circumstances a few months later when we celebrated my 81st birthday at Tickle Pink in Carmel, CA. Having had such a good time the previous year, we brought back most of the same people for another round of drinks, golf, good food, and hikes. Betty did fine, but it was clear she needed more than occasional guidance and reassurance. I felt her leaning on

81st birthday: Betty, JoAnn, Kathy Wreden, Herm Bleibtreu, Toby, Nick, me, David and Carie Boesch, and Suzi

me in ways I had not experienced during the first 10 years of our relationship. We still had a very good time, but I was gradually assuming the role of caregiver.

Toward the end of the summer, I took Cody on a fishing trip on the Yampa River. We hired Johnny Spillane to be our guide. Johnny was a three-time Olympic silver medal winner in nordic combined events. He had just retired as a professional athlete the year before and had purchased a recreational fishing business in Steamboat Springs. He knew the Yampa like the back of his hand, and he could see that Cody was an eager student who really wanted to excel at fly fishing. I was delighted. Under Johnny's guidance, Cody caught several really nice fish. I caught a few myself. We had a great time together and returned to the river the following year to float and fish again. By then, Cody was the master. I fished in his shadow.

The winter of 2014–2015 was the next to last trip Betty and I took to Kailua and the Davie house. Those Hawaii weeks revealed again how our lives would be changing in the future. For reasons that neither we nor the doctors could figure out, Betty experienced pain in the vicinity of her bladder within days of arriving in Hawaii. She was treated for a UTI infection, but lab tests showed no suspicious bacteria. The pain lasted for most of our four-week stay and didn't entirely go away until we had been back in Colorado for a month. Very strange. The cause of her discomfort had to be related to something in the Hawaiian air, water, or foods, because the pains returned like clockwork when she made her final visit to Hawaii. There might have been a connection between the malfunction of her innards and her dementia, but I was always suspicious of her radical change in diet, in particular papaya. Even her son, Dr. Dan, was flummoxed.

Because of her not feeling well, I wasn't sure she would be able to help me host Alejandro, Kim, Ainsley, and Andon who had been invited to Kailua for a week. At one point, I suggested to Kim that they might consider canceling their trip. Fortunately, she remained positive and offered, as she always does, to help out with all household chores. Cristina also joined us. We had a great time. Not the first salt water experience for the grandchildren, but one of the best. The waves at Kailua beach are always small, and the water is warm. They swam a lot, visited Hanauma Bay for their first snorkeling experience, and chilled out for hours on the lanai playing board games with Mama and Papa; a lovely family scene that gave me great pleasure. For the most part, Betty was fine.

My second ukulele, purchased from Kanile'a Ukulele in nearby Kaneohe also gave me pleasure. In the spring of 2014, I had bought my first quality uke made from koa. It had a low G string. It was what I played when our Steamboat group convened. But I also wanted to learn to play a baritone uke, which is strung exactly like the lower four strings of a guitar (DGBE). Fingering for chords is different, but the sound is deeper, richer, more mellow. I actually picked out the piece of koa wood that would comprise the body of this baritone uke and when the instrument was completed and sent to me in Steamboat, I was ecstatic. From then on, I pretty much just played the baritone. I'm glad I did, because the transition I made to the guitar in the spring of 2018 was a lot easier than it would have been had I not been familiar with the first four strings of that 6-string instrument.

Soon after we returned to Steamboat from Hawaii, I thought about how Betty would be best cared for as her illness worsened. I decided to begin simplifying my own life, the first step being to get rid of the 1956 MGA which had been a great source of pleasure for almost 10 years.

I decided to gift it to Philip. I don't think the underlying reason for the gift is a secret anymore, but if so, Philip, please forgive the conspiracy. Nick was hoping the MGA might lure Philip out of Los Angeles where the bad air provided no benefits for Philip's sensitive lungs. Austin, where Nick had been living, not only had better air, it also had a dynamic music scene which would have appeal to the founder of Louder Space. And Nick is a great mechanic! We agreed that he would garage the MGA at his place, although he had to grit his teeth. A Triumph-man does not easily accommodate an MGA in his stable of vehicles. The transfer of ownership became an adventure in itself.

With Betty following me in her Lexus, which she drove pretty darn well, we departed Steamboat in May 2015 for her condo at The Spire in Denver. A second parking space we hardly ever used was a great spot for the MGA until Nick arrived with his pickup.

Philip flew to Denver. Nick and I picked up a U-Haul trailer, and I brought the car to Alejandro's house where we loaded it on the trailer. With Nick driving and Philip riding shotgun, we headed south on I-25, destination Austin.

Unexpectedly, a spring hail storm passed over Colorado Springs just as we arrived at the north edge of town. Worried about the soft top on the MGA, we pulled off the highway under an overpass to await better weather. It didn't come soon. While Nick watched a car doing 360s in his rearview mirror, the hail piled up several inches on the highway. We suffered no damage, but we were lucky. Cars and trucks unable to gain shelter got badly beaten up.

We had no special place to stop for the night; no defined destination, so we just kept on going—not my thing. By the time we got to Texas, our cell phones were no longer operable; something had happened to Verizon service. We had no maps and were not sure where we were. We stopped in a small town where Nick engaged a local rancher who had a very old map in his truck which he gave us. I'm not sure the lesson was learned by everyone about having backup maps when your principal guide is a GPS app on your cell phone. But I now make sure I have maps when I drive long distance. It's like the lesson I learned in the Air Force: instruments are fine, but you better know where you are via dead reckoning if the electrical system fails!

Around midnight we passed a motel with its lights still on. I knocked on the door and was told that all rooms were occupied. The manager said that there was another motel 10 miles down the road where we might find vacancies. Fortunately, we were in luck. Five hours of sleep later, we were on the road again, arriving in Austin in the late afternoon.

I know Philip appreciated the car, but he was then very

attached to the LA scene, and I could tell that he was conflicted about how he was going to enjoy a car parked 1,400 miles away from home and girlfriend, Tara. He spoke a few times of having the car delivered to LA, but I think we all knew that if it left Nick's garage, it would probably not be running for very long. While in Austin, we drove it around, had a few beers, and enjoyed catching up. When I left, I said goodbye to Albert, never thinking that down the road, he might once again share space in my garage.

Back in Denver, I had the pleasure of attending Alejandro's graduation with a Master's degree in secondary education from the University of Phoenix. Having left the University of Houston when the faculty associated with his Ph.D program in statistics revealed flaws in direction and leadership, Alejandro had set his sights on teaching high school math. After doing his student teaching at Arapahoe High School, he was offered a contract at Heritage High School in Littleton. A year there proved satisfying, but when Arapahoe had an opening the next year, they asked him to return. Colleagues at Arapahoe were delighted when he accepted. The decision was not easy. But his fellow teachers are good friends and now that he has tenure, he can rest easy that conflicts with the principal won't mean he might have to look for another job. Alejandro is a born teacher, a perfect combination of intellectual integrity, common sense, and a no-nonsense approach to distraught students and parents. He's using his talents in the best way possible, and he is inspiring a good number of students.

In the fall of 2015, I underwent Altemeier surgery in Denver for what is referred to as rectal prolapse. No need to describe this in any detail. Suffice to say, the prolapse was making it more difficult for me to walk the golf course, and I knew that it wasn't going to get better.

The surgery went well, but I ended up contracting C. difficile, a bacterial infection, at the hospital. The bacteria that causes this condition frequently invade a wound after an overdose of antibiotics. Under doctor's orders, I had taken a lot of antibiotics prior to surgery. Because the condition is prevalent in hospitals, patients try to go home as soon as possible after surgery. I didn't know I had it when I left the hospital, and when I later asked the doctors why I was so bloated and uncomfortable, they led me to believe that it was just the impact of surgery and that all would be fine shortly.

So Betty and I embarked on a driving trip to Dallas where her best friend, Betty Avril, was celebrating her 80th birthday. It was a Halloween birthday, and we had costumes. I had to make quite a few unplanned stops on the way, occasionally flirting with dust storms, cacti, and rattlesnakes, but we got to the party relatively unscathed. Finding our hotel in Dallas proved challenging and once again, I learned how Betty's once flawless skill with maps and road signs had all but vanished. Her directions were no longer of much use to me as driver, mainly because she could no longer process what she read.

We spent a couple of nights in Dallas before visiting Nick and Suzi in their new Austin home. I didn't feel great and ended up in a nearby hospital twice: once because of the C. diff and a second time because I had been given so much fluid that my legs had swollen up. We weren't very good guests and when more antibiotics seemed to have knocked out the C. diff, Betty and I headed home.

My gut gradually settled down somewhat, but the Altemeier procedure, along with the brachytherapy I underwent several years earlier for prostate cancer, combined to make things a little dicey in my lower intestines. I had days of low energy and nights of discomfort, but I decided to treat symptoms with exercise and a blander diet. I lost weight, which I still haven't gained back entirely, and I have experienced a certain amount of apathy from doctors who just don't know how to treat irritable bowel syndrome. Hopefully, this will change as I begin a new series of tests and nutrition-based programs with a functional medicine practitioner. But in 2016, I wasn't too sure about returning to Hawaii with these symptoms. Betty was already there along with her cousin, Ann Kelleher and husband Pete. At my request, they had flown with her to the Islands. They were staying in the Davie's house until I arrived. Unfortunately, Betty's UTI symptoms came back almost immediately, forcing Pete and Ann to take on the role of daily caregiving. By the time I arrived, they were frustrated by having to spend so much time around the house with Betty. Within hours of my landing, they announced plans to go elsewhere. They had been invited to stay at Patty Henshaw's sister's house for their remaining week in Hawaii. And by the way, they said, Betty had a doctor's appointment with a urologist the next day. Boom! I had to get up to speed fast.

The urologist did a swabbing and sample taking to see if he could determine the cause of Betty's discomfort. A few days later, she was in greater pain. I took her back to the clinic, but they didn't have any answers and by the time we got home, she had spiked a fever and was shaking violently.

Dr. Dan finally showed up, recognized that his mother was quite sick, and took her to the nearby Adventist Health Castle Hospital. From blood work, it was determined that the invasive procedures of the urologist had somehow caused sepsis, i.e., blood poisoning.

The hospital care she received was excellent, but it took several days before she could return home and when she arrived, she was weak and without much appetite. The Henshaws and I decided she should have home care, so they hired a service that contracted wives from the nearby Kaneohe Marine Base to act as caregivers in homes of elderly people. They had little training and didn't do much, but their presence allowed me to get away for a few rounds of golf. Betty was an accommodating patient, but her recovery was slow, and her confusion from the dementia was pronounced.

I had long talks with the Henshaws during this time. I felt that we would need a better arrangement than what I could provide for Betty in Steamboat. Ann Kelleher suggested we look at a facility in Omaha near where she and Pete lived. She all but offered to be Betty's advocate if we placed her in that assisted living facility.

Shortly after Betty and I flew home, Dan arrived and the three of us flew to Omaha. Betty was not happy with the plan. She and I had been through a bad experience the previous year when I made a reservation for both of us at newly constructed Balfour Assisted Living near Union Station in downtown Denver. I furnished the place with the help of a professional designer, but when it came time to try it out for two weeks, Betty wouldn't go. All of the furnishings had to be removed from the room, so I hired a truck and sent everything to Cristina in New York. What was intended initially for Betty has made its way with Cristina in her moves to Seattle and finally to 8888 Snowball Way in Parker, CO. Betty's reluctance to relocate in an independent living facility was mostly based on a fear that I would abandon her once we settled in. She far preferred living on the 36th floor of The Spire when we were in Denver. Additionally, she was on edge, because she felt that her son Dan and I might be conspiring to place her in memory care. Omaha was not a good setting to gain her cooperation, no matter how nice that facility seemed to be.

But we gave it a shot. I let Dan Henshaw take the lead. He and the facility director toured the building and ended up in a conference room where Betty basically said that if she were to be incarcerated in that facility she would stop eating. They finally called me into the meeting, but Betty's mood didn't change. She was angry. I really don't blame her, but we had to begin looking for a modification of our Steamboat-Denver lifestyle and even though this was a harsh moment for all concerned, I knew that a change was necessary. Dan Henshaw was devastated by what he witnessed, not so much because of his mom's negativity and threatening comments, but because he now realized firsthand how complex and deeply emotional decisions can be when they involve a loved one with dementia. For years, he had managed to remain distant and somewhat aloof. Now, probably for the first time, the reality of his mom's dementia got to him. It wasn't fun to see him break down. There would be no easy answers going forward, but in Omaha I think we found a level of mutual understanding that had been previously absent.

The three of us returned to Steamboat. For several days, we attempted to return to a normal and relaxed routine, but the dementia gorilla never left the room. On the day Dan Henshaw was to leave, I took my usual morning soak in the hot tub before anyone else was up. I won't say that it hit me like a rock, but I felt more comfortable with the idea of selling my home and moving with Betty into the assisted living facility, Casey's Pond, across the valley. I told Dan that this was what I was going to do. He was very relieved. It had been clear for some time that he and Patty were at odds over Betty's future. Dan knew that he had the principal responsibility for taking care of his mother. But Patty knew that Doctor Dan would continue to prioritize his work as a radiologist at Kaiser Permanente, delegating to Patty the myriad chores of running a household. If Betty were to be brought to Hawaii to spend her last years with her only child, Patty concluded, she would be doing the caregiving. With her own mother in her nineties, Patty was leery of any plan that would settle Betty nearby. And they both knew that Betty wanted to stay with me. Period! Any changes would have to wait until Dr. Dan retired.

It was a dilemma for all of us; one that occasionally became contentious. I decided to sell the home I had built in order to resolve what had become a real standoff. Casey's Pond had a nice apartment with a view of the ski mountain so we signed a lease, and I put the house up for sale. It sold relatively fast. We moved into Casey's Pond in September 2016.

Betty liked Casey's Pond. I hired several caregivers who took her on outings, and we both still did a few things together in the town. But I never felt comfortable in that facility. We made a few friends, but overall I felt constricted, not quite ready to call assisted living my home. On a trip to The Spire in Denver, I booked a tee time at an executive golf course called The Links. Coming up the 16th fairway, with Betty riding shotgun in the golf cart, I saw a sign on a house saying "For Sale By Owner." I called the owner and arranged for a tour the next day. The house was smaller than my Steamboat home and on a golf course. Betty could be comfortable there, knowing that I would be golfing close by and able to return quickly if she needed me. I didn't tell her what I was doing, but I made an offer on the house, and it was accepted in November 2016. A month later, Betty was en route to Hawaii to spend Christmas with her family. While she was gone, I moved us out of Casey's Pond and hired a moving company to transfer all our stored possessions from a Steamboat warehouse to the garage of my new home, 15 Canongate Lane in Highlands Ranch. The warranty deed to my new home was executed in January 2017.

Betty returned from Hawaii in January. We moved into her condo in The Spire. Things had not gone too well in Hawaii, and Betty was going to need daily care. Patty had found a lady by the name of Margo Allman who had a stable of caregivers. I made contact with Margo, and we decided to set up a weekly program that would provide Betty with company while I gradually worked on remodeling the living room and master bath at 15 Canongate.

This was the spring of 2017. In March, Betty and I took a trip to Tucson to get out of the cold. We stayed a month in a comfortable condo near The Lodge at Ventana Canyon. A good friend, John Morrison, whose company I enjoyed in Steamboat, had purchased a house near the resort which had two tough golf courses. We played together a number of times. When not golfing, Betty and I enjoyed eating at nearby restaurants. We took tours to the Arizona-Sonora Desert Museum, the University of Arizona, and to Sabino Canyon for short hikes. We also drove to the top of Mt. Lemon.

When we returned to Denver, we settled into a routine at The Spire. I left after breakfast in the morning to work at 15 Canongate; Betty was accompanied for most of the day by a caregiver. The arrangement worked well, but it wasn't a good permanent solution. I continued to play with Gary Jugert's Ukulele Orchestra every Monday night, including several concert performances. It was great fun. Betty accompanied me to our Monday night uke practices in Lakewood. She sat next to me and turned pages of the musical numbers we were playing. She was very helpful and followed along pretty well. The only part of the orchestra experience she did not like was driving to and from Lakewood in the dark during the late fall, winter, and early spring. I was learning that people with dementia feel uneasy in the dark.

In May, Betty and I worked with Laurie Hunter of Wade Ash

Woods Hill & Farley to bring her estate planning documents current. Among those documents was a joint medical POA which gave me the power to make decisions regarding Betty's health, so long as I consulted with her son. It wasn't long before the efficacy of this document was tested. Dan and Patty, for reasons I still don't comprehend, decided to take the advice of Margo Allman who had been providing caregivers for Betty. Margo recommended placing Betty in a small (8–10 residents) home for people with various forms of dementia. Margo, of course, would get a kickback. She never asked for my advice, assuming that Dan Henshaw's financial power of attorney was all she needed to move Betty out of The Spire into a small home.

I contacted Laurie Hunter who immediately pointed out that my joint medical POA was sufficient to block this very sudden and thoughtless move. Betty never knew what was going on, but Dan Henshaw ultimately backed down.

All of this came to a head in the summer of 2017. I had a hard time wrapping my head around the situation, not only because I had worked so hard to help Betty feel safe and loved during a difficult period, but also because I was unable to understand how anyone could treat Betty that way, given the generosity she had always shown to her family and the gentle manner she always manifested in her dealings with other human beings.

Dan Henshaw and I have never exchanged harsh words. He actually called and apologized for attempting to move his mom without input from me. I give him credit for that and even though the scars associated with these events remain, I am better able to understand his actions now that I am more familiar with the emotional complexities associated with dementia. Dan and Patty were trying to simplify their responsibilities, but their distance from

Colorado, Dan's work responsibilities, and Patty's aging mother made things complicated.

I did not forgive Margo Allman, however. Her attempt to lock Betty up and make a few bucks in the process really offended me. And she lied about the reasons for her wanting to place Betty in a small home. Partly in response, I hired a psychotherapist to visit with Betty on 2–3 occasions to see if she could help me persuade Betty to enter an established assisted living facility. Ultimately, we all knew, Betty would be better off being cared for in an established care facility with a good reputation.

Fortunately, Beverly Essex, who had helped us when I had the Altemeier surgery, was available for a few days a week, so I brought her back for as many days as she could work. What a lovely woman! She and Betty got along really well. Meanwhile, I initiated a formal complaint against social worker Margo Allman with the Colorado Department of Public Health. It is illegal under Colorado law to place people in care facilities without a proper license. My complaint was referred to the Department of Regulatory Agencies, where it moved very, very slowly. Exactly one year later, I received a letter stating that Margo Allman had been issued a warning, but nothing of consequence happened. I wasn't surprised. Perhaps she at least had a few months of worrying about losing her social worker license.

Once Betty had agreed to look at a few facilities, we toured the Denver area: Holly Creek, The Vi, Windcrest, etc. She was pretty negative about them all, obviously preferring that we just stay at The Spire. She wasn't angry; sad, really, and maybe just disappointed in me. But at the same time, I sensed in her a growing awareness of her condition. I worried about the health issues I might face were I to continue as her primary companion and caregiver. Existing literature makes clear the health risks involved when family members assume the responsibility of caring for someone with dementia.

When I had the opportunity, I attended an Alzheimer's support group in Highlands Ranch on Saturday mornings. I went to half a dozen meetings and heard about Ginny Davie who helped place people in assisted living and memory care facilities. She worked for Senior Path and was licensed to do this. Members of the group raved about her. I met with Ginny and a Senior Path attorney to explain my situation and to get advice on how to move forward without causing additional problems with the Henshaws. Ginny wanted to show me three places she thought might work. The third one we toured was Cherry Hills Assisted Living, a relatively new facility that had assisted living upstairs and memory care downstairs. Ginny was cautious due to CHAL's untested newness, but I was impressed with all the large glass windows, the location next to a very large park near the historic High Line Canal, and an available room which was located close to the front desk. I contacted Dan Henshaw and told him we should grab it.

He was glad to oblige. We settled on an October 2017 move-in date when he could join us. I found a moving company that would re-create Betty's Spire apartment ambience by transferring furniture that would fit the space, along with pictures on the walls that would be hung in the same manner in which they had been hung at The Spire. The best part was that the moving and set-up would take place in one day.

On the designated date, Dan and I took Betty for a tour of Rocky Mountain National Park. We were instructed to arrive at CHAL around 6 p.m. Sure enough, when we came through the door to her suite (bedroom, bath, and sitting room), everything from the bed to the pictures and even the items Betty had on her bedside table at The Spire were in the same place. I'm not sure Betty felt 100% comfortable, but Doctor Dan and I dined with her at CHAL and spent the night, Dan sleeping on the sofa. We continued the same togetherness for the next few days, hoping that Betty would gradually feel that she was home. Unfortunately, Dan experienced a severe A-fib (atrial fibrillation) attack on the third day. He had medication which helped relieve the symptoms, but it was clear that the experience of putting his mom into CHAL was taking an emotional toll on him. The a-fib attacks happened at CHAL on two other occasions.

When Dan returned to Hawaii, I remained with Betty for another 10 days until one of the managers suggested it was time for me to leave. Betty had a tough time with this, but there was no other option. It was the beginning of a new relationship between us that continued for four and a half years until Dan and Patty came to pick her up and take her to Hawaii in June 2022.

Reflections

Looking back, I think we made the right decision to put Betty in Cherry Hills Assisted Living in 2017. It was hard on both of us in different ways, but overall it meant safety and security for Betty and a better chance for me to have time for myself. Even with Betty at CHAL, however, there were many responsibilities connected with her new life: doctors, mail, room cleaning, clothing, laundry, taxes, hygiene, etc. Over the four and a half years she was there, I joined her at meals, took her on walks in the park which she loved, went on ice cream excursions, and ventured out on occasion to museums and other cultural venues.

Dementia destroys many, but not all, of the connections that bind two people together. Betty's decline was slow, and her lovely essence came to the surface in warm and unexpected ways. But the give and take enjoyed by us as equal partners disappeared under these trying circumstances, leaving one of us dependent and trusting; the other committed to advocacy and reassurance. There was still plenty of love that flowed both ways, but it was marred by sadness which at times, dipped into depression—what could have been! I'm not ashamed to say that I wept a lot over the past decade.

The CHAL experience was good for me. I have often been reminded of the silent promise I made to Betty's late husband during my first few days with her in Cincinnati. Before and after CHAL, I felt the stress of honoring that vow while at the same time respecting the warnings of experts that caregivers, prone to various levels of worry and frustration, are susceptible to strokes, heart attacks and other age related infirmities. With Betty at CHAL, those strains were somewhat reduced, but they didn't go away entirely. I tried to help her adjust to an assisted living facility, but because of her pride and her unique life experiences, she tended to be somewhat standoffish with other residents in noteworthy contrast to her gregarious, outgoing self before the dementia took hold.

Consequently, her focus on me became more intense. I tried to be in touch with her daily. The old Blackberry she carried with her was our conduit for texts, poems, phone calls, and pictures. During her last year at CHAL, she lost the ability to use it. I also tried to improve her daily life by suggesting to her caregivers a variety of better activities, more exercise, and interesting excursions. But like most facilities, CHAL is shorthanded. The staff focuses on bingo and board games which don't interest Betty. When we hired Danielle Schmidt in the fall of 2019 to work one-on-one with Betty several days a week, things improved immensely.

Danielle had imagination, energy, and affection for Betty. When it became apparent that Betty's worst times were in the evenings, when there were no activities or people around to keep her distracted, I asked Danielle if she would consider spending time with Betty five days a week during that "sundowning" period. She agreed, and Dan Henshaw was willing to pay for the service. Danielle became part of our lives. She kept Betty's spirits in good order, taking her for walks, engaging her in discussions about family and travels, and finding puzzles and other games to occupy Betty's mind. Fortunately, Danielle was viewed as an essential worker during the COVID-19 pandemic, and we had high hopes she would be able to continue her good work. Her anti-vaccine views, however, put her at odds with the authorities at CHAL, so we had to let her go. For the last two years of her stay at CHAL, Betty was pretty much on her own. My visitations were curtailed, and we could find no one to replace Danielle. It was a very difficult period for all concerned.

My involvement with CHAL also included raising Christmas cash for all the hourly caregivers while Betty was there. They show a lot of kindness to the residents for not much more than minimum wages. Some are better than others, but as a group they provide much needed support and empathy. With donations from residents and family, I was able to raise enough money so we could hand out $100 to each of approximately 80 hourly employees in 2017, $150 in 2018, $175 in 2019 and $200 in 2021. I skipped 2020. The smiles, tears, and hugs we received when we passed out the money intensified and made meaningful the spirit of Christmas. Those caregivers, many of whom are recent immigrants to the United States, have a hard job which they perform with little thanks.

I have not had to worry about paying Betty's bills. Dan Henshaw has written the checks. Betty had the assets—now under Dan Henshaw's control—to pay the cost of assisted living and because Dan relied on me and hired caregivers to keep his mother well and reasonably happy, he was almost always amenable to whatever I suggested. Although there might have been a little tension in the air at times, we got along well, and we respect each other. When Dan retired in 2022 from his medical practice at Kaiser Permanente in Honolulu, he decided that it was time to take Betty to Hawaii.

He announced this decision while sitting in my living room after a day-long visit with his mom. I was shocked. It had seemed to me that the obstacles were too great, and Betty's limited mobility and declining mental acuity were such that the risks of failure seemed high. But without the daily responsibilities of his work to distract him, Dan considered the possibility of having Betty in Hawaii. It had become clear that the distance between Denver and Hawaii and the awkwardness of trying to keep up with all the decisions he was required to make were good reasons to revisit the possibility of bringing Betty home.

Consequently, after finding a memory care facility for her in Hawaii, Dan and Patty came to Denver to empty her apartment and take her on a plane to Honolulu. It was an extremely stressful experience. Betty actually traveled quite well, but Dan came down with COVID-19 on the return flight. He was forced to quarantine at his home in the basement, while Patty assumed the responsibility of taking Betty to the new facility. Confused and frightened, Betty was furious at having to be locked into a strange room because of her recent exposure to Dan. She pounded on the door most of the night, demanding that she be released. Patty had to come get her the next day. They returned to the Henshaw home where Betty remained for six weeks. Dan recovered from COVID-19, then experienced a bad case of shingles, while Patty, exhausted from assuming most of the chores along with Betty's care, fell and broke her wrist. It was not the best of times.

But things improved. The Henshaws received a call from Hale Ku'ike, a small memory care facility 10 minutes from their home. A private room had opened up, and Betty was next in line to be admitted. She adapted well, having missed the noisy comings and goings to which she had become accustomed at CHAL. The staff made sure she integrated with the small group already there and within a few weeks, she had made friends and was settling in. Dan and Patty visited once or twice a week and took pictures which they sent me. From what I could see, and from what they tell me, Betty is in the best place she could be. Although her cognitive skills have deteriorated, she is happy in the mild climate, has regular visitors, and appears to be accommodating well to a smaller facility. This, of course, makes me happy. I miss her, but I realize that what I really miss is the lady she was before the onset of dementia. I think I fulfilled my commitment to her husband. The age-related infirmities created a different sort of relationship, but even that had its moments of pleasure. When she left Denver, I said goodbye to a wonderful woman.

Reflecting on my own life in Denver after saying goodbye to Steamboat in 2016, I still miss that wonderful home I built and the friends I made in the Yampa Valley. I remember when Grampy sold the ranch in 1967; it felt like a piece of my heart was being removed. I think my siblings felt the same way. Shortly after the sale, in an attempt to salvage something, I told the purchaser, Phil Anschutz, that there were 15 acres at the north end of the ranch which we hayed every summer with great difficulty. Getting water on that piece of land and getting mowers, rakes, bailers, and hay trucks over and back without an accident were weighty tasks not worth the harvest of a few hundred hay bales. I asked Anschutz if I could buy that land so I might build a house there one day. He was polite but non-committal, so I was left with an awareness that I would never again be a part of the place which had no small impact on my physical and emotional development.

I have similar feelings of loss regarding 34630 Country Green Lane in Steamboat. That was the first and only house I built. During 15 years as a resident, I packaged a lot of good memories there. I expected to die in that house, but it was not to be. Moving to Denver was a struggle for me, but it was part of the commitment I made to Betty and when all is said and done, that move has worked out pretty well. More than anything, I am so glad to be close to Kim, Alejandro, Ainsley, Andon, and Cristina. I have been able to function as a real "Grandude" for Ainsley and Andon, and the time spent with Alejandro's family has been rewarding and meaningful.

I do like my new home on the 16th fairway of The Links Golf Course. Living in an over-50 community has pros and cons; the people are nice, albeit a little nosy, and golf is near at hand, on a well-maintained golf course. The house has been hit by errant balls a dozen times in the five years I have lived here, but the upside is that I have had fun conversations with many of the golfers who come by and glance enviously at the sight of a few neighbors and me drinking beer on the back porch. The traffic noise from E-470 can be bothersome when the wind blows from the north, but the early mornings in the hot tub are relatively peaceful, even though the maintenance guys roar by on their machinery before the sun is up, on a day when golfers are expected on the first tee by sunup. I do yoga at the Glen Eagles Village club house, attend an occasional neighborhood cul-de-sac party, play my guitar on the sidewalk or on my back porch, and try to cultivate sunflowers, wild flowers, phlox, and sage in the few planters and pots that surround my house. I know about a dozen neighbors by name, some of whom I consider good friends. They would provide assistance in a heartbeat if I need it.

During the worst of the pandemic in 2020 and 2021, socialization became difficult. I wore a mask and gloves when I left the house and for the most part, I tried not to enter public buildings. Groceries were ordered for pickup at King Soopers or Whole Foods; liquor was ordered for pickup at Davidsons, and almost anything else I needed I ordered through Amazon Prime. I made a couple of trips to Barnes and Noble, FedEx, and Ace Hardware, but I mostly sheltered in place since returning from Arizona on March 10, 2020. It was frustrating seeing people of all ages flouting the gravity of COVID-19; ordinary citizens paid the price, however, as the number of infections ebbed and flowed. But with the absence of national leadership and the duels between state, municipal, and county governments to develop and/or ease restrictions, the average citizen became confused, frustrated, and hostile. What a mess! Alejandro didn't know when or how a school plan for one day might be amended the next day as the virus evolved, mutated, and strengthened. The turmoil in schools for a good two years had a huge impact on the entire educational system. We still don't know the extent to which students lost ground, but all signs indicate that losses in academic skills, maturity, socialization, and emotional stability are huge.

A silver lining for me was the chance to work with Ainsley and Andon on their writing skills. Via FaceTime and Google Docs, we were able to share a lot of creative ideas. I would never have had this opportunity without the pandemic. Ainsely and Andon completed fairly long and creative narratives: Andon focused on the bloody rivalries of his video game characters; Ainsley crafted a teenage romance with a lot of shape-shifting. Grandude was challenged, but it proved to be a great way for me to get to know my grandchildren.

As I look back at the pandemic in 2023, my 90th year, I see and feel the changes it has wrought. Freedom as we knew it has been compromised. But I subscribe to the belief that perhaps this pandemic will serve as a turning point for humans who may be willing to address our broken medical system, our politicized immigration policy, our reliance on fossil fuels, our disrespect for climate change, our cowardice regarding gun control and the racial tensions that never seem to go away. The Black Death from the bubonic plague pandemic led to the Renaissance. Maybe something similar might happen worldwide in the 21st century. But as I write these words, Putin is in his second year of leveling Ukraine, the refugee crisis due to war and climate change has escalated,

Republicans and Democrats have increased the ugly rhetoric in their culture wars, and mass shootings have become more popular (647 in the US in 2022). I am skeptical about the world's ability to fix its problems; I don't see the kind of leadership that would be required, and I fear that a revived sense of community could easily be eclipsed by innate human greed, selfishness, and a continuation of the ugliness, vulgarity, hate speech, and prevarication of which Trump is only a pathetic symbol. There are good people in this country, but will they lead?

Meanwhile, I have tried to use some of the resources made available by the business successes of the Elkins and Tyler families, and I have taken considerable satisfaction in being able to assist those who were especially hard hit even before the pandemic. As previously mentioned, during the 2008–2009 recession, I established the Gateway to Graduation scholarship at CSU. The idea formed when CSU President Tony Frank came to Steamboat, as he did every summer, to connect with alums. He spoke of the increasing number of seniors who were dropping out of school, because neither they nor their parents had sufficient resources for both education and basic necessities of life. I started the Gateway scholarship for them and was bowled over when Tony and his chancellor, Joe Blake, each pledged $12,500. Ten years later, the scholarship has grown to over $250,000, making approximately $10,000 available annually for financial assistance. I also established a scholarship for young musicians and their parents, in Steamboat. After attending several performances of the Steamboat Symphony Orchestra, in which I noted a sea of gray hair and white skin, I established a scholarship that seeks out minority children interested in music and offers them and their parents free tickets to concerts. I also funded a matching grant in 2020 that enabled SSO musicians, whose livelihood has been severely eroded by the cancellation of performances, to receive a cash stipend with the understanding that they would be available when musicians were authorized once again to gather and play. I am hopeful that throwing them a lifeline has made a difference in their commitment to Director Ernest Richardson and the SSO.

Having the financial benefit of trusts established by Grampy and his father, I have tried to focus on stewardship of the assets through philanthropy. I have not preached these principles to my own children; I think the desire to lift up others less fortunate is very personal, and we all have different causes in which we believe. But I have found the experience very rewarding, beginning with the establishment of the Daniel Tyler Health and Education Foundation in 2005. With Nick as co-trustee, the plan was to invest in researchers who made progress in finding a cure for CF. Over the years, we invested in various individuals and organizations, and we may have done some good. In 2021, Philip assumed the task of directing the balance of assets to the Keck School of Medicine at the University of Southern California. It was a good thing for him to do, not only as an example of what significant philanthropy feels like, but as a chance to support the folks who have worked with him all his life. The foundation is now closed.

I have also worked with Fountain Valley School. Beginning when I was on the Board of Trustees, I have made significant gifts to my old alma mater. Alejandro, Cody, and Jesse are all graduates who can look back on the incredible experience they had at FVS. I don't know if the school can survive going forward. With tuition approaching $75,000 per year, I fear that the pool of prospective students will shrink to those of extreme wealth, along with families from Europe and Asia who have bottomless pockets and want their children to learn English. Average, middle-class, American families won't be in consideration; there aren't enough scholarships available, and many families with bright, multi-talented sons and daughters will have to save money for college. The student body may very soon reflect only the very richest people in the US, Europe, and Asia. This is not a good model going forward.

I am also a regular contributor to PBS and NPR. While the bias of the media remains a criticism heard from both sides of the political aisle, I feel that both of these publicly funded news outlets do a great job of attaining balance. I support their work.

Perhaps the greatest impact on me during the pandemic happened when I received an early morning phone call from Cristina on February 23, 2021. She had broken her ankle and was going to have surgery two days later in a Seattle hospital. Loss of balance on slippery ground while walking her new, two-month old, husky mix, Cash, had resulted in the accident. It was serious.

Surgery went well. A plate and screws were inserted in the wound area to help the bone heal correctly. A good friend brought her home to her three-story house. But right away, it was evident that she could not function in that house alone, even with crutches. Alejandro and I urged her to fly to Denver where she could recover and rehabilitate in Alejandro and Kim's second floor guest bedroom, while continuing her computer-based work with Framework. We picked her up at the Denver International Airport on March 7.

Without Cash or her car! Fortunately, old friends from Steamboat volunteered to fly to Seattle and pick up both. Except for not wanting to pee on the Seattle-Denver drive, Cash did fine. He took up residence with Cristina at Alejandro and Kim's house.

For the next two months, Cristina healed, and Cash made the best of his hosts' over-the-top generosity. Growing fast and being mostly husky, Cash desperately needed to be outdoors, moving around. Cristina found someone to walk him five days a week, and Andon helped a lot by romping with him in the back yard. But his energy level was high. He also loved to be with people, and when he observed Kim and me doing yard work below his second-story window, he decided to join us. With no warning, Cash lurched through an open window, determined to join the adults on the ground below. Out of the corner of my eye, I saw the window screen come flying out with Cash not far behind. The landing was rough, but nothing broke. We all learned quickly that Cash would do whatever was necessary to be a part of a social group.

Sometime in May, the three of us headed back to Seattle in Cristina's car. Cash was still stubborn about peeing, holding back throughout the entire first day of driving until we were about ready for bed. But other than that, he was a model passenger, content to sleep in the back seat as we completed the 1,300 mile drive.

I stayed a few days in Seattle, then flew home. It was clear by then that Cristina was considering leaving Seattle to be close to her family. She looked at houses for sale online. Prices were high in the Parker area where we thought she might relocate. Her agent, Diane Kreider, sent us listings which Alejandro and I checked out. Nothing really rang our bell until Father's Day when Cristina found a listing she liked on Snowball Way. Diane rejected it at first, because the listing address showed the house to be on a very busy cross street: Cottonwood Drive. I went over to take a look at it. The listing address was incorrect and from everything I could see, the house was in a great location on a corner lot, backing up to a park with a fenced yard, minimal landscaping to care for, and great views to the east.

I called Diane. She contacted the listing agent and learned that bids were being accepted until 4 p.m. that same day. I grabbed

Alejandro. We met Diane at the house and kicked off a Facetime-driven perambulation of the property with Cristina on the other end oohing and aahing. There was nothing not to like. The house is relatively new with lots of space on the upper living level, a huge basement with good light, a graveled outside area with no grass to mow, a raised flowerbed, covered porches on east and west sides and a three-car garage. We agreed that a bid of $15,000 over the asking price was probably needed to purchase the house. We were correct. The owner accepted our bid and returned $5,000 for future repairs of the fence. Unheard of!

I can't speak for Cristina, but I was ecstatic. I think she was, in fact, a degree higher than ecstatic, even though she was far away and had only the Facetime images to work with. But it really was a perfect find. The location is excellent: about 15 minutes from me, 10 minutes from Alejandro and Kim, and 5 minutes to the town of Parker, where just about anything can be found: Costco, pilates, yoga, dog grooming, grocery shopping, Starbucks, and everything in between.

By late July, Cristina had finished packing up the Seattle house and had hired a moving van. Alejandro flew to Seattle and drove with her and Cash to the new home, arriving July 31, 2021. This was a watershed moment for us all. Because "Dr. Kim" had approved in-the-bubble family gatherings, we were able to visit each other without the discomfort and strain of wearing masks. The pandemic was still a serious threat. We all got vaccinated and masked up when we entered closed-in public spaces, but even though the data showed a gradual decline in infections, the curve was mercurial at best, requiring constant vigilance and the use of masks away from home in closed spaces. That limitation on our freedoms and social interactions made family time even more rewarding.

I had done a lot of work organizing a family reunion in Redstone, CO. We had tried to gather everyone on Grampy's branch of the family tree in 2020 and canceled due to concerns about travel and hotels. For pretty much the same reasons, we canceled again in 2021. My hope was to present a verbal portrait of my grandfather, George Frederick Tyler, believing that my generation and all the children and grandchildren had little knowledge of him and his talented wife, Stella VanTuyl Elkins. Because of the two cancellations, I had time to extend my research beyond the anecdotal level. I hired a CSU graduate student to assist me with archival research and tracking down GFT's activities and accomplishments from his birth in 1883 to his death in 1947. I received good help from a few cousins and learned a great deal from newspapers, historical societies, private clubs, and archives. Impediments developed as a result of institutional employees not being allowed to do their jobs because of COVID-19 fears, but I think I found enough evidentiary material to flesh out a reasonably good biography: *Bucks County's Benevolent Squire. In Search of George Frederick Tyler* (Denver: Spring Cedars, 2022). The principal theme of the book is that GFT, born into wealth and marrying into even greater wealth, decided to use the family fortune to create something beneficial to society. The Tyler family crest motto is *Esse Quam Videri* (To Be Rather Than To Seem [To Be]). GFT, however, was interested in more than just being; he also wanted to be a doer. Neshaminy Farms, the agricultural community he created, produced world-class dairy animals, beef cattle, and a special wheat used for making matzah, an unleavened flatbread. His voluntary dedication to the governance of Abington Memorial Hospital, the Boy Scouts, the American Legion, an early iteration of the United Way, Temple University, the Philadelphia Symphony Orchestra, and the Westminster Choir were examples of his quiet leadership and his commitment to the regional community during the worst years of the Great Depression. In addition to the farm's national and international success, the Tyler School of Art and Architecture, Tyler Park, and Bucks County Community College represent the legacy of deeds he and Stella gifted to future generations.

For me, writing *Bucks County's Benevolent Squire* was a powerful antidote to the depressing restrictions caused by the pandemic.[10] As the virus assumed new variations every few months, we learned more about the unexpected consequences associated with getting and recovering from COVID-19. I became even more determined to protect myself. I hardly traveled at all. No movies, few restaurants, limited social occasions, and an embarrassingly frequent refusal of invitations to participate in conferences where my fading expertise in water history might have been useful. I wasn't a hermit; there was still plenty of golf to play, hiking, chauffeuring grandchildren, and wonderful mornings with Cash, romping in Cherry Creek Park. But there has been a significant amendment to the carefree, eclectic life I had enjoyed prior to the onset of the pandemic.

Playing the guitar assuaged the in-house loneliness. When the pandemic hit in 2020, I practiced a finger-style technique for classical guitar just about every day. The melodic sound of that instrument served as a calming distraction that helped me get through the days of isolation when I couldn't visit Betty at Cherry Hills Assisted Living, and when a self-imposed quarantine of sorts forced me to spend a lot of time at home. I continue to practice, but old fingers, demanding chords, and a capricious memory continue to present ongoing obstacles. My crazy goal is to master Beethoven's "Moonlight Sonata" before I have to quit playing forever. If the index and pinky fingers on my left hand appear deformed at my death, you will know they fought the good fight to the end.

KT Tunstall opened her rendition of *Through the Dark* with words that seem appropriate to me as I terminate this memoir: "As I walk away, I look over my shoulder to see what I'm leaving behind."

I too look back—a long way! And what I focus on most often is the children and grandchildren that became a part of my life. You have all done me proud; you have made me feel that even with my own missteps, questionable behaviors and decisions, I can still rejoice in the accomplishments of all 10 of you, begot by my marriages to Jean Ames Theopold and Silvia Ruíz Sahagún. What a diverse group you are! But you share more than blood; you have found ways to be successful, to speak your own truths, and to achieve goals each of you determined for yourselves.

Dan Jr., with your doctorate in meteorology and your great love of the Weminuche Wilderness, you added a love of flying. Not just fixed-wing, single-engine aircraft, but that very personal, open-air kind of flying called hang gliding. And you have not only enjoyed the wind in your face, on the ground and at altitude, you have taught us to be better stewards of this earth, which may be as I write, way beyond repair. We will probably all be dead when the apocalypse occurs, but knowing how we contributed to the earth's destruction has been partially a result of your constant and immutable warnings.

Nick, you have taken off in directions for which this family has no precedent. Your struggles to succeed in construction, leading to a CSU degree in construction management, brought out your leadership, planning, and negotiating talents. You made a huge success of your years in California and then made the decision to settle in Austin where you and Suzi could own twice the house for half the money. Well, almost! You continue to be a leader in the construction industry, while your talents as a British car guru are hardly less distinguished. Along with the memorable trips I have taken with Dan—Cycle Oregon and backpacking in the Weminuche—I will carry to my death the memories of the Great Race in your TR3 from Philadelphia to San Rafael, CA. Those were 14 days of pain, laughter, fatigue, and success. Will you ever forget Motor Mouth's compliment to you and Victoria (TR3) as we ended our day on the bridge over the Mississippi River into St. Louis? "Best British car ever in the Great Race!" That was a well-deserved accolade, and I am glad you are now in possession of a TR6, as well as a Triumph GT. Your love of British cars added an unexpected pleasure to my own life. And now that you own an MG Midget, perhaps you will feel more charitable toward MGs in general? I know that Suzi hasn't shown great affection for riding around in these little British cars, but maybe she will enjoy the GT? She deserves the best. You married well, and she has been such a wonderfully energetic and enterprising part of your life through its various stages. Her horsemanship, entrepreneurial talent, and parental dedication are so very admirable. You were smart to capture her when you did, because the two of you have been a mutually supportive team which has produced nothing but admiration from me.

Kit, I want to begin by recognizing your great success in overcoming significant odds. You mastered complex and intricate aircraft manuals to become an aviation mechanic. You learned about and maintained aircraft systems, and you earned the confidence of a businessman who put you in charge of his life, i.e., his private plane. When you and Trina found each other, you saw the opportunity to put the talents you both possess into the kind of work that utilize your respective skills. You did well with the Westcliffe Motel during good years and bad. Your mechanical aptitude has done nothing but increase over the years. You could probably build a spaceship if you had the parts and the funds, but I just want to see the 1974 Ford Bronco finished in my lifetime. Most of all, I applaud the business instincts you have developed while keeping your love of the outdoors and the Colorado mountains part of your life. Trina has been a great complement to your own skills. She is that hard worker you were always looking for, and she has impeccable instincts in the hotel business based on years of work and observation. And she too loves the Colorado mountains. Your concern for me and our relationship has always meant a lot and even though there are invariably hiccups in any relationship, you should know that I am so very proud of how you have pursued a meaningful life without crutches to lean on. Truly, a triumph with a small t, because you are a muscle-car guy, and I expect that you may soon develop a competitive drag racer made out of a lawn mower and V-12 engine.

Alejandro, I am so glad that you decided to bag the Ph.D and go into high school teaching. You are a born teacher! For many years, while you were growing up, it was difficult to discern a direction which you might pursue, and the only really powerful signal Mom and I received was when you performed as Joseph in *Joseph and the Amazing Technicolor Dreamcoat*. But we knew you wouldn't be a professional singer, so what direction would you go? Apparently, you had something of a burning bush experience at JHU when you found statistics. That area of study fits you like a glove and now that you have shown such awesome ability teaching AP stats at Arapahoe High School, you are a happy camper. I hope you will endure the rigors of public school teaching for many years to come. For all the immature and coddled students you have had to deal with, plus demanding parents who don't have a clue about teaching children responsibility, you have created a cadre of grateful teenagers who have appreciated your knowledge, your prods, challenges, and sense of humor. When things seem gloomy, focus on them. You are making a difference in their lives and in the lives of your own family. You are an exceptional husband and father, and Kim is such a very talented and loving partner for you. What a superb choice you made for a lifelong mate. My hat is off to you both. You have an enviable family, a future that has no limits, and the respect of folks like me who didn't come up to that high bar. And to you, Kim, know that I am forever in your debt for being such a generous and loving daughter-in-law.

Cristina, I hardly know where to begin. Five children, and you are not only the last but the only female. Thank you, Mom, for a gift I didn't expect and a love I had not previously known. Like those who preceded you in the family, you have made me very, very proud. Who would have thought that a young lady whose casual relationship with checkbooks and money as a youngster would become a financial consultant in a firm whose mission is to persuade the corporate world that their bottom line can grow if they marry money making to government regulations, environmental laws, and social justice? You have a heady responsibility, and you have earned respect from your peers. I salute you. Not an easy challenge in what must be a male-dominated environment, but you have become tough and resilient. Just what I had hoped you would become when I saw you take on those soccer players who were bullying you at a game in Monument. I'm sure Addison "Snort" was your true partner in more than a few teary moments when your career progress seemed stalled. But I know now, with great confidence, that you can handle the curveballs life throws at you, especially now that Cash has taken over as your canine partner. You have everything it takes to persevere: courage, determination, smarts, and a sense of humor. Perhaps we are alike in some ways. That reality has always made me smile. But you are your own person, and you have made the leap to professional status with little help from me. As you grow older, don't forget Ebon. He taught you a lot about persistence in the pursuit of worthwhile goals. Persistence, perseverance, and tenacity are the *sine qua non* of achievement.

Philip, I am in awe of what you have done, how you have grown in so many ways, and how you have found a voice for so many of society's ills. Geography and life's circumstances have diminished the amount of time I would have enjoyed spending with you, but I will never forget chasing the cats when you were young, forays on the tennis court, a few golf games, hikes, baseball, and the trampoline. But what will always remain deeply etched in my mind is the trip you and your music buddies made to Hawaii. The four of you on Lanikai Beach at dawn, playing your songs in Kailua and at the beach house where Betty and I were staying—these are images that are etched deeply in my memory bank, along with your sensitive response to Uncle Sid's death. Letting me play "Hallelujah" with you guys was generous on your part and deeply emotional for me. You know the power of music, and you have pursued it with high standards and considerable talent. You have also discovered how to use your computer engineering degree in a business that had a major impact in the medical field during this pandemic. Keep doing what you are doing. You and Tara are now married. I wish you both the best and hope that all your future plans are realized.

Cody, you have the charm and sensitivity to accomplish just about anything. There were times early on, as you well remember, when those qualities were in evidence without any true direction. But you took on Fountain Valley School with energy and enthusiasm, not only making lots of friends but proving that your intellect could catch up with your charm. And then you went on to CSU, majoring in a science that required additional fortitude and perspicacity. Your graduation was, I believe, a milestone in your growth and for me, a quintessential memory. Your accomplishment made me very proud. Now that you have found employment in a field which you enjoy and understand, your life has become stable and productive. You are near Crested Butte and Monarch Pass for winter riding and the Gunnison River for floating and fishing. Nirvana? Pretty close. And when you go back to Steamboat for a few runs, remember that day when we rode and skied together, and you caused me no little worry as you darted in and out of the trees. Talent was evident that day; I could see it, so I'm not at all surprised that today you are a snowboard instructor. Keep on fishing, Codeman! You have a special touch which I hope you will again put to work on the Yampa River when I am gone. We had fun on those excursions, and I was never so happy to be out-fished as I was with you on those occasions. Onward!

Jesse, you have surprised me on so many occasions. I had no idea when you were young that you were so well organized and driven to be productive and a forward-looking thinker. Your time at FVS served you well, and your degree in construction management at CSU was a great choice. Clearly, you have settled into a career that suits you. I know you had desires to play Division I football, but the Tylers aren't really big enough for that level. You handled the disappointment well, studied hard, and graduated with a good record. That you were almost immediately employed in a competitive industry is testimony to your internal drive, and I am delighted that you had the ability to save enough money to become a homeowner when you moved to Denver. With your equally talented and successful bride, Kendall, you will always have wonderful companionship and support. My hope is that you work to become a leader in your profession and in whatever community you live in. You have the personality and the perspective to guide others less talented, especially young people who have made wrong turns or have lacked role models. I think you could make a huge contribution to society in general by using your skills to help disadvantaged kids turn their lives around. Whatever you decide, know that I have especially appreciated your courtesies and expressions of gratitude for giving you a leg up in your education. You have paid me back tenfold by setting your sights high and maintaining standards that I respect. Don't settle for mediocrity, ever!

Ainsley, you are truly amazing. I remember singing songs to you when you were a baby, supposedly going to sleep while I was lying on the floor next to your crib. I nodded off after the songs and when I awoke, you were staring at me over the side of your crib, not too sure who I was and what I was doing there. But I think our relationship has been one of mutual joy. As hard as it was for me to leave Steamboat and come to live in Denver, that move has allowed me to spend quality time with you. I have watched how conscientious you are at home and at school. I have reveled in the many cards and letters you have sent me, expressing love and gratitude. I have taken enormous satisfaction out of seeing you turn into a young lady, and I am in awe of your smarts, your maturity, and your strong family ties. Bravo! I wish the world was less messy and disorganized. You may have issues with people who aren't as reliable and dedicated as you, but don't despair. We humans are mostly imperfect and complicated. I am so happy that you are putting energy into your skating; you have achieved so much in that sport, because you have the discipline to demand more of yourself. In the past few years, you have shown the willingness to take on challenges that you might have ducked earlier, afraid that you might not succeed. No longer, or not so much anymore. Perhaps you have recognized that a full life requires trying lots of new things, even those we don't have a chance of mastering. I predict you will always be an academic whiz kid, and I hope you will take my comments about your writing skills to heart. There is more than one story in that imaginative brain of yours, and perhaps they are worth telling. *The Peanut and the Dude* provided for such great fun. *Forsan et haec olim meminisse iuvabit.* Perhaps some day it will please you to remember these things.

Andon, you are a lot of energy: physical, emotional, creative. I used to think you would really dominate a traditional team sport like baseball, soccer, or basketball. But it seems that you are happiest with individual sports. Fencing proved such a success for you. You have the moves, the touch, the quick reflexes. I also watch you climb and twist and pirouette around every obstacle, making me wonder if one day you might want to try gymnastics. I think you would be a natural. You have a great imagination, so I don't think you will ever be bored. And, of course, you have a special love of the ladies in your life. I don't know where you get that trait, but I suspect it may be a gene that found its way down through a generation or two into your own genetic makeup. Handle with care and treat as a privilege! Include your extraordinary warmth and sense of humor in all your relationships. I predict that you will have a most interesting and unpredictable life, and I hope you will look back on our time together with a smile on your face. If I have tried to teach you anything, it is to seek excellence in what you do. Excellence is an attitude, not a skill, and you have a great attitude.

That's a wrap, everybody. Take care of each other.

Cash

About The Author

Daniel Tyler is a retired history professor. Born before WWII, he grew up on a ranch in Colorado prior to studying at Harvard College. After receiving a degree in political science and a commission in the USAF, he served as a jet flight instructor and taught history in Hawaii. Tyler returned to ranching for a few years then earned a Ph.D. in American History. He taught in Mexico, Argentina, and at Colorado State University where he researched the West's water development and resulting conflict. Previous publications by Daniel Tyler include, *The Last Water Hole in the West*, *W.D. Farr, Cowboy in the Boardroom, Silver Fox of the Rockies*, *Love in an Envelope*, and *Bucks County's Benevolent Squire*.

Notes

[1] Sidney F. Tyler, <u>A Joyful Odyssey</u>, Part Two, p. 30. I have used my father's recollections to enhance my own recall of Rydal days.

[2] Cristina's godfather.

[3] Schaefer: <u>The Great Endurance Horse Race</u>, <u>Shane</u>, <u>Monte Walsh</u>; Waters: <u>The Man Who Killed the Deer</u>, <u>Pumpkin Seed Point</u>, <u>People of the Valley</u>, <u>Book of the Hopi</u>.

[4] <u>Sources for New Mexican History, 1821-1846</u>. (Santa Fe: Museum of New Mexico Press), 1984.

[5] <u>The Mythical Pueblo Rights Doctrine</u>. (El Paso: Texas Western Press), 1990.

[6] Gorham Bacon, Mum's great uncle. See Daniel Tyler, <u>Mum: The Life and Extended Family of Constance Harper Tyler</u> (Denver: E&R Publications, 2013), Chapter III and p. 126.

[7] See Daniel Tyler, <u>Mum. The Life and Extended Family of Constance Harper Tyler</u> (Denver: E&R Publications, 2013).

[8] It can be seen at https://youtube/u-ZBGmSL0bg. <u>The Little Dancin' Boy</u> (Raleigh, NC: Lulu Publishing Service, 2015).

[9] Secklin, Barbara J.,<u>The Long Goodbye: Lewy Body Dementia Alzheimer's First Cousin</u> (Scotts Valley, CA: Createspace Publishing, 2015).

[10] <u>Bucks County's Benevolent Squire. In Search of George Frederick Tyler</u> (Denver: Spring Cedars, 2022) is dedicated to Sid.

www.ingramcontent.com/pod-product-compliance
Lightning Source LLC
Chambersburg PA
CBHW050515170426
43201CB00013B/1963